CANNABIS MARIJUANA

GANJA

CANNABIS ✿ MARIJUANA

GANJA

THE JAMAICAN AND GLOBAL
CONNECTION

DR HENRY I.C. LOWE, OJ | PROF. ERROL Y. ST. A. MORRISON, OJ

PELICAN PUBLISHERS LIMITED
Kingston, Jamaica W.I.

First Published in Jamaica, 2013 by Pelican Publishers Limited

44 Lady Musgrave Road
Kingston 10, Jamaica, W.I
Tel: (876) 978-8377 | Fax: (876) 978-0048
Email: pelicanpublisers@gmail.com
Website: www.pelicanpublishers.com.jm

ISBN: 978-976-8240-09-5 (paperback)
      978-976-8240-14-9 (hardback)

Cover design by Pelican Publishers Limited

DEDICATION

To all those who have striven to present an objective picture of the Cannabis plant and its chemical components and to those who have helped to develop the medicinal potential of the Cannabinoids. Importantly also, to those who have benefited from the scientific study of the Cannabis and its educes...

Net proceeds from this publication will fund further research on the Cannabis plant and its chemical components.

AUTHOR'S EARLY WORDS | Henry I.C. Lowe • Errol Y. St. A. Morrison   X

PREFACE | Emeritus Professor Manley West   XI

FOREWORD | Professor Barry Chevannes   XII

ACKNOWLEDGMENTS   XIV

ABBREVIATIONS USED IN THIS BOOK   XV

INTRODUCTION   XVI

1. CANNABIS - THE PLANT, ITS BOTANY AND CHEMISTRY   1

2. TOXICOLOGY AND PHARMACOLOGY   8

3. HISTORY OF THE USE OF MARIJUANA   13

4. IS MARIJUANA SAFE?   29

5. MAJOR EFFECTS   37

6. POTENTIAL APPLICATIONS OF CANNABIS AS MEDICINE   46

7. METHODS OF APPLYING CANNABIS AS A MEDICINE   89

8. CANNABIS - DERIVED DRUGS IN FORMAL MEDICINE   92

9. **RECREATIONAL USE OF CANNABIS** 104

10. **CANNABIS AND SOME LEGAL CONSIDERATIONS** 110

11. **SUMMARY AND THE WAY FORWARD** 139

APPENDIX 1 157

- The Jamaican Legal Position BY DR. VELMA BROWN HAMILTON
- Dangerous Drugs Act of Jamaica: The Background
- Summary of the Legislation
- Drug Offenses (Forfeiture of Proceeds) Act, 1994
- Interpretations of the Courts
- Duty of the Judge
- Medicinal Preparations
- Mutual Assistance (Criminal Matters) 1995
- The Drug Court (Treatment and Rehabilitation of Offenders) Act 1999
- International Obligations
- Money Laundering Act

APPENDIX 2 174

Marihuana - Hashish Epidemic And its Impact on United States Security
- DR. JOHN HALL

APPENDIX 3 — 188

- The Mental Health Perspective of Cannabis Use in Jamaica
  - PROFESSOR FREDERICK HICKLING

APPENDIX 4 — 199

A   The Use of Certain Cannabis Derivatives (Canasol) in
    Glaucoma - PROFESSOR EMERITUS MANLEY WEST

B   The Potential Use of Cannabis sativa in Ophthalmology
    - A.B.LOCKHART, M.E. WEST AND H.I.C. LOWE

APPENDIX 5 — 213

- Medical Marijuana: The Continuing Story - BY BRIGID KANE

APPENDIX 6 — 223

- Books published on Marijuana by Jamaican Authors

APPENDIX 7 — 225

- Selected Journal Articles Published on Ganja

APPENDIX 8 — 228

- Selected Articles Published in The Jamaica Daily Gleaner
  on Marijuana
  (1950-2013)

APPENDIX 9 — 253

- Selected Articles Published in the Jamaica Observer on Marijuana
  (1998-2013)

APPENDIX 10-A   263

- A Weed of Many Names

APPENDIX 10-B   263

- Legalize It - Songs with lyrics that call for the legalization and or glorification of Marijuana

APPENDIX 11-A   264

- Articles published in The Daily News in Jamaica on Marijuana

APPENDIX 11-B   264

- Websites relevant to Marijuana

GLOSSARY   266
BIBLIOGRAPHY   269
REFERENCES   273
AUTHOR'S INTRODUCTION   278

AUTHORS' EARLY WORDS

This book intends in a few chapters to capture the history of this enigmatic plant *Cannabis sativa*. That history speaks to its discovery, its use in folklore, its scientific study, medicinal potential and possible adverse health outcomes. No plant in Christendom has been so exhaustively studied; some 20,000 publications attest to that, and growing!

With the laws changing in countries both north and south of the equator, new evidence is coming forth from the laboratories of renown Scientific institutions. This has increased the clamour for access to its medicinal promises. Cannabis sativa has found new life and it is chronicled here in these pages.

That aspects of the book may seem repetitive must be recognised that, for example, to deal with the mental effects of the smoked preparation, there was an early era clouded by superstition and folklore, then the medical observations, then the scientific pursuit and now amazing claims for therapeutic efficacy in a cross section of disease states. This is absolutely overwhelming and each era has to be taken in relation to the knowledge status of the time.

This is a fascinating read, factual and objective. What seems clear at this point in time is much scientific data must be obtained to give policymakers a balanced approach as they seek to protect the vulnerable from adverse health outcomes, the populace from the avarice of illegal traders, and to encourage the scientific enquiry to shed light on the dark ages of the past and provide a guiding beacon for the future.

Enjoy reading!
HENRY LOWE & ERROL MORRISON

PREFACE

The controversy and issues about the good and evil effects of cannabis have grown exponentially over the last 20 years. Some of the findings have shifted from the issues of criminalization to focus on its potential as a medicinal agent. This has led to exploratory studies into the therapeutic utility of cannabis. At this time a number of areas of potential medicinal applications have been identified and investigated; for example, glaucoma, asthma, pain, epileptic seizures and multiple sclerosis, to name a few.

The present knowledge about these issues is scattered all over the literature. This book is an attempt to collate a reader friendly account of the knowledge and issues at this time, with emphasis on the knowledge and experience of the subject as it relates to Jamaica.

The variability of the results from cannabis research should not be surprising, especially when one considers that the plant has over 400 chemicals and as shown by Professor Michael Paris of the University of Paris, variation of the degree of humidity, light and heat can change the cannabinoid content and nature within a few hours.

Rubin and Comitas, two of the early leading researchers on cannabis, concluded that 'chronic use of potent cannabis is not toxic to the human mind and body'.

As the story goes two 'stoned' cannabis users were watching a jet plane streaking through the sky; "Man" one smoker said to the other 'I thought he'd never leave'.

EMERITUS PROFESSOR MANLEY WEST (1929-2012)

Pharmacology Section, Department of Basic Medical Science,
University of The West Indies, Mona, Jamaica

FOREWORD

Cannabis sativa, easily the most widely used and controversial illicit plant consumed by mankind, is used in over 130 countries across the world. It has attracted more research and literature than any other as many tracts, books, pamphlets and scholarly papers have been written against its use as well as for it, and there are now web sites on the Internet to inform as well as to lobby.

The controversy has been raging from the first ever Commission of Enquiry set up by the British Colonial Government over 100 years ago, known as the India Hemp Commission, to that set up by New York Mayor La Guardia in the 1940s, to the Jamaica National Commission on Ganja in 2000. It is therefore reasonable to suggest that this very timely and useful review by two of the Caribbean's eminent scientists is not likely to be the final word. Indeed, the authors make no such claim, their intent clearly being to offer the reading public a summary of the health-related literature on ganja, with an introduction to its ancient origin.

Why is so ancient a substance the subject of such intense controversy? It might help to consider that the controversy is a modern one. On the one hand, as the authors show, its use among the folk, in ways similar to the use of other herbs and natural substances reputed to have therapeutic or beneficial effects, spread freely from China and India across the world.

In colonial times, on the other hand, when opinions began to surface attributing to ganja responsibility for anti-social behaviour in Jamaica as far back as the 1870s when its use was still mainly East Indian, and not well known or used throughout the populace, ganja was being blamed for murder and it is at such a point that a state will adopt measures to control social practices, without waiting to base its action on scientific evidence. There is ample proof that the ban placed on certain substances came first and the scientific evidence came after. Some even point to the fact that the scientifically undisputed proof of the harmfulness of a substance does not necessarily lead to its suppression, as is the case with tobacco.

At the root of the controversy over ganja is fear. There are those who see ganja as part of a growing culture, and fear it as a gateway to other more harmful substances. Then there is the fear that it produces indolence, and fear also of its psychoactive properties. Nevertheless, in the likely event that science were to settle the controversies about ganja, the use of it would remain fairly widespread. It is better then that up-to-date knowledge about its properties and its effects be available so that people may make informed decisions and conscious decisions about their health. This is what, *Cannabis, Ganja: The Jamaican and Global Connection* seeks to provide.

PROFESSOR BARRY CHEVANNES (1940-2010)

Dean of the Faculty of Social Sciences
University of the West Indies. Mona, Jamaica

ACKNOWLEDGMENTS

We owe our deepest appreciation to the many persons who contributed materials and articles to make this publication possible. They are Emeritus Professor Manley E. West and Professor Barry Chevannes for the Preface and the Foreword respectively; and Professor Emeritus Manley West, Dr A.B Lockhart, Dr. John Hall, Professor Frederick Hickling, and Velma Brown-Hamilton for contributing articles.

The authors also acknowledge the assistance of the Jamaica Constabulary Force, in particular Deputy Sergeant A.J. Forbes and Detective Sergeant Llewellyn for some of the pictures used in the publication; Ellen Grizzle and the staff at the Drug Abuse Secretariat; The Gleaner Company of Jamaica for the Leonardo cartoons; the Jamaica Observer and Clovis Brown for their kind permission to include the Clovis cartoons; the National Library of Jamaica and the Medical Library of the University of the West Indies for facilitating data gathering efforts, as well as family and friends who have helped in many ways.

We would also like to thank the many publishers and individuals who gave us permission to use their materials. Thanks also to the many other individuals whose names are not mentioned, but who have offered encouragement and made significant contributions in a variety of ways to the writing and publication of this book.

Finally, to the Environmental Health Foundation- a special appreciation for its financial support; and to the Pelican Publishers team, and Shanika Allen for their invaluable help in researching, editing and designing this book.

ABBREVIATIONS

ADD	Attention Deficit Disorder
AIDS	Acquired Immune Deficiency Syndrome
BBC	British Broadcasting Corporation
BC	Before Christ
CBD	Cannabidiol
CBN	cannabinol
CNS	Central Nervous System
CSA	Controlled Substance Act
DEA	Drug Enforcement Agency, USA
DHH	Department of Health and Human Services, USA
FDA/USFDA	Food and Drug Administration
GLC	Gas-liquid Chromatography
HIV	Human Immunodeficiency Virus
IOM	Institute of Medicine, USA
IOP	Intraocular Pressure
MS	Multiple Sclerosis
NIDA	National Institute of Drug Abuse, USA
NIH	National Institute of Health
PAG	Peri Aqueductal Gray Area
PMS	Premenstrual Syndrome
POAG	Primary Open Angle Glaucoma
THC	Delta-9-trans-tetrahydrocannabinol
USA	United States of America
UCSF	University of California, San Francisco, USA

INTRODUCTION

"Even while we speak, time, the churl, will have been running. Snatch the sleeve of today and trust as little as you may to tomorrow."

HORACE, 65-8 B.C

Cannabis sativa L., (source of marijuana), which was so named by the famous Swedish botanist Carl Linnnaeus in 1753, is an herbaceous annual plant that is cultivated or grows wild in most tropical and temperate regions of the world. Currently, the cannabis plant is thought of mainly in the context of a psychoactive drug, Delta-9-trans-tetrahydrocannbinol (THC), but this versatile plant has played an important role in human agriculture for thousands of years. In fact, *Cannabis sativa,* which is one of man's oldest cultivated non-food plants, was cultivated for three main purposes: hemp fibre from its stem, oil from its seed and the psychoactive substances from its flowering top.

The terminologies ganja, cannabis, marijuana tend to be confusing. The plant has been called many different names in different parts of the world. It is popularly referred to as 'kiki', 'high grade' and 'ganja' in Jamaica, 'bhang' in India, 'kief' in Morocco, and 'dagga' in southern Africa. It is also known as 'sinsemilla', 'weed', 'grass', 'pot', 'Mary Jane', 'dope', 'bush', 'tea', 'boo', 'reefer', and 'shit'. However, marijuana is the generic name for preparations of variable potency made from the dried flowering tops of both the male and female plants of *Cannabis sativa.* Ganja, Indian hemp and cannabis (in addition to the other names given in Appendix 11-A) are often used as synonyms for marijuana. These terms are mainly used in Jamaica and the Caribbean .

Cannabis sativa is an adaptable species with many variables, due to its genetic flexibility, environmental influences and human manipulations. Additionally, research has shown that the leaves and buds of the cannabis plant have natural therapeutic properties that have been used for centuries in the treatment of numerous illnesses.

The intoxicating substances derived from Cannabis sativa vary greatly in potency depending on the variety of the plant, the varying mixtures of the plant and the technique of preparation as shown in Table 1. Consequently, the uses of the cannabis plant cover a wide range of activities, from the fibres to psychoactive principles from selected varieties.

TABLE 1 | PREPARATIONS FROM CANNABIS

NAME	PART OF PLANT	THC CONTENT (%)
MARIJUANA/GANJA	Leaves, small stems, compressed sterile female flower heads	1.0 - 3.0
SINSEMILLA	Sterile female flower heads	3.0 - 6.0
HASHISH	Cannabis resin	10.0 - 15.0
CANNABIS OIL	Alcoholic extract of resin	20.0 - 60.0

The cultivation of Cannabis sativa for its THC property is illegal in many countries. A few countries and states in the US have legalized the possession, cultivation and use of cannabis for medicinal purposes upon sanction from a physician. It is otherwise illegal to possess, sell or consume cannabis products in most countries.

Cannabinoids, the primary psychoactive ingredient in marijuana, are produced most abundantly in the flowering tops in the female plants that are grown mainly in tropical climates. Cannabinoids also play an important role in protecting the plant against heat. Advances in cannabinoid science have given rise to an abundance of new opportunities for the development of medicinally useful cannabinoid-based drugs. The compiled data suggest a variety of uses, particularly, for pain, nausea and appetite stimulation, for patients with AIDS, or those undergoing chemotherapy and who suffer simultaneously from severe pain, nausea, and appetite loss. Cannabinoid drugs might also give relief not found in any other single medication. Many persons also believe it relieves pre-menstrual syndrome (PMS), itching, insomnia, arthritis, depression, pain associated with childbirth, attention deficit disorder (ADD) and ringing in the ears.

The debate continues as to whether marijuana is safe for medicinal use. Is it substantially effective and better than medicines already available? Societal views and social concerns (often conflicting) fuel the debate, especially as it relates to the non-medicinal use of marijuana.

There are those who argue against the legalization of marijuana for medicinal use, as they believe that it would result in more liberal use of the plant. They further argue that with the persistent drug abuse problem, especially among young people, legalization would potentially provide a gateway to even more harmful substance abuse. This often casts a shadow on the medicinal use of the plant. However, there is much scientific evidence that proves its potential value in traditional medicine, and more recently in alternative complementary medicine. In addition, a report presented by the Institute of Medicine (USA) entitled "Marijuana and Medicine: Assessing the Science Base", (1999) concluded that there is no evidence that the drug effects of marijuana are causally linked to the subsequent use of other illicit drugs.

Meanwhile, the dedication and resolution of several scientists worldwide have resulted in significant discoveries being made regarding the benefits of marijuana to medicine. There have been remarkable and increasing advantages in the molecular and behavioural studies, showing interesting physiological effects of cannabinoids.

What is most effectively demonstrated by the current research is the vast potential of the plant in terms of its medicinal benefits as well as

Cannabis sativa L.

(1) TOP OF MALE PLANT, IN FLOWER; (2) TOP OF FEMALE PLANT, IN FRUIT; (3) SEEDLING; (4) LEAFLET FROM LARGE, 11-PARTED LEAF; (5) PORTION OF A STAMINATE INFLORESCENCE, WITH BUDS AND MATURE MALE FLOWER; (6) FEMALE FLOWERS, WITH STIGMAS PROTRUDING FROM HAIRY BRACT; (7) FRUIT ENCLOSED IN PERSISTENT HAIRY BRACT; (8) FRUIT, LATERAL VIEW; (9) FRUIT, END VIEW; (10) GLANDULAR HAIR WITH MULTI-CELLULAR STALK; (11) GLANDULAR HAIR WITH SHORT, ONE-CELLED INVISIBLE STALK; (12) NON-GLANDULAR HAIR CONTAINING A CYSTOLITH. ILLUSTRATION BY E. W. SMITH.

EXTRACTED FROM *THE GREAT BOOK OF HEMP*, ROBINSON, 1996

its uses for food and fibres. These developments remain stifled because of the socio-political and legal issues surrounding the plant.

However, it should be remembered that the marijuana extractive is not a benign substance. It is a powerful drug with a variety of effects. Although marijuana smoke delivers THC and other cannabinoids to the body, it also delivers harmful substances, including many of those found in tobacco smoke. In addition, the plant contains a variable mixture of biologically active compounds and cannot be expected to provide a precise drug effect. **For these reasons, the future of cannabinoid drugs lies not in smoked marijuana, but in chemically-defined drugs that act on the cannabinoid systems that are a natural component of human physiology.**

The focus should not only be on the potentially harmful effects of recreational use of ganja but also on the advantages of its medical applications, thus establishing a balanced approach.

It is recognized, however, that the governments typically accept or reject scientific studies based on their impact on policy, so medical and other issues are doomed if governments choose not to support them.

The purpose of this book is not to persuade or encourage the reader to join either side of the debate, but rather to inform by presenting the history and socio-cultural impact of marijuana. The primary focus of the book is the current research on the medical aspects of ganja. The appendices expand the offering of the book. These include lists of publications, books, journal articles and newspaper articles, which are provided to lead interested readers to further information on the subject.

It should also be noted that the title of the book *Cannabis Marijuana, Ganja: The Jamaican and Global Connection* is designed not only to give a world view on the subject but the scientific and socio-cultural uses as they relate to Jamaica through narrative illustrations.

A GANJA TREE GROWING GROWING FRESH OUTSIDE OF KINGSTON, JAMAICA

THE GLEANER Friday, July 27, 2001

The Gleaner

The ganja culture

We note that the National Commission on Ganja is nearing the end of its work. Some nine months of hearings have been held in all parishes aimed at framing recommendations about possible decriminalisation of the drug.

As we understand it, the objective is to determine whether the drug should be decriminalised for limited personal use. The Commission, headed by Professor Barry Chevannes, was asked by the Prime Minister to examine the possible economic, cultural, social and international effects if a positive recommendation is instituted.

Professor Chevannes has stated that a majority of some 250 persons appearing before the seven-member Commission were in favour of decriminalisation; but the Commission would not necessarily be swayed by that.

Even before a final determination is reached we think it is important to recognise some current realities. Firstly, neither law nor gentle persuasion will ever eradicate the growth and use of ganja in this society. One remote possibility is the upgrading of legal farming activity to make it a more attractive economic alternative. We doubt that even the affable Roger Clarke as Minister of Agriculture is that optimistic.

Secondly, chasing spliff smokers, as happens so often, is futile and counter-productive law enforcement. Policemen must know that the pungent aroma of the weed at pop music sessions and political rallies is more the rule than the exception. It is a part of the popular entertainment scene. In short, ganja is part of Jamaican culture even beyond the ritual usage that is fiercely defended on religious grounds.

The negative side of ganja, of course, is the trafficking which is a major part of the crime scene. It will be difficult to separate this illegal aspect from the recreational or religious usage; which is what decriminalisation is all about. But the effort must be made.

Maintaining a purely hardline stance against ganja is no more tenable than the 1919-33 Prohibition against alcohol was in the USA.

The opinions on this page, except for the above, do not necessarily reflect the views of **The Gleaner.**

1

CANNABIS
THE PLANT, ITS BOTANY AND CHEMISTRY

"Chance favours the prepared mind"
- LOUIS PASTEUR 19TH CENTURY

THE PLANT AND ITS BOTANY

It is believed that the *Cannabis sativa* originated in Asia, and more specifically in the Himalayas and Afghanistan. It is an annual, which can grow in any type of soil. However, since it can deplete the soil nutrients rapidly, good crops require fertilizers. The plant can grow at a rate of 7 centimetres per day. The average time for maturation is 4 to 10 months.

The botanical classification has almost been as varied and controversial as the origins and uses of cannabis. This issue continues to attract several scholarly reviews.

Cannabis sativa has in recent years been placed in the family Cannabaceae and not in others as was the practice in previous years. Linnaeus in his *Species Plantarum* in 1753 gave the plant the Latin name *Cannabis sativa*. The genus name Cannabis means 'canelike' and the species name sativa means 'planted or sown'. There are several types (subspecies and varieties) of *Cannabis sativa*, which have created great difficulties for taxonomists throughout the world. In fact, in recent years this has complicated legal issues relating to identification of plant residues. In most countries marijuana is recognized as an extractive from the *Cannabis sativa* plant.

TABLE 2 | THE TAXONOMIC CLASSIFICATION OF CANNABIS. BASED ON THE DESCRIPTIONS OF QUIMBY (1974) AND SMALL AND CRONQUIST (1976)

KINGDOM	Plant
DIVISION	Tracheophyta
SUBDIVISION	Pteropsida
CLASS	Angiospermae
SUBCLASS	Dicotyledonae
SUPERORDER	Dilleniidae
ORDER	Urticales
FAMILY	Cannabaceae
GENUS	Cannabis
SPECIES	Sativa

SUBSPECIES

C. sativa L. subsp. sativa (L.) Small et Cronquist

C. sativa L. subsp. indica (Lam) Small et Cronquist

VARIETIES

C. sativa L. subsp. sativa (L.) Small et Cronquist
var. sativa (L.) Small et Cronquist
taxon 25 (1976) 421.

C. sativa L. subsp.sativa (L.) Small et Cronquist
var. spontanea Vavilov
taxon 25 (1976) 423.

C. sativa L. subsp. indica (Lam.) Small et
Cronquist var. indica (Lam.) Wehmer
Die Pflanzenstoffe (1911) 248.

C. sativa L. subsp. Indica (Lam.) Small et
Cronquist var. kafiristanica (Vavilov) Small et
Cronquist
Taxon 25 (1976) 429.

The sex of the plant is usually determined when flowering begins. The male flowers (inflorescence) have several individual flowers on branches up to 20 centimetres long. The female flowers do not project beyond the surrounding leaves.

The male plant is not regarded as being pharmacologically active. In fact, it is called 'mad' because of its relatively low THC content and the headaches it can cause when smoked.

Cannabis farmers have suggested that in an average field approximately 40 percent of the plants are male and 60 per cent are female. They have also stated that the male plants need to be uprooted and destroyed at an early stage of development (as soon as flowering begins), otherwise the crop will be contaminated and will result in low yields. However, the male plant normally dies much earlier than the female, especially after fertilization.

The cannabis plant is typically covered with tiny hairs (called trichomes), some of which are glandular and produce and contain resinous substances, which have been identified chemically as THC and non-narcotic cannabinoids and cannabidiols. The resin typically contains high THC concentration and is mostly found on flowers. These are often used, with the aid of a microscope, to identify the plant. The unfertilized flowers from the female plant are highly prized and are called 'sinsemilla' (which means without seeds).

The female flowers, leaves and resin are the materials usually harvested for non hemp purposes, and in general different harvesting methods are used for these products depending on whether they are used for 'narcotic' or medicinal purposes. Scientists have determined that marijuana may contain up to 10 per cent of THC, hashish up to 15 per cent and hash oil up to 65 per cent.

Storage conditions (heat and light reduce the THC content) and the age of the materials have been found to influence the quality of the material, mainly because of chemical changes to the THC. Usually, a one-year old material will on average have lost only 10 per cent of its potency, but after two years, without storage, it maintains only about 10-12 per cent of its original potency. However, when stored in a cool, dark area its potency can be effectively maintained for about two years, but begins to fall off rapidly thereafter.

THE CHEMISTRY OF CANNABIS

In terms of its chemistry, cannabis has been described as one of the most studied plant materials in history. A recent count has indicated that more than 7,000 scientific papers have been published on this subject area, along with related pharmacological activities. This is not surprising since the phyto-chemistry of *Cannabis sativa* has so far identified more than 400 different chemical compounds, with a variety of interesting chemical, pharmacological and physiological principles.

Of these many chemicals identified, the one that has been of major interest is THC, which was first isolated in 1964. THC and its relatives (over 60 compounds) are chemical compounds typically with 21 carbon atoms, which are referred to as cannabinoids. These cannabinoids are exclusively found in cannabis. However, interestingly, several non-cannabinoid compounds have been found in *Cannabis sativa,* but these are generally widely distributed throughout the plant kingdom. They include enzymes, glycosides, vitamins, acids, alcohols, amino acids, proteins, sugars, alkaloids and terpenes. It is believed that it is these terpenes that attract sniffer dogs to marijuana.

It has been observed that the concentration of the various chemicals, particularly THC, varies significantly in plants taken from different parts of the world. This has, to an extent, allowed for the chemical classification of the cannabis plant based on their chemical constituents. These different types are called 'chemovars'. However, they do not represent different varieties or species of the plant but, instead, breeding and climatic effects. Recent scientific studies have also indicated that relatively high temperature, sunlight and rainfall can stimulate a higher concentration of THC in *Cannabis sativa* plants.

delta-9-THC

delta-8-THC

Cannabidiol

Cannabinol

NATURALLY OCCURRING CANNABINOIDS IN CAANNABIS EXTRACTS

SUMMARY AND EXPLANATION OF THE TEST

Cannabis sativa is a weedy annual which grows readily in both tropical and temperate areas of the world. Δ^9- Tetrahydrocannabinol (THC) is the primary psychoactive ingredient found in leaves and flowering tops of the plants, preparations of which are commonly referred to as marijuana. It has been suggested that chronic use of marijuana can interfere with tasks involving complex psychomotor skills, such as driving and flying. Synthetic cannabinoids, such as nabilone and levonantradol, have been used therapeutically to prevent the nausea and vomiting associated with cytotoxic drug therapy, and to reduce intraocular pressure in glaucoma. Marijuana is usually either ingested orally or inhaled by smoking. THC, being very lipophillic, accumulates in body fat, a property which contributes to the very long urinary elimination times seen with this drug. Storage of the drug in body fat may be faster than elimination in chronic users, and this may lead to longer elimination times in these individuals compared to occasional users. When smoked, THC rapidly enters the blood-stream in 1-3 minutes whereas taken orally, the absorption is considerably slower (1.5-3 hours). Once in the bloodstream, it is quickly transformed by liver enzymes to several metabolites, the foremost being 11-nor-Δ9 THC-9-carboxylic acid. In man, two-thirds of the dose is excreted in the feces and a third in the urine, almost entirely as metabolite. THC itself is detectable for a few hours in blood, but because of its rapid metabolism and distribution little unchanged THC appears in the urine.

PRINCIPLE OF THE PROCEDURE

DPC's Double Antibody Cannabinoids procedure is a competitive radioimmuno-assay in which I-labelled THC competes with cannabinoids in the patient sample for antibody sites. After incubation for a fixed time, separation of bound from free THC is achieved by the PEG-accelerated double-antibody method. Finally, the antibody-bound fraction is precipitated and counted. Patient sample concentrations are read from a calibration curve.

PROCEDURE

The assay requires a total incubation time of only 75 minutes. An experienced technician with proper equipment can prepare a calibration curve and 20 patient samples for counting in 2 hours, using less than 1 hour of bench time. Sample and tracer addictions can be handled simultaneously, if desired, with the help of an automatic pipettor-diluter.

SEPARATION

Separation is by a single-reagent precipitating solution consisting of second antibody and dilute PEG. This method has been shown to yield more consistent and reproducible results than other liquid phase techniques. The flocculation reaction is complete in just minutes at room temperature. The precipitate packs to a firm and easily visible pellet, and nonspecific binding is at least as low as in separations employing second antibody alone.

DATA REDUCTION

Conventional RIA techniques of calculation and quality control are applicable. The assay has been optimized for linearity in a logit-log representation throughout the range of its calibrators.

CALIBRATION

The kit is equipped with human urine matrix calibrators having THC metabolite values ranging from 10 to 250 ng/mL of 11-nor-Δ9-tetrahydrocannabinol-9-carboxylic acid. The calibrators are lyophilized for maximum stability.

COUNTS

The tracer has a high specific activity, with total counts of approximately 110,000 cpm at iodination. Maximum binding is approximately 50-60%. Nonspecific binding and patient blanks are negligible.

PRECISION

CVs are low and uniform, and the Quantitative Procedure can detect as little as 1.1 ng/mL.

SPECIFICITY

The antiserum is highly specific for cannabinoids, with very low cross reactivity to other compounds that might be present in patient samples.

ACCURACY

The assay calibrators have been checked against the Bureau of Standards Standard Reference Material for THC Metabolite in Urine. Extensive recovery experiments have shown that the assay is accurate over a broad range of THC metabolite values. Its accuracy has been further verified in patient comparison studies against another immunoassay for cannabinoids.

COURTESY OF CENTRAL MEDICAL LABORATORIES, KINGSTON, JAMAICA

TOXICOLOGY
AND PHARMACOLOGY

" A man so various, that he seemed to be
Not one, but all mankind's epitome
Stiff in opinions, always in the wrong;
Was everything by starts, and nothing long;
But, in the course of one revolving moon,
Was chemist, fiddler, statesman and buffoon".
- JOHN DRYDEN 1631-1700

The effect of the pharmacological properties of cannabis depends on how it is administered, whether it is smoked or taken orally. Smoking marijuana can transmit various substances into the lungs which enter through the blood-stream more quickly than when taken orally.

OVERVIEW

Though there are more than 400 chemical compounds in the cannabis plant, the cannabinoids have been the most studied; especially delta-9-tetrahydrocannabinol (THC), delta-8-tetrahydrocannabinol (delta-8-THC), cannabidiol (CBD) and cannabinol (CBN). THC produces most of the well known effects of marijuana, but it interacts with the others to modify the results. THC, the most psychoactive ingredient of the plant, is a part of some of the preparations made from the plant. However, the percentage varies.

Natural and most synthetic cannabinoids are oily and soluble in fat, but only slightly soluble in water. The pharmacological effects of cannabinoids depend on the medium used to administer them.

In order to understand the effects of substances derived from cannabis, the dosage has to be controlled. The quantity of THC present in a sample delivered by smoking depends on the genetic background (the genotype) of the plant, the sex of the plant, conditions of growth and storage, and sample preparation. Also, a significant proportion of the THC that is found in the fresh leaves is in the inactive carboxylated form and this can be detected by gas-liquid chromatography (GLC). Decarboxylation to the active THC occurs slowly during storage and rapidly during heating, as in smoking or in GLC analysis. Moreover, the way a cigarette is smoked determines the amount of THC absorbed by the smoker.

METABOLIC EFFECT

When THC is ingested, very little reaches the brain, but most is accumulated in the liver, kidneys and lungs. As THC is fat-soluble, some of it tends to accumulate longer in the fat deposits in the body, hence the complete elimination of a single dose of the drug takes about one week and it is eliminated mostly in the urine and faeces, but not through the salivary glands.

Cannabinoid metabolites can be found in the blood and urine for up to one month after exposure to marijuana. The test can be positive for three days after a single use of cannabis. Secondary exposure to the smoke through inhalation is enough to produce positive urine test results. In chronic cannabis users, a urine test can detect residual positive levels for up to six weeks after the last use. As a result, a positive urine test for a chronic user does not necessarily indicate recent or continued use. A test was recently developed by Schwilke et al. which allows the differentiation of residual cannabinoid excretion in chronic users and new cannabis use.

PHARMACOLOGY

Pharmacologically THC is not a narcotic, although considered so by law. In the pharmacological sense, a narcotic induces trance-like or calm state and allows one to become indifferent to pain. Marijuana is therefore better described as an intoxicant, a hallucinogen or a euphoriant. To eliminate the unwanted effects of the drug, the molecule can be modified. Some of the synthetic analogues are even more potent than THC itself.

The intensity and duration of effects in relation to dosage is still to be determined. These factors depend on the concentration of the drug, which is determined by the dose, the route of administration and the mechanisms of interaction. Another important determinant is the physiological state of the person being affected and the sensitivity of relevant cells.

THC interacts with common drugs. It increases the depressive effects of psycho depressants like alcohol, sedatives and opiates. These interactions are most likely mediated by the brain. Interactions of THC and stimulants like caffeine, nicotine and cocaine are complex, with occurrence of addictive and conflicting effects, depending on dosage and time intervals between ingestion.

A notable and rapid tolerance to most of the physical (functional) and psychological effects of THC develops in animals and man. This tolerance, which has a metabolic and tissue component, may not develop into some of the non-specific cellular effects of the drug. There is some cross-tolerance between THC and ethanol, and between THC and barbiturates. Withdrawal symptoms develop after termination of heavy cannabis administration on a daily basis. These symptoms are more noticeable after pure administration.

THC has been classified among the dependence-producing drugs that have the following characteristics. They:

- induce symptoms of reversible neuropsychological and neurobehavioural toxicity;

- induce a primary pleasurable reward and diffuse unpleasant feelings;

- intensify or induce craving for the drug and drug-oriented behaviour; and

- Induce tolerance.

Abrupt interruption is associated with some withdrawal symptoms. Long-term use is associated with increased incidents of mental impairment.

PHARMACOKINETICS

The absorption, distribution, metabolism and elimination of delta-9-THC is dependent on the length of time that THC and its metabolites remain in the body. No significant difference has been found in the metabolism, disposal and kinetics of THC between the human male and female. The absorption, distribution, metabolism and secretion of cannabis within the human body depend on the method of administration and potency of the specific plant. THC is absorbed into the blood faster when marijuana is smoked than when it is taken orally because of the large surface area of the lungs.

TOXICITY

Cannabis has been in use for about 6,000 years and it still remains a relatively safe drug. The toxicity of the cannabis resin and of THC is low. There have been very few reports of death by overdose. Furthermore, there was no proof that these deaths were due to THC.

In Britain, for example, more than 100,000 alcohol-related deaths and at least as many tobacco-related deaths occur each year. Also, commonly used drugs such as aspirin, paracetamol and some non-steroidal anti-inflammatory compounds are not safe in some cases as they may cause gastric bleeding and liver damage. It should be noted though, that no drug is free of toxic effects, so the risks always have to be balanced against the benefits.

Most pharmacological studies have focused on the toxic effects of cannabis on the central nervous system (CNS) and as such, acute cannabis toxicity results in difficulty with coordination, decreased muscle strength, decreased hand steadiness, postural hypotension, lethargy, decreased concentration, slowed reaction time, slurred speech and conjunctival injection.

Continued research is needed on other cannabinoids and more acceptable administration of cannabis to prevent the adverse pulmonary effects, associated with smoking. However, these research developments have to be balanced against the restrictive public policy decisions of government agencies.

3
HISTORY
OF THE USE OF
MARIJUANA

"What experience and history teach is this-that people and governments never have learned anything from history, or acted on principles deducted from it!"
- GEORGE HEGEL, 1770-1831

Historical data on the many uses of cannabis date back as far as 6,000 years. In fact, the first real description was given in a medical book prepared by the legendary Chinese Emperor, Shen Nung in 2737 B.C.

Cannabis is thought to have originated in Central Asia or China. Its use spread very quickly to Africa, India, Arabian countries, and Mediterranean countries, where it was mostly used for religious purposes. The Spaniards introduced it to Mexico and Peru, the French to Canada and the English to North America. It has been adopted everywhere, except in the Arctic regions and the wet, humid tropical forests.

Though cannabis or 'ta ma' was first used as food in China, generally its earliest uses

CHINESE EMPEROR SHEN NUNG, AUTHOR OF THE OLDEST KNOWN PHARMACOPEIA were as fibre, especially in India and North America, where it was used to make cord, ropes, threads, fabric, paper and oil. Medicinally, it was used as an all-purpose drug and especially as a sedative.

Cannabis was also used and is still being used in religious worship. Eastern Shirva worshippers, the Rastafarians in Jamaica and certain West African and Brazilian tribes seek a chemically mediated transcendence from the use of the drug which they believe will lead to insights and experiences not normally perceived. It is also used extensively as an aid to manual labour for example in India, Jamaica and Morocco.

The medicinal use of cannabis declined in the late nineteenth century because of the emergence of more effective medications the dosages of which were easier to control. Consequently, it began to lose the support of the medical profession and was left with the image of an intoxicant.

JAMAICA

The use of marijuana in Jamaica has been the subject of much research by a number of eminent scientists and researchers. Not only have they generated useful knowledge about this preparation and its effect on the

body, they have also brought new scientific insight into the traditional usefulness of this versatile plant. In fact the literature dates as far back as 1951 when W. Barrett published a book titled *Ganja*.

Several other authors, particularly Vera Rubin, have contributed significantly to the development of the literature. Her works include The *Ganja Vision in Jamaica* and *Ganja in Jamaica: A Medical -Anthropological Study of Chronic Marijuana Use*. The latter represents the first comprehensive account of the effects of chronic marijuana use in the Caribbean. The study has been frequently cited in the United States to support the view that chronic marijuana use is relatively harmless. Melanie E. Dreher has also done extensive study on marijuana's disadvantageous effects, marijuana use in rural Jamaica and child health.

The liberal use of marijuana is perhaps more widespread in Jamaica than any other Caribbean country. In fact, it was brought to Jamaica in the mid-nineteenth century by the Indian indentured workers and has since been part of our popular culture.

FOLK USE

In Jamaica, cannabis is popularly known as marijuana or ganja, and is an established folk medicine. It is brewed and the tea taken as a tonic or crushed and applied as an ointment to cure many common and some serious conditions. There are many Jamaicans who have cooked with marijuana or used it in baking. It is important to note that the ardent ganja users and many other people have sanctioned the use of these ganja preparations and many have testified to their effectiveness.

Many common preparations include:

- Soaking the bud or the green leaves in white (overproof) rum to be used for the relief of stomach ache, toothache and the symptoms of asthma. For those who have an aversion to the taste of white rum, this preparation is usually mixed with fruit juice. For the treatment of toothache, cotton is usually soaked in the mixture and placed on the tooth, or the fingertips are wetted in order to massage the mixture into the gum surrounding the tooth.

- The leaves are brewed to make tea which many use as a tonic or for the relief of common ailments such as those described above.

- The leaves are crushed and pureed with butter/margarine to make marijuana butter, as a spread for bread or to bake cakes and cookies.

- The leaves are also used in the making of soup.

THE RASTAFARIAN LINK

In an important sense, marijuana use is a 'normal' part of Rastafarian culture. Rastafarianism, which was founded in the late 1930s, represents the most obvious example of the use of cannabis for religious purposes. In other words, the smoking of marijuana or ganja lies at the core of this movement. The movement celebrates the heritage of African-Jamaicans and has spread from Jamaica to the African Diaspora, particularly Ethiopia. In fact, Marcus Garvey, through his teachings paved the

SOME HOME-MADE GANJA PREPARATIONS

way for Rastafarianism by identifying Ethiopia as a symbol of freedom, sovereignty and African spirituality.

Rastafarians use ganja as an aid to work. It is described as the 'healing of the nation,' the 'wisdom weed' of divine origin and as an 'elixir vitae.' These views are substantiated by alleged references in the Bible and by any favourable social commentary. But the connection between Rastafarianism and the ritual/spiritual smoking of ganja may be more profound than it appears to be, in the sense that they believe that the smoking of marijuana in a ritual manner cleanses both the body and the mind. It prepares the user for meditation, prayer, the reception of wisdom, and communal harmony with others.

As a result, over the years, Rastafarians have validated and fortified their commitment to its usage and have continued to argue for its legalization as a religious sacrament. In many instances, they have challenged the legal system in this regard.

REGGAE MUSIC AND THE LEGALIZATION DEBATE

However, one of the more popular approaches is the use of reggae music to argue for the legalization of this herb. Reggae music, which has achieved international acclaim, was made popular on the world stage by the late Bob Marley, and others who followed in his footsteps. Noted reggae artistes, such as Peter Tosh, Jacob Miller, and more recently Bounti Killa, have been at the forefront of using the music to make the argument for legalization. The late Peter Tosh, in particular, has received much publicity in this regard, and some may argue that this was his major cause.

It is interesting to note that many songs were banned from Jamaican airwaves because the lyrics advocated the legalization of marijuana. (See Appendix 11-B for a list.)

Marijuana is grown in Jamaica on steep tiny fields unsuitable for mechanized cultivation. In the first three weeks, the seedlings are watered daily and protected with pesticides. All that is required thereafter is occasional budding until the plant reaches maturity. Two crops per year are possible.

The various grades of marijuana are as follows:

KALI
Matured plant, having seeds and strong scent. This type is the most potent and expensive.

SEEDED BUSH
The stage before full maturity. This is better for smoking but not as potent as Kali.

GREEN GANJA
This refers to the freshly cut bush and can be of the Kali or seeded bush variety. Greatest use is in medicinal prescriptions and teas.

BUSH WEED
Immature, pale green. This is less potent and not as smooth for smoking.

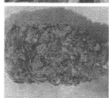

CURED GANJA
Kali or seeded bush dried by sunlight for about three months. This enhances its potency.

THE REST OF THE WORLD

The first ethnographic description of a cannabis-smoking device in world literature was found in Central Asia. Accordingly, the ritual intoxicant use of cannabis to communicate with spirits or ward off evil is found in ancient China, India, Central Asia, and Europe before the Christian era.

The Scythians may have introduced the ritual use of cannabis to the Middle East, but it was the Greeks and Romans who mostly spoke of cannabis as a fibre and as medicine.

CHINA

Ancient books on China state that the cannabis seed was eaten as food. According to legend, even Buddha existed for six years under the Bo Tree awaiting enlightenment, eating one cannabis seed per day. The early Chinese thought that if they ate cannabis, it would result in hallucinations and help them to communicate with spirits. This belief gave rise to its religious use.

AN 1843 HASHISH SMOKER FROM M. VON SCHWIND'S *ALBUM OF ETCHINGS*

Hua Ta'o, the founder of Chinese surgery (A.D. 110-207) used a mixture of hemp and wine as an anaesthetic during surgery. The world's oldest Chinese pharmacopoeia listed more than 100 illnesses treated with cannabis, such as female weaknesses, gout, rheumatism, malaria, beri-beri, boils, constipation and absent-mindedness. Later in the tenth century, it was described as having a spicy taste and being toxic. It was used in the treatment of wasting diseases and injuries, cleansing the blood, cooling temperature and discharging pus.

Cannabis was also used as an antiemetic, antibiotic, antihelmintic, leprosy treatment, and for healing haemorrhages.

INDIA

Cannabis has been associated with magical, medicinal, religious and social customs in India for thousands of years. It is thought that the religious use of cannabis preceded its medicinal use. The Indians believed that it promoted good health and long life. It was also used as an intoxicant and as incense.

Cannabis was recorded as being used as an appetite stimulant, digestive aid, analgesic, sedative, fever reducer, diuretic, tonic, disinfectant, an aphrodisiac and a food and supplement creator. It was also used to dry the mucous membranes, relieve congestion and diarrhoea, control dandruff and cure venereal disease.

There are testimonies of its therapeutic uses in the treatment of cramps, spasms, convulsions, headache, hysteria, neuralgia, sciatica, tetanus, hydrophobia, ague, cholera, dysentery, leprosy, brain fever, gonorrhoea, hay fever, malaria, asthma, whooping cough, earaches, hunger, stress, toothaches and extractions, bronchitis, tuberculosis, flatulence, dyspepsia, diabetes, delirium tremens and impotence.

However, despite its many uses, the Indian Hemp Commission was established, in 1893-1894, to examine the full use of cannabis because of concerns about its use as an intoxicant.

ANCIENT MIDDLE EAST

The first recorded use of cannabis in the Ancient Middle East was as an eye medication. The drug was also used extensively in salves for swellings and bruises, for impotence, arthritis, kidney stones, female ailments, in childbirth, as an ointment for bandages and for the elimination of witches. It was also used as incense.

Hemp has been used for over a thousand years as a textile and as medicine in Arabia, Mesopotamia, Persia, and Egypt. Arabian scientists were several centuries ahead of the current knowledge of the curative powers of cannabis. Therefore information found in Arabic literature could be considered as a possible basis for future research on the potential uses of cannabis and hemp seeds.

Arabian physicians knew cannabis and used it as a diuretic, anti-emetic, anti-epileptic, purge, carminative, anti-inflammatory, painkiller and anti-pyretic, anti-parasitic, treatment of ear and skin diseases, abscesses and tumours, vermicide and vermifuge, liquification and purging of humors, treatment of the hardening and contraction of the uterus.

According to Simon Wills in the book, *Cannabis,* there are no obvious references to cannabis in the Bible. However, he stated that the neighbouring Assyrians were known to have used cannabis widely for a variety of medicinal purposes.

Cannabis was administered orally for a variety of reasons including the treatment of impotence and depression, topically for bruises, by inhalation for a disease assumed to be arthritis, and in various forms to ward off evil. In the later stages of the Roman occupation, cannabis was used in Jerusalem.

MODERN MIDDLE EAST

It has been said that cannabis relieves earaches, epilepsy, seizures, dystonia, flatulence, dandruff and other convulsive and neurological disorders. It is thought that it can be used as a diuretic and to aid digestion.

ANCIENT GREECE AND ROME

Cannabis was not used much as an antioxidant or grown as a plant for fibre in Ancient Greece and Rome. However, it was sometimes drunk with wine and myrrh to give 'visions'. It was also used for inflammations, appetite stimulation, earaches, joint pains, gout, gas and burns. Greeks and Romans were of the view that cannabis would lessen one's sexual potency and cause headaches

EUROPE

Europe knew little about cannabis during the Renaissance period in the Middle Ages, even though hemp had been cultivated in Europe since Roman Times. However, the demand grew in England during the Elizabethan period, though it was said to cause sterility. It was later used to treat dry cough, jaundice, diarrhoea, colic, gout, hard tumours, joint pain, burns, worms and also as an antibiotic. Yet it was not until 1798 that there was serious investigation of the social, religious and medicinal uses of cannabis. In the eighteenth century, the fibre was used to make sails for ships, textiles and rope.

During the nineteenth century it was used to treat rheumatism, convulsions, vomiting and diarrhoea associated with cholera and muscle spasms of tetanus and rabies. The first mention in European clinical literature of cannabis was an antiemetic. Cannabis was also used as an appetite stimulant, analgesic, antidepressant, tranquilizer, antiasthmatic, antiepileptic, antispasmodic, prophylactic, neurological disorders, childbirth analgesic, topical anaesthetic, antibiotic, oxytocic (stimulates uterine contractions in childbirth and as a withdrawal agent for opiate and alcohol addiction.

Queen Victoria's physician found that it was useful in cases of senile insomnia, dysmenorrhoea, neuralgia, migraine headaches, and muscle spasms. He thought it was not as useful in asthma, alcoholic delirium and depressions, joint pains, and epilepsy.

AFRICA

The inhabitants of Africa have been smoking cannabis for at least six centuries. The plant was used as a remedy for snakebites, malaria, fevers, blood poisoning, anthrax, dysentery and asthma.

Women also used cannabis to induce partial stupefaction before childbirth.

THE AMERICAS

The English spread hemp cultivation among their colonies; first in Canada in 1606, to Virginia in 1611 and then to New England in 1632. Before the revolution, hemp fibre was used to make clothes in North America. Cannabis was already in general usage on Central and South America when the Spanish Conquistadors arrived in the sixteenth century. The Spaniards led the cultivation of cannabis for its fibre in Chile from 1545.

THE DECLARATION OF INDEPENDENCE. IT WAS SUMMER OF 1776 AND HEMP MADE HISTORY BY PROVIDING THE PAPER ON WHICH THE DECLARATION WAS PRINTED. *THE GREAT BOOK OF HEMP,* 1996

Ganja smoking in the United Kingdom

BRIXTON, ENGLAND is now an official Ganja Smoking Zone. Put that in your pipe and smoke it! It's true, you will no longer be arrested for smoking ganja in Brixton. Even in public. Neither will you be charged for possession of small amounts of ganja, deemed for personal use. On the surface the British government say this is so that the Police Force can concentrate or a crack down on crack cocaine and other more serious drug trades. But I say halleluiah, it's about time! Frankly it's a victory for Jamaican culture versus English law. It just goes to prove how via a process of attrition you can change perceptions and law, even in another man's country, to accommodate your own way of thinking. It also shows how white guilt can play a part in such an issue.

YARDIE: "Yow! Dis a fi we culture, awhoa!"

ENGLISHMAN: "It may be against our laws but those chaps are perfectly entitled to celebrate their culture! After all Britain is culturally diverse and we did take them from their homeland." And why not? Everyone allows the English to visit a country, lose at sports, then drink till drunk, fight and throw up all over the place. So what's wrong with us calmly smoking a spliff and listening to some Reggae music? Credit where credit is due, Rastafarians have made the difference. Decades of dreadlocks standing in British docks, pleading religious grounds for their possession of ganja, has finally paid off.

RASTA: I & I just have a likkle personal herb which I smoke because it is my religion to get irie, your honour.

JUDGE: But you have three kilos in your possession.

RASTA: I & I are very devout and need to meditate a lot your honour. The question of legalisation and decriminalisation has become such a burning issue in Britain it's been debated in the House. Tony Blair's father-in-law

JAMAICAN PALEFACE

TONY HENDRIKS

admitted smoking it upstairs in his daughter's house. And Tory leaders have been filling papers with ganja recently. Newspapers, not rolling papers. It certainly would be huge if Britain did decriminalise Ganja. We might even see someone actually "Lightin' up a chalice inna Buckingham Palace".

Instead of merely banning our bananas the EU might finally buy some herb. Quick Jamaica, before it's too late, we gotta get there first and legalise the Collie Weed and cultivate it. Face it, our agricultural sector went to pot ages ago! Sugar salt from time! While ganja is a hardy perennial cash crop, the best of which makes Blue Mountain Coffee look ordinary. Legalising ganja is the best chance we have of paying off the debt we owe to the IMF, World Bank and MCC. (Medellin & Cali Cartels) Forget NAFTA, let's sign GANJA, the Ganja Agriculturalist's National Jamaican Association. If we don't capitalise on it others will! We can't trust the USA. Their President's name is Bush Coincidence? I think not. One minute it'll be 'Vote Bush' the next it'll be 'Smoke Bush'! Before you know it the USA will be growing the crop they've demanded we destroy for years and push us out of the market.

The DEA and CIA will deal in drugs, overtly for a change rather than as a smoke screen, but it'll be too late for us to cry foul! In case you wonder why I'm not writing about Jamaica's mayhem, it's because war is everywhere. Bradford burns by Muslim hands while Ulster Christians celebrate their Peace Treaty and Ceasefire by throwing petrol bombs and shooting each other. Summer's always a riot in Europe. The weather's warmer for one thing and winter clothes restrict your throwing arm for another.

■ *Tony Hendriks can be reread at www.JamaicanPaleface.com or e-mailed androundly chastised via JamaicanPaleface@aol.com 2001.TonyHendriks.*

It seems that the early colonists did not use hemp for its psychoactive effects. It is evident though that people like George Washington were aware of its medicinal properties. During the nineteenth century, cannabis was used (but rarely) as an antispasmodic. However, its popularity waned during the mid-nineteenth century and was only used regularly in a few large cities by local groups of Mexicans and by African American jazz musicians.

The first American clinical conference on medical marijuana held in 1860 noted that cannabis was found to be useful for treating stomach pain, childbirth psychosis, chronic cough, and gonorrhoea, loss of appetite, sleep disorders, muscle spasms, nerve disorders and general pain.. It was also found to be an aphrodisiac, and an analgesic for inflammatory or neuralgic pains. It was recommended specifically for neuralgia, gout, rheumatism, tetanus, hydrophobia, convulsions, cholera, hysteria, mental illness, delirium tremens, uterine haemorrhage, childbirth, depression, cough, and bladder problems, sexually transmitted diseases, eczema, hypnosis, sedatives and diarrhoea.

During the early decades of the twentieth century, immigrants from Mexico brought marijuana with them when they migrated to the USA, which consequently led to its prohibition. It came first to New Orleans and some other southern cities and then slowly spread to some of the major cities.

In the early twentieth century cannabis was used as a sedative or hypnotic in insomnia, senile insomnia, melancholia, mania, delirium tremens, chorea, tetanus, rabies, hay fever, bronchitis, pulmonary tuberculosis, coughs, paralysis agitans, exophthalmic goitre, bladder spasms and gonorrhoea. It was also used as an analgesic in headaches, migraine, eye-strain, menopause, brain tumours, tic douloureaux, neuralgia, gastric ulcer, indigestion, tabes, multiple neuritis pain, nodular lesions, uterine disturbances, dysmenorrhoea, abortion, postpartum haemorrhage, acute rheumatism, eczema, senile pruritus, tingling, gout and dental pain. Other uses were to improve appetite and digestion, anorexia, gastric neuroses, dyspepsia, diarrhoea, dysentery, cholera, nephritis, hematuria, diabetes mellitus, cardiac palpitations, vertigo, sexual atony in females and male impotence.

Medicinal use of cannabis decreased in the 1930s, as it was replaced by synthetic drugs. Strong public reaction and a campaign by the media led to a federal anti-marijuana law in the USA. In 1937, the Marijuana Tax Act was passed despite the 28 medicinally approved marijuana preparations and the medicinal potency reported by organizations such as the American Medical Association. However, the drug had already been made illegal in many states. In 1994, the U.S. District Court of Appeals in Washington DC, issued findings that cannabis has no medicinal value.

The Controlled Substances Act of 1970 placed illegal drugs in one of five schedules. Cannabis and its derivatives were placed in Schedule 1, which include drugs with a high potential for abuse, having no medicinal use and not prescribable. Subsequently, it was found to be beneficial in glaucoma and cancer treatment. The successful use of cannabis in cancer treatment led to the marketing of an expensive synthetic tetrahydrocannabinol, Marinol. This drug was listed as a Schedule 11 drug, having potential abuse but prescribable for specific indications although tightly regulated and though the plant and THC extracted from the natural sources remained in Schedule 1.

The proven antiemetic value of cannabis led to its use by AIDS patients in the1980s. Cannabis is now on the list of approved medicines in California and Arizona, among other states of the USA, which means that it is legal for doctors to prescribe it and patients to use it. The situation is complicated by Federal Law which prohibits its use

TODAY

Today, marijuana is mostly used for its psychoactive effects. It is also widely used for its folkloric traditions. There is limited medicinal use of cannabis outside an experimental context. Although cannabis had been reported to produce a great deal of possibly useful medicinal effects, these have either not been sufficiently investigated, or have been replaced by the use of other more readily available and convenient drugs. However, it is because of its complexity, its physiological unreliability and instability of the potency of the natural products that has led to the disapproval of ganja in modern western medicine.

Finally, cannabis and its products are not receiving the expected medical applications because established drugs have become cheaper, and in some cases other natural medical drugs, purer and much easier to study. The medicinal uses of marijuana that are now being researched include the treatment of the following:

- Vomiting and appetite loss
- AIDS Wasting Syndrome
- Anticonvulsant effects
- Epilepsy
- Multiple Sclerosis
- Spinal cord injuries, Paraplegia and Quadriplegia
- Other Movement and Muscle Spasm Disorders
- (Menstrual Cramps, Labour Pains, Intestinal Cramps,
- Tourette's Syndrome, Dystonia, Black Widow Spider Poisoning)
- Intra-ocular Pressure (Glaucoma)
- Bronchospasm (Asthma)
- Analgesia and inflammation
- Migraine
- Arthritis and Rheumatism
- Psychological disorders

- Clinical depression

- Anxiety

- Insomnia

- Drug and Alcohol Dependency

- Autoimmune inflammatory diseases

- Infections

- Tumours

- Choreas, Parkinson's Disease and Cerebral Palsy

- Fibromyalgia

IS
MARIJUANA
SAFE?

The question concerning the safety of marijuana is coloured by issues of morality and public policy. It can be argued that scientists, who should be objective in their approach in the answering of this question, have consciously or unconsciously designed and manipulated their research in the quest for fame and fortune, or more importantly have been guided by a moral commitment to prove that cannabis is harmful or unharmful to mankind. According to a National Household Survey on Drug Abuse, kids who frequently use marijuana are almost four times more likely to act violently or damage property and also five times more likely to steal than those who do not use the drug. Due to tolerance build up, marijuana can lead users to consume stronger drugs to achieve the same unwanted conditions that prompted him to take marijuana in the first place.

Marijuana itself does not lead the person to the other drugs: people take drugs to get rid of unwanted situations or feelings. Marijuana masks the problem for a time (while the user is "high".). When the "high" fades, the problem, unwanted condition or situation returns more intensely than before. The user may then turn to stronger drugs since marijuana no longer "works".

As a result, much warning has been given to the effect that cannabis is an extremely dangerous drug that can cause chromosomal damage, impotence, sterility, respiratory damage, depressed immune response, personality changes and permanent brain damage.

However, most of these claims were refuted by Lynn Zimmer and John P. Morgan in their book entitled *Marijuana Myths, Marijuana Facts* (1997).

TOXICITY

THC, which is the psychoactive ingredient in cannabis, is a relatively safe drug. It has an extremely low toxicity and the amount that can enter the body through the consumption of cannabis plants poses no threat of death. Research has shown that laboratory animals (rats, mice, dogs, monkeys) can tolerate doses of up to 1000 milligram per kilogram (1000 mg/kg). This is equivalent to a person weighing 70 kilogram (70 kg) swallowing 70 grams (70 g) of the drugs. Despite the widespread and illicit use of cannabis, there has been very few, if any, documented evidence of people dying from an overdose. Long-term exposure to cannabis has also been studied and there is no evidence to support any adverse side effects of toxicity on the organs of the body.

"The toxicity levels of cannabis compounds are estimated at 40,000, meaning that a subject would have to ingest 40,000 times the regular dose to induce death. "In layman's terms," according to *The New England Journal of Medicine,* 'a smoker would theoretically have to consume nearly 1500 pounds of marijuana within about fifteen minutes to induce a lethal response. "While that amount of consumption is certainly an impossible feat, in comparison, legal prescription medications cause thousands of deaths per year. Common household drugs are much more lethal than marijuana. For instance, a lethal dose of caffeine is equal to about 100 cups of coffee. In 2008, The Canadian Medical

Association Journal published a review of research spanning 30 years, concluding that there are no serious adverse effects of cannabis use. Contaminants, however, are known to be hazardous, especially to those suffering from immune disorders. The United Kingdom government reported in 2006 that the use of tobacco, alcohol and prescription drugs are more harmful than that of cannabis, but a study published in 2007 comparing the properties of mainstream and sidestream cannabis smoke and that of tobacco concluded that cannabis had more hydrogen cyanide, ammonia and nitrogen oxides than tobacco.Tobacco however, contained higher levels of polycyclic aromatic hydrocarbons (PAHs), and other studies have found that some harmful compounds found in tobacco such as lead, arsenic, nicotine and polonium-210 are either non-existent or of small amounts in cannabis while refuting the difference between ammonia and hydrogen cyanide levels in cannabis and tobacco.

EFFECTS ON MENTAL ILLNESS OR MENTAL HEALTH

Cannabis use has been assessed by several studies to be correlated with the development of anxiety, psychosis and depression. Some studies assess that the causality is more likely to involve a path from cannabis use to psychotic symptoms rather than a path from psychotic symptoms to cannabis use. However, other studies assess the opposite or hold cannabis to only form parts of "casual constellation", while not inflicting mental health problems that would not have occurred in the absence of the cannabis use.

As much as 60 per cent of the mentally ill are suspected to be substance abusers, and many seem to prefer cannabis and alcohol. Dr. Stanley Zammit of Bristol and Cardiff universities reported, "Even if cannabis did increase the risk of psychosis, most people using the drug will not get ill."

"Nevertheless," he added, "we would still advise people to avoid or limit their use of this drug, especially if they start to develop any mental health symptoms or if they have relatives with psychotic illnesses." A recent study also showed that after a first psychotic episode following cannabis use, an individual is not likely to have recurring episodes if he/she discontinues its use.

In 2007, a meta analysis was published in the Lancet which concluded that cannabis users are 40 per cent more likely to be sufferers of a psychotic illness than non-users. In comparison, alcohol, as the only intoxicating drug with similar levels of popularity, has been linked to more than 65 percent of all suicides (UK study) and to general psychiatric mental health problems including depression, anxiety, schizophrenia, psychosis, psychoneurosis, post traumatic stress disorder, physical brain damage and more.

Over the past few years, research has strongly suggested that there is a clear link between early cannabis use and later mental health problems in those with a genetic vulnerability - and that there is a particular issue with the use of cannabis by adolescents.

BEHAVIOURAL EFFECTS

Socially deviant behaviour may be found more frequently in individuals of the criminal justice system compared to those in the general population, including non users. In response, independent studies have shown that there was no difference in grade point average, and achievement, between marijuana users and nonusers, but the users had a little more difficulty deciding on career goals, and a smaller number were seeking advanced professional degrees. Laboratory studies of the relationship between motivation and marijuana outside of the classroom, where volunteers worked on operational tasks for a wage representing a working world model, also fail to distinguish a noticeable difference between users and non-users.

CO-OCCURRENCE OF MENTAL ILLNESS

Studies have shown that a risk does exist in some individuals with a predisposition to mental illness of developing symptoms of psychosis.

The risk was found to be directly related to high dosage and frequency of use, early age of introduction to the drug, and was especially pronounced for those with a predisposition for mental illness. These results have been questioned as being biased by failing to account for medicinal versus recreational usage –critics contend it could be a causal relationship, or it could be connected to the criminalization of cannabis. Others contend that in some cases the effect of marijuana on an individual may be directly related to the reasons he/she smokes it, whether for social or medicinal purposes and that those who smoke it for social reasons are more likely to be mentally affected than those who do it for medicinal or religious purposes.

MEMORY

Studies on cannabis and memory are hindered by small sample sizes, confounding drug abuse, and other factors. The strongest evidence regarding cannabis and memory focuses on its short-term negative effects on short-term and working memory. Evidence also suggests that long-term effects exist, but these appear to be reversible except in very heavy users.

A 2008 review of the evidence surrounding the acute impact on memory concluded that cannabinoids impair all aspects of short-term memory, especially short-term episodic and working memory. One small study found that no learning occurred during the 2 hour period in which the subjects were "stoned". Long-term effects on memory may be balanced by neuroprotective effects of THC against excitotoxicity. Another 2008 study suggests that long-term, heavy cannabis use (5 joints daily/ 10years) is associated with structural abnormalities in the hippocampus and amygdala areas of the brain. The hippocampus, thought to regulate emotion and memory, and the amygdala, involved with fear and aggression, tended to be smaller in heavy and long term cannabis users than in controls (volume was reduced by an average of 12 per cent in the hippocampus and 7.1 per cent in the amygdala).

RESPIRATORY SYSTEM

Quantitative studies on the smoking of marijuana have suggested that when compared with tobacco smoking, marijuana smoking is associated with nearly a five-fold greater increase in the blood carboxyhaemoglobin level, and an approximately three-fold increase in the amount of water inhaled and retained in the respiratory tract. These observations may account for the previous findings that smoking only a few marijuana cigarettes per day (without tobacco) has the same effect on the prevalence of acute and chronic respiratory toxicity and the extent of tracheobronchial epithelial histopathology, as smoking more than 20 tobacco cigarettes per day without marijuana. Recent studies have also found that there may be adverse pulmonary effects associated with marijuana inhalation such as impaired lung function and respiratory infection, among others. Other studies maintain however, that there is no risk for lung cancer and other pulmonary diseases and there was even evidence of anti-cancer effects of cannabis in lung cancer.

PREGNANCY

Studies have been carried out to assess the potential damage on the developing foetus that has been exposed to cannabis or cannabinoids during pregnancy. The findings have revealed that it neither affected birth weight nor caused any abnormalities when the child is born. In fact, one study claimed that babies that are exposed to these two substances tend to be more advanced in their intellectual abilities

However, further studies of marijuana use and pregnancy suggested that infants whose mothers had positive urine assays for marijuana, when compared with infants of non-users, showed impaired foetal growth, characterized by lower birth weight, decrease in length and a slight deficit in visual responsiveness. No additional differences were found up to 24 months of age. At age 3, however, children of 'moderate' smokers had superior psycho-motor skills. At age 4, children of 'heavy' marijuana users (averaging 18.7 joints per week) had lower scores on one subscale of a standardized test of verbal development. By the age of 6, these same children scored lower on one computerized task- that measured 'vigilance'. On other scales and subscales, no differences were ever found.

Another study, where IQ tests were administered to marijuana exposed and unexposed three years old children, revealed that among African-Americans only, scores were lower on one subscale in those exposed during the 2nd trimester than those exposed during the 1st trimester.

An initial unconfirmed case-control study suggests that there is a 10-fold increased risk of leukaemia in the offspring of mothers who had smoked marijuana just before or during pregnancy.

Although it is sensible to advise pregnant women to abstain from using most drugs - including marijuana, the weight of scientific evidence indicates that marijuana has few adverse consequences for the developing human foetus.

INGESTION BY CHILDREN

The ingestion of cannabinoids by children can be potentially life-threatening. A 250-1000mg ingestion of hashish (up to 20% THC concentration) can result in obtundation within 30 minutes, apnea, bradycardia, cyanosis or hypotonia in children. Cannabinoid hyperemesis was recently defined in the literature to occur in adults and is characterized by severe nausea and hyperemesis (excessive vomiting) associated with chronic marijuana use, but in 2010, 2 cases of pediatric cannabinoid hyperemesis were also reported.

Canabis ingestion should be suspected if a combination of the following clinical signs are present:

- rapid onset of drowsiness,

- moderate pupillary dilation,

- marked hypotonia with other neurologic involvement

- presence of small dark particles (e.g., granules, leaves, or resin) in the mouth,

- significant lag in the eyelids,

- the absence of a history and/or symptoms indicative of trauma, central nervous system infection or seizures.

EARLY AMERICAN CHILDREN'S MEDICINE CONTAINING CANNABIS.
Photograph by Andre Grossman
THE GREAT BOOK OF HEMP, ROBINSON, 1996, P.44

MAJOR
EFFECTS

Fat man to thin man: "Hey there, from the looks
of you,
It seems that where you come from there is a famine"
Thin man to fat man: "And from the looks of you, you
caused it!"
   - ANONYMOUS

Legislation activists and many marijuana users believe smoking marijuana (pot) has no negative effects even though scientific research indicates that marijuana use can cause many different health problems.

The acute effects of a drug are short term (minutes to hours to days), while the chronic effects are long-term (days to weeks to months). The objective effects are readily observable and quantifiable, while the subjective effects are less obvious.

The most familiar short-term effect of cannabis is to give a "high" – a state of euphoric intoxication. This is precisely the effect sought, similar to the effect of alcohol.

In the case of marijuana, the following have been reported but not always substantiated.

SHORT-TERM EFFECTS

The short-term effects of cannabis are dependent on the method through which it is introduced into the body, whether smoked or orally, and the potency of the dose. The psychoactive effects usually take longer to manifest and last longer when taken orally as opposed to when smoked. Marijuana is more potent today than it was in the past. Growing techniques and selective use of seeds have produced a more powerful drug. This has increased the number of young pot smokers. Smokers tend to experience a few if not all of the following:

- Distorted perception (sights, sounds, time, touch)

- Problems with memory and learning

- Loss of coordination

- Trouble with thinking and problem-solving

- Increased heart rate, reduced blood pressure

- Dry mouth

- Reddening of the eye

Sometimes marijuana use can also produce anxiety, fear, distrust or panic.

EFFECTS ON THE BRAIN

The active ingredient in marijuana, delta-9-tetrahydrocannabinol or THC, acts on cannabinoid receptors on nerve cells and influences the activity of those cells. Some brain areas have many cannabinoid receptors, but other areas of the brain have few or none at all. Many cannabinoid receptors are found in parts of the brain that influence pleasure, concentration, memory, thought sensory and time perception, and also coordinated movements.

High doses of marijuana, when consumed via food rather than smoked can cause the following to the user:

- Hallucinations

- Delusions

- Impaired Memory

- Disorientation

According to an imaging study published in *the Journal of Psychiatric Research* (January 2009), adolescents and young adults who are heavy users of marijuana are more likely than non-users to have disrupted brain development. Pediatric researchers found abnormalities in areas of the brain that interconnect brain regions involved in memory, attention, decision-making, language and executive functioning skills. As adolescence is a crucial period for brain development and maturation, these findings are of particular concern.

The researchers caution that the study is preliminary and does not demonstrate that marijuana use causes the brain abnormalities. However, "Studies of normal brain development reveal critical areas of the brain that develop during late adolescence, and our study shows that heavy cannabis use is associated with damage in those brain regions," said study leader Manzar Ashtari, Ph.D., director of the Diffusion Image Analysis and Brain Morphometry Laboratory in the Radiology Department of The Children's Hospital of Philadelphia.

Ashtari and his colleagues performed imaging studies on 14 young men from a residential drug treatment center in New York State (all had a history of heavy cannabis use during adolescence), as well as 14 age-matched healthy controls. All the study subjects were males, with an average age of 19. On average, they had smoked marijuana from age 13 till age 18 or 19, and reported smoking nearly 6 marijuana joints daily in the final year before they stopped using the drug.

The study team performed a type of magnetic resonance imaging scan called diffusion tensor imaging (DTI) that measures water movement through brain tissues.

Among limitations of the study, such as a small sample size, five of the 14 subjects with heavy cannabis use also had a history of alcohol abuse, which may have contributed an effect. Also, it is possible that the brain abnormalities may have predisposed the subjects to drug dependence, rather than drug usage causing the brain abnormalities.

However, the research reinforces the idea that the adolescent brain may be especially vulnerable to risky behaviors such as substance abuse, because of crucial neural development that occurs during those years.

EFFECTS ON MENTAL HEALTH

Scientific evidence continues to support the fact that though many believe cannabis is relatively safe, there may be some potentially harmful effects associated with its long-term use. The effect of cannabis on mental health is probably the most researched area on the plant and its derivatives. Psychosis has long been known to be an effect but recent studies have further explored the relationship in depth. They have shown that there is a relationship between cannabis use and earlier onset of psychotic illness and also that its use plays a causal role in the development of the condition in some patients. Genetics also plays an important role in cannabis associated psychosis as evidenced in a few studies. It is apparent that there is a higher risk for the onset of schizophrenia and other psychotic disorders in some individuals than in others. One such investigation conducted by Ho and colleagues and presented in Schizophrenia Research in 2011, concluded that specific CB1 receptor (Primary mediator of marijuana effects in the brain) genotypes had more white matter insufficiencies with the use of the drug than in others. Therefore, some individuals are already genetically predisposed to mental illness and cannabis use may augment incidences.

The pro-psychotic effects of THC were found to possibly be related to impaired network dynamics and communication between different parts of the brain, specifically the right and left frontal lobes. Interestingly, another study in mice conducted by Assaf et al. In 2011 revealed that a pre- or post- conditioning treatment with extremely low doses of THC, several days before or after brain injury, may provide safe and effective long-term neuroprotection. The use of marijuana during the crucial period of adolescent brain maturation is also said by research-ers at the University Of Iowa Carver College Of Medicine in 2011, to possibly enhance schizophrenia susceptibility by neuro-modulatory influences of endocannabinoids. Furthermore, Meta analysis of these investigations conducted by researchers at the University of the Basque Country in 2011 concluded that the long-term effects of cessation of cannabis use after a first psychotic episode are positive. While some studies highlight the negative effects of cannabis and its derivative on mental health, others have sought to weigh them against the beneficial properties as it relates to its use in medicine.

EFFECTS ON THE HEART

One minor toxic side-effect of taking cannabis which merits attention is the short-term effect on the heart and vascular system. Within a few minutes after smoking marijuana, the heart rate increases (20-50 bpm) and the blood pressure drops. The heart rate can increase even more if other drugs are used at the same time. Due to the lower blood pressure and the high heart rate, risks for a heart attack are four times higher within the first hour after smoking marijuana. There is an elevated risk for stroke among young marijuana users, which is said to be a rare side effect and which was found in a 36-year-old man who after smoking a large amount of marijuana on 3 different occasions suffered a stroke. This was reported in a 2005 article in the Journal of Neurology, Neurosurgery and Psychiatry. Ischemic stroke is also associated with marijuana smoke but findings suggest that combustion products may be the cause as there is a similarity in the increase of the condition and heart disease with tobacco smoke.

The National Institutes of Health Biomedical Research Centre in Balti-more in 2008 found that there was a change in blood proteins associated with heart disease and stroke with the chronic smoking of marijuana.

EFFECTS ON THE LUNGS

Smoking marijuana, even infrequently, can cause burning and stinging of the mouth and throat, and cause heavy coughing. Scientists have found that regular marijuana smokers can experience the same respiratory problems as tobacco smokers do, including:

- Daily cough and phlegm production

- More frequent acute chest illnesses

- Increased risk of lung infections

- Obstructed airways

Marijuana contains more carcinogenic hydrocarbons than tobacco smoke and because marijuana smokers usually inhale deeper and hold the smoke in their lungs longer than tobacco smokers, their lungs are exposed to those carcinogenic properties longer.

One study found that marijuana smokers are three times more likely to develop cancer of the head or neck than non-smokers. Researchers believe that smoking marijuana is overall more harmful to the lungs than smoking tobacco.

OTHER HEALTH EFFECTS

Research indicates that THC impairs the body's immune system from fighting disease, which can cause a wide variety of health problems. Other studies have found that marijuana actually inhibited the disease-preventing actions of key immune cells and that THC increases the risk of developing bacterial infections and tumours.

Marijuana smoking has had repeated effects such as hunger, mood changes such as spontaneous laughter and drowsiness. These effects are thought to be related to the presence of cannabinoids.

The relationship between cannabis use and ischemic stroke was evaluated by Wolff V. et al. in 2011 and it was found that in young people, multifocal angiopathy (disease of the blood vessels) associated with consumption of the drug could be an important cause.

Additionally, Cannabinoid Hyperemesis is a recently described clinical syndrome characterized by the hyperemesis and severe nausea associated with chronic cannabinoid use. There is an increase seen in the number of reported cases of late.

LONG-TERM EFFECTS

Long-term use of marijuana can cause psychotic symptoms. It can also damage the lungs and heart, worsen the symptoms of bronchitis and cause coughing and wheezing. In addition, it may reduce the body's ability to fight lung infections and illness.

Cannabis can have long-term effects on cognitive performance, i.e. the performance of the brain, particularly in heavy users. While users may show little or no impairment in simple tests of short-term memory, they show significant impairments in tasks that require more complex manipulation of learned material (so-called "executive" brain functions)

All of the long-term effects of marijuana use are not yet known and there are studies showing serious health concerns. For example, a group of scientists in California examined the health status of 450 daily smokers of marijuana but not tobacco. They found that the marijuana smokers had more sick days and more doctor visits for respiratory problems and other types of illness than did a similar group who did not smoke either substance. However, findings so far show that the regular use of marijuana or THC may play a role in cancer and problems in the respiratory and immune systems.

CANCER

Many people today who smoke marijuana also smoke cigarettes and use other drugs. So it is somewhat difficult to determine whether marijuana alone causes cancer. Marijuana smoke contains some of the same cancer-causing compounds as tobacco, sometimes in higher concentrations. Studies show that someone who smokes five joints per day may be taking in as many cancer-causing chemicals as someone who smokes a full pack of cigarettes every day.

Tobacco smoke and marijuana smoke may work together to change the tissues lining the respiratory tract. Marijuana smoking could contribute to early development of head and neck cancer in some people.

University of Leicester researchers writing in the journal *Chemical Research in Toxicology* say they have found "convincing evidence" that cannabis smoke damages DNA and it could potentially increase the risk of cancer development in humans.

Using a newly developed highly sensitive liquid chromatography-tandem mass spectrometry method, the University of Leicester scientists found clear indication that cannabis smoke damages DNA, under laboratory conditions.

Researcher Raj Singh said: "There have been many studies on the toxicity of tobacco smoke. It is known that tobacco smoke contains 4000 chemicals of which 60 are classed as carcinogens. Cannabis in contrast has not been so well studied. It is less combustible than tobacco and is often mixed with tobacco in use. Cannabis smoke contains 400 compounds including 60 cannabinoids. However, because of its lower combustibility it contains 50% more carcinogenic polycyclic aromatic hydrocarbons including naphthalene, benzanthracene, and benzopyrene, than tobacco smoke."

It is well known that toxic substances in tobacco smoke can damage DNA and increase the risk of lung and other cancers. However, scientists were unsure whether cannabis smoke would have the same effect. The University of Leicester research focused on the toxicity of acetaldehyde, which is present in both tobacco and cannabis.

The researchers said that the ability of cannabis smoke to damage DNA has significant human health implications especially as users tend to inhale more deeply than cigarette smokers, which increases respiratory burden. "The smoking of 3-4 cannabis cigarettes a day is associated with the same degree of damage to bronchial mucus membranes as 20 or more tobacco cigarettes a day," the team adds.

These results provide evidence for the DNA damaging potential of cannabis smoke, implying that the consumption of cannabis cigarettes may be detrimental to human health with the possibility to initiate cancer development, the researchers wrote.

It was also theorized that marijuana use may have an effect on bone loss through a study done in rats at the University of Manitoba published in 2011.

IMMUNE SYSTEM

Our immune system protects the body from many agents that cause disease. It is not certain whether marijuana damages the immune system of people. But both animal and human studies have shown that marijuana impairs the ability of T-cells in the lungs' immune defense system to fight off some infections.

LUNGS AND AIRWAYS

People who smoke marijuana regularly may develop many of the same breathing problems that tobacco smokers have, such as daily cough and phlegm production, more frequent chest colds, a heightened risk of lung infections, and a greater tendency toward obstructed airways. Cancer of the respiratory tract and lungs may also be promoted by marijuana smoke, since it contains irritants and carcinogens.

Marijuana smokers usually inhale more deeply and hold their breath longer, which increases the lungs' exposure to carcinogenic smoke. Thus, puff for puff, smoking marijuana may increase the risk of cancer more than smoking tobacco does.

6

POTENTIAL
APPLICATIONS OF
CANNABIS AS MEDICINE

"O for a muse of fire, that would ascend
The brightest heaven of invention..."
- W. SHAKESPEARE (KING HENRY V)

Marijuana has been used medicinally around the world for thousands of years, and in Jamaica and the United States, in particular, for over 200 and 150 years respectively. In fact, it was listed in the US Pharmacopoeia until 1942 after which it was removed due to federal legislation which made the drug illegal in that country. Cannabis extracts and tinctures have also appeared in the British Pharmacopoeia and were available for more than 100 years (Table 3).

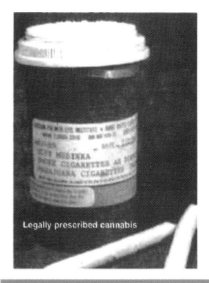

Legally prescribed cannabis

Photograph by Andre Grossman
THE GREAT BOOK OF HEMP, 1996 P. 49

TABLE 3 | BRITISH PHARMACEUTICAL CODEX 1949

EXTRACTUM CANNABIS | (Ext. Cannab.)

EXTRACT OF CANNABIS:	Cannabis in coarse powder 1000g Alcohol (90%)....a sufficient quantity Exhaust the cannabis by percolation with the alcohol and evaporate to the consistence of a soft extract. Store in tightly-closed containers, which prevent access of moisture. Dose: 16 to 60 milligrams

TINCTURA CANNABIS | (Tinct. Cannab.)

TINCTURE OF CANNABIS:	Extract of Cannabis 50g Alcohol (90%) to 1,000 ml

DISSOLVE

Weight per ml at 20, 0.842g to 0.852g
Alcohol content 83% to 87% v/v
Dose 0.3 to 1 ml

The wide range of the proposed therapeutic indications of marijuana (Table 4 & 6) has rivaled those of patent medicines in the first half of the twentieth century. However, like patent medicines, most if not all the proposed indications were based on anecdotal evidence and folklore (Table 5).

TABLE 4 | PROPOSED THERAPEUTIC INDICATIONS OF MARIJUANA

• Antiemetic	• Neuralgia
• Appetite Stimulant	• Antispasmodic, Muscle Relaxant
• Antitussive	
• Analgesic	• Antineoplastic
• Bronchodilator	• Antipyretic
• Anti-convulsant	• Topical Antibiotic
• Sedative, Hypnotic	• Anti-inflammatory
• Alcohol withdrawal	• Obsessive-compulsive disorder
• Anti-hypertensive	
• Melancholia	• Dysmenorrhoea

It should be noted though that it was not until the mid 1960s that a more formal pharmacologically-based study became possible. This was due primarily to the isolation and synthesis of THC component (Gaoni and Mechoulam, 1964; Isbell et al, 1964). Subsequently, most studies of medicinal marijuana have used THC or its homolog rather than smoked marijuana. It is the belief that this oversight has created and/or contributed to the current climate of controversy that surrounds the medicinal uses of marijuana.

TABLE 5 | CHAT 'BOUT MARIJUANA

Marijuana interferes with male and female sex hormones

Marijuana-related hospital emergencies are increasing

Marijuana is more damaging to the lungs than tobacco

Marijuana use during pregnancy damages the foetus

Marijuana use is a major cause of highway accidents

Marijuana's harms have been proved scientifically

Marijuana is more potent today than in the past

Marijuana offences are not severely punished

Marijuana causes Amotivational Syndrome

Marijuana policy in the Netherlands failed

Marijuana impairs memory and cognition

Marijuana impairs the immune system

Marijuana has no medicinal value

Marijuana gets trapped in body fat

Marijuana use can be prevented

Marijuana causes impotence

Marijuana is a gateway drug

Marijuana is highly addictive

Marijuana causes madness

Marijuana kills brain cells

Marijuana causes crime

The controversy originated from the various interpretations of the medicinal literature as it relates to the use of this substance. It ranged from those who, on the one hand, 'believed it to be a cure-all' given to us by nature to alleviate whatever ails mankind, to those who, on the other hand, strongly believe that the acceptance of any medicinal use would send the wrong signal to young people. The latter consider marijuana to be a menace and a stepping stone to the use of more dangerous drugs.

The primary focus of this review is on clinical studies, published in refereed medical journals which have evaluated the proposed medicinal uses of marijuana.

TABLE 6 | MEDICINAL AND QUASI-MEDICINAL USES FOR CANNABIS AND ITS DERIVATIVES

INDICATIONS FOR WHICH ONLY ANECDOTES OR REPORTS OF TRADITIONAL USE EXIST:
Aphrodisiac, muscular spasm, Huntingdon's chorea, jaundice, toothache, rabies, tetanus, earache, tumour growth, cough, hysteria, insanity, menstrual cramps, rheumatism, movement disorders, gut spasm, pyrexia, migraine headache, increasing urination, inflamed tonsils, uterine contractions, bladder retention, childbirth, spasm, parasite, fatigue, allergy, fever, herpetic infection, hypertension, joint pain, diarrhoea, malaria, forgetfulness, inflammation
INDICATIONS FOR WHICH THERE IS GENERAL ACCEPTANCE OF EFFICACY, AT LEAST IN SOME SPECIFIC PATIENTS, AT SOME STAGE OF THEIR DISEASE:
Glaucoma, chemotherapy, relief of muscle pain, lost appetite, induced nausea, anorexia, vomiting, spasms in particular in multiple sclerosis, AIDS patients

ANALGESIA

Pain is the most common symptom for which patients seek medical assistance. Pain associated with either structural or psycho physiological disorders can arise from somatic, visceral, or neural structures. Somatic pain results from the activation of receptors outside the brain and is transmitted back to the brain via peripheral nerves. Visceral pain results from the activation of specific pain receptors in the gut. It is characterized by a deep aching or cramping sensation. However, the source of the pain is often experienced at sites far removed from the site of the receptor activation. Neuropathic pain results from injury to peripheral receptors, nerves, or the central nervous system. It typically has a burning sensation and the skin feels abnormally unpleasant when gently touched, and often occurs in an area of sensory loss.

All of the currently available analgesic or pain-relieving drugs have limited effectiveness for some types of pain. Some are limited by dose-related side effects, and some by the development of tolerance or dependence. Cannabinoids, or any new analgesic, could potentially be useful under one of the following circumstances.

- They are medicinal treatments that are more effective than any currently available medication;

- They have a broad clinical spectrum of effectiveness and a unique side effect profile that differs from other analgesics;

- They have chemical interactions with other analgesics;

- They exhibit "side effects" which are considered useful in certain clinical situations;

- Their effectiveness is enhanced in patients who have developed tolerance to opioids.

Opiates, such as morphine and codeine, are the most widely used drugs for the treatment of acute pain. However, they are not consistently effective in chronic pain, as they often induce nausea, sedation and tolerance in some patients.

There have now been extensive animal and clinical studies which explore the efficacy of cannabinoid therapy in analgesia. The range of these studies includes conditions such as fibromyalgia, neuropathic pain, rheumatoid arthritis and multiple sclerosis among others. In general, cannabinoids were found to be mildly to moderately analgesic in most conditions but some studies reported excellent pain relief with administration . In light of the solid evidence that cannabinoids can reduce pain both in animals and humans, it is important for continuing research focused on exploring its application in other pain-related conditions and to gather further information on the already identified ones. This will facilitate the formulation of new drugs which are effective in pain relief and which lack some of the unwanted side effects associated with conventional drugs.

CLINICAL STUDIES WITH CANNABINOIDS

There have been three types of studies on the effects of cannabinoids on pain sensitivity in human volunteers:

- studies of experimentally-induced acute pain
- studies of post-surgical acute pain
- studies of chronic pain

EXPERIMENTALLY- INDUCED ACUTE PAIN

Early studies of cannabinoids in human volunteers using experimental models did not demonstrate consistent analgesia effectiveness. The studies suffered from two major procedural problems. First, they measured only the extremes of pain sensation-threshold (the lowest intensity at which a particular stimulus is perceived as painful) and tolerance (the maximum intensity of pain that a subject can withstand).

Most pain is experienced at the intermediate stage, where effects on pain suppression are most detectable. Modern methods of pain assessment in humans typically use ratings of the intensity of the sensation of pain, a measure that has been found to be superior to assessing the effects of a drug on the extremes of pain. The second problem was that they did not include a positive control, That is, they did not demonstrate the adequacy of their methodology by showing that an established analgesic, such as an opiate, was effective under the study conditions.

CANCER PAIN

The most encouraging clinical data on the effects of cannabinoids on chronic pain are from studies on pain associated with cancer. Cancer-associated pain can be as a result of inflammation, nerve injury, mechanical invasion of bone or other pain sensitive structure. It is severe, persistent, and often resistant to treatment with opioids. It is interesting to note that there were no reports of nausea and vomiting in this study. In fact, at least half of the patients reported increased appetite. A common limitation, however, is that there were no positive controls. That is, other analgesics that could provide a better measure of the degree of analgesia produced by THC were not used.

SURGICAL PAIN

No analgesic effect of THC has been found on surgical pain such as that induced by tooth extraction. However, that study had serious limitations:

- the tooth extraction included treatment with the local anaesthetic, lidocaine,

- the pain experienced during the procedure was assessed 24 hours later,

- there was no positive control,

CASE REPORTS AND SURVEYS

The few case reports of clinical analgesia trials for cannabinoids are not convincing. They are anecdotal surveys that raise the possibility that there might be a role for cannabinoids in certain patients who experience chronic pain syndromes with prominent spasticity.

MIGRAINE HEADACHES

There is clearly a need for improved migraine medications. Sumatriptan (Imitrex) is currently the best available medication for migraine headaches but fails to completely eliminate migraine symptoms in about 30 per cent of migraine patients. Marijuana has been proposed on many occasions as a treatment for migraine headaches but there is almost no clinical data on the use of marijuana or cannabinoids for migraine. There is, however a possible link between cannabinoids and migraine that is suggested by the abundance of cannabinoid receptors in the periaqueductal gray (PAG) region of the brain. The PAG is part of the neural system that serves to suppress pain and is thought to be involved in the generation of migraines. The link or lack thereof between cannabinoids and migraines might be illustrated by examining the effects of cannabinoids on the PAG. Recent results indicating that both cannabinoid receptor subtypes are involved in controlling peripheral pain, suggest that this might be possible. Nonetheless, the PAG offers only a weak structural association between cannabinoid effects on the brain and their possible role in migraine relief.

BASIC PAIN RESEARCH

A key question to address is whether there is any receptor selectivity for the analgesic efficacy of cannabinoids. Are the unwanted side effects (amnesia and sedation) caused by the same receptors in the same brain regions as those producing the analgesia? If the answer is yes, enhancing effectiveness will not solve the problem of sedation. Similarly, are the pleasant side effects due to an action at the same receptor? Can the feelings of well-being and appetite stimulation be separated by molecular design? The recent results indicating that both cannabinoid receptor sub-types are independently involved in controlling peripheral pain suggest that this might be possible and that further research in this area is clearly needed.

The variety of neural pathways that control pain suggests that an analgesic mixture might be effective.

CLINICAL PAIN RESEARCH

Clinical studies should be directed at patients who experience intense pain, especially where there is a demonstrated need for improved

management and where the particular side effect profile of cannabinoids holds promise of a decided benefit over current approaches.
The following patient groups should be targeted for clinical studies of
cannabinoids in the treatment of pain:-

- Patients on chemotherapy, especially for the treatment of
  mucositis, nausea and anorexia,

- Postoperative patients, as an opioid accessory to determine
  whether nausea and vomiting from opioids are reduced,

- Patients with spinal cord injury, peripheral neuropathic pain, or
  central post-stroke pain,

- Patients with chronic pain and insomnia,

- AIDS patients with cachexia, AIDS neuropathy, or any other
  significant intense pain.

In any patient group, an essential question to be answered is whether
the analgesic effectiveness of opioids can be enhanced. The strategy
would be to find the threshold analgesic effect with an opioid (as determined by pain intensity and tolerability of side effects) and then add
a cannabinoid to determine if additional pain relief can be obtained.
This would begin the investigation of potential drug combinations. As
with any clinical study on analgesic drugs, it will be important to investigate the development of tolerance and physical dependence. These
are not, of themselves, reasons to prevent the use of cannabinoids as
analgesics, but such information is essential to the management of any
drug to which patients develop tolerance or physical dependence.

Another question is to determine whether THC is the only or the best
component of marijuana for analgesia. How does the analgesic effect of
the plant extract compare to that of THC alone? If there is any difference,
it will be important to identify which combinations of cannabinoids
are the most effective analgesics. Some researchers have suggested a
combination of different cannabinoids after assessing them individually and finding that they had some effect.

In conclusion, the available evidence from both animal and human studies indicates that cannabinoids can produce a significant analgesic effect. One exception is the lack of analgesic effect in studies on experimentally induced acute pain. However, these studies were inconclusive due to limitations in their design.

Further clinical work is necessary in order to establish the magnitude of this effect in different clinical conditions and to determine if the effect is maintained over time. Although the usefulness of cannabinoids appears to be limited by side effects, notably sedation, there are other effects, such as anxiolysis, appetite stimulation, and perhaps antinausea and antispasticity effects that should be studied in randomized, controlled clinical trials. It is this particular combination of effects that might necessitate the development of cannabinoid drugs for certain clinical use.

ASTHMA

Asthma is a breathing disorder that arises when bronchial muscles go into spasm and the pathway to the lungs is blocked by mucus and swelling. A number of antiasthmatic drugs are available, but they all have drawbacks, limited effectiveness or side effects. As marijuana dilates the bronchi and reverses bronchial spasm, cannabis derivatives have been tested as antiasthmatic drugs.

In the nineteenth century, marijuana was prescribed as a bronchodilator. However, by the early twentieth century, its medicinal value declined with the introduction of synthetic drugs. During the last 20 years, potentially beneficial effects of smoked marijuana, oral, inhaled synthetic and inhaled delta-9-THC in asthma have been investigated in human volunteers.Smoking marijuana would probably not be a good way to treat asthma because of the chronic irritation of the bronchial tract by tars and other substances in marijuana smoke. Hence through research a better means of administration was found - THC in the form of an aerosol spray, which has been investigated extensively.

Asmasol, an extract from *Cannabis sativa*, is also used to treat coughs, colds and bronchial asthma. Asmasol was evaluated both in animal studies and in asthmatic patients in the Department of Pharmacology, Physiology and Medicine at the University of The West Indies at Mona, Jamaica. Oral administration resulted in improvements in breathing function from 30 minutes onward to a maximum of 60 minutes. Its actions are through beta-receptors and the active principle is a cannabinoid.

A limited amount of a modified form of Asmasol is now used in the management of chemotherapy-induced nausea and vomiting.

CHRONIC PAIN

Many persons live with chronic pain and many of these persons suffer from neuropathic pain (nerve-related pain). Neuropathic pain is a condition that is associated with numerous diseases, including diabetes, cancer, multiple sclerosis, and HIV. In most cases, the use of standard analgesic medications such as opiates and NSAIDS (non-steroidal anti-inflammatory drugs) is ineffective at relieving neuropathic pain.

Survey data shows that the use of cannabis is common in chronic pain populations, and recent clinical trials indicate that marijuana can significantly alleviate neuropathic pain. Recent clinical trials also demonstrated that smoking cannabis reduces neuropathic pain in patients with HIV by more than 30 per cent compared to placebo.

Researchers concluded: "the use of a standardized extract of Cannabis sativa...evoked a total relief of thermal hyperalgesia, in an experimental model of neuropathic pain ... ameliorating the effect of single cannabinoids." Collectively, these findings strongly support the idea that the combination of cannabinoid compounds, as present in (plant-derived] extracts, provide significant advantages in the relief of neuropathic pain compared with pure cannabinoids alone.

FIBROMYALGIA

Fibromyalgia is a chronic pain syndrome of unknown etiology. This disease is characterized by widespread musculoskeletal pain, fatigue, and multiple tender points in the neck, spine, shoulders and hips. Millions of persons, mostly Americans, are afflicted by fibromyalgia, which is often poorly controlled by standard pain medications.

Fibromyalgia patients frequently self-report using cannabis therapeutically to treat symptoms of the disease, and physicians – where legal to do so – often recommend the use of cannabis to treat musculoskeletal disorders. To date, there are a few clinical trials available in the scientific literature assessing the use of cannabinoids to treat the disease.

An evaluation, done by investigators at the Germany University, evaluated the analgesic effects of oral THC in nine patients with fibromyalgia over a 3-month period. The subjects in the trial were administered with daily doses of 2.5 to 15mg of THC, and received no other pain medicaton during this time. Among those who completed the trial, all reported a significant reduction in daily recorded pain and electronically induced pain.

Clinical and preclinical trials have shown that both naturally occurring and endogenous cannabinoids hold analgesic qualities, particularly in the treatment of cancer pain and neuropathic pain, both of which are poorly treated by opioids. As a result, some experts have suggested that cannabinoid agonists would be applicable for the treatment of chronic pain conditions unresponsive to opioid analgesics, such as fibromyalgia, and theorize that the disease may be associated with an underlying clinical deficiency of the endocannabinoid system.

Continuing studies on the effect of marijuana on Fibromyalgia has shown that it relieves some of its symptoms including pain and stiffness. Concurrent studies on the efficacy of cannabinoids in the treatment of fibromyalgia and other chronic pain conditions including rheumatoid arthritis and neuropathic pain further provide evidence that it is safe and works in pain relief.

DIABETES

Recent research has suggested that CBD has potential in the treatment of diabetic complications. It was also implicated in the treatment of cardiovascular disorders through its action on inflammation, cell death and fibrosis and the reduction of oxidative/ nitrative stress in a study done by Rajesh et al. in 2010.

GLAUCOMA

Glaucoma, after cataracts, is one of the leading causes of blindness around the world. In this disease, fluid pressure within the eyeball increases until it damages the optic nerve. The most common form of glaucoma is primary open-angle glaucoma (POAG), which is a slow progressive disorder that results in loss of retinal ganglion cells and degeneration of the visual fields and, ultimately, blindness. The mechanisms behind this disease are not understood but three major risk factors are known. They are age, race and elevated intraocular pressure (IOP).

The eye's rigid shape is normally maintained, in part, by IOP which is regulated by the circulation of a clear fluid, called the aqueous humour, which is located between the front of the lens and the back of the cornea. An elevated IOP is a risk factor for glaucoma as a result of obstruction to the outflow of aqueous humor fluid from the anterior chamber of the eye. However, the mechanism by which it damages the optic nerve and retinal ganglion cells remain uncertain.

The two leading possibilities are that elevated IOP interferes with the nutrient blood flow to the region of the optic nerve, and the transportation of nutrients, growth factors and other compounds within the optic nerve axon. If this interference continues, it will permanently result in atrophy and consequently blindness. As elevated IOP is the only known major risk factor that can be controlled, most treatments have been designed to reduce IOP. Reducing the rate of the fluid formation in the eye or increasing the drainage of fluid away from the eye will reduce IOP. Unfortunately, reducing IOP does not always arrest or slow the progression of visual loss.

Symptoms associated with the acute attacks of glaucoma include severe headaches and vomiting, halos and blind spots.

MARIJUANA IN THE TREATMENT OF GLAUCOMA

Both marijuana and THC have been shown to reduce IOP by an average of 24 per cent in people with normal IOP that have visual field changes. Topical treatments of cannabinoids have been ineffective in reducing IOP. Therefore, cannabinoids or marijuana can only reduce IOP when administered orally, intravenously, or by inhalation. An important factor in slowing the progression of glaucoma by the use of medications that reduce IOP is patient compliance with dosing regimens . In addition to lowering IOP, marijuana reduces blood pressure, palpitations and psychotrophy in glaucoma patients who inhale marijuana. There have also been reported cases of increased anxiety and tachycardia when an intravenous infusion of THC is given. All of these side effects are problematic, particularly for older glaucoma patients with heart and blood vessel disease.

The reduction of blood pressure can be substantial, and might adversely affect blood flow to the optic nerve. Many people with systemic hypertension have their blood pressure reduced to manageable and acceptable levels through medication, but this does not seem to affect IOP. In contrast, there is evidence that significant reduction in blood pressure (below normal levels) will adversely influence IOP. Reduced blood flow to the optic nerve of an eye with elevated IOP, or an optic nerve in poor condition makes it vulnerable to damage which could compromise a functional retina and be a factor in the progression of glaucoma.

Marijuana causes a dose-related, clinically significant drop in intraocular pressure that lasts several hours in both normal subjects and those with the abnormally high ocular tension produced by glaucoma. Oral or intravenous THC has the same effect, which seems to be specific to cannabis derivatives rather than simply a result of sedation.

Cannabis does not cure the disease, but it can retard the progressive loss of sight when conventional medication fails and surgery is too dangerous.

THERAPY FOR GLAUCOMA

| PRESENT THERAPY|

There are many effective options to choose from today to slow the progression of glaucoma. One such option is reducing IOP. The medicine is administered directly to the eye by drops or ointment. This makes it easier to control the dosage. These methods of administration also reduce many of the side effects of other medicines given by mouth. Currently, there are six classes of drugs used to treat the progression

of glaucoma, all of which reduce IOP. None of the early inhibitors are popular today because of their side effects, such as pupil constriction or dilation, brow ache, tachycardia and diuresis. Additionally, there are surgical options available today to lower IOP, including laser trabeculoplasty, trabeculectomy/sclerostomy, drainage implants, and cyclodestruction of fluid-forming tissues.

Dr. Manley West and Dr. Henry Lowe pioneered the research and development of medicinal marijuana for the treatment of glaucoma: Canasol and Cantimol. However it was Dr. Manley West and Dr. Albert Lockhart who finalized the commercial development from the original research. Cantimol is a combination of Canasol, an alpha agonist, and Timolol Maleate, a beta-blocker. It was formulated to give a rapid onset and long-term management of glaucoma. It is one of the world's first combinations of an alpha agonist and a beta-blocker in one bottle for the treatment of glaucoma. Both Canasol and Cantimol have proven to be effective in the treatment of glaucoma.

According to Dr. Lockhart, a consultant ophthalmologist, "Most patients with glaucoma have had to use two or more different drugs to control the condition. This new formulation makes the treatment simple, more effective and economical."

Canasol, which is also a cannabis-based drug, was developed in 1987. The research started some 10 years earlier after Professor West noticed that Jamaican fishermen who used ganja before going out to sea, claimed that they had better vision. A scientific paper presented by Dr. Lockhart, indicated that persons using cannabis had lower intraocular pressure than non-users,

Other effective medicines include the acetylcholine-like drugs pilocarpine or carbachol, which stimulate fluid outflow; the noradrenaline beta-receptor blocker, timolol; the alpha-adrenocepter drugs that reduce fluid formation; prostaglandin analogues that increase fluid outflow; and inhibitors of the enzyme carbonic anhydrase associated with ocular fluid formation.

| FUTURE THERAPY |

The next generation of glaucoma therapies will, in all likelihood, deal with neural protection, rescue, regeneration, or blood flow, where the optic nerve and neural retina are treated directly, rather than just lowering IOP. There is some evidence that a synthetic cannabinoid, HU-211, might have neuro-protective effects in vitro, which presents a potentially new approach that has nothing to do with IOP. HU-211 is commonly referred to as a cannabinoid, because its chemical structure is similar to THC. However, it does not bind to any known cannabinoid receptors.

Cannabinoids do substantially lower IOP. Yet it is not known if the endogenous cannabinoid system is a natural regulator of IOP. In summary although one of the most frequently cited medicinal uses of marijuana is the treatment of glaucoma, many deny its effectiveness. High intraocular pressure (IOP) is a known risk factor for glaucoma and can, indeed, be reduced by cannabinoids and marijuana.

The potential harmful effects of chronic marijuana smoking outweigh its modest benefits in the treatment of glaucoma. Attempts to make a topical preparation of THC or other cannabinoid that is easily tolerated by patients have had limited success to date.

The treatment of glaucoma is a lifetime proposition; therefore clinical studies should focus on systemic therapy. It is also hoped that future research will reveal a therapeutic effect of isolated cannabinoids. For example, it might be possible to design a cannabinoid drug with longer lasting effects on IOP and with less psychoactivity than THC.

CANCER

The potential of cannabinoids in the therapy of cancer attracts ongoing research worldwide as the disease is one of the leading causes of death. There is evidence from in vivo and in vitro studies that the endocannabinoid system has anti-tumor action in breast, prostate and bone cancers as summarized in an article by Guindon et al. in the British Journal of Pharmocology in 2011 which highlights its therapeutic implications. Endocannabinoids have been shown to inhibit cell proliferation and migration, induce apoptosis (cell death) and reduce tumor growth. Clinical cancer studies have also shown cannabinoids to have considerable anti-emetic and anti-tumor properties in recent times. Fewer studies have focused on its analgesic properties and those which have, did not find them to be as effective in pain relief as in other aspects of the disease. Further research examining the effects of pharmacotherapies which target the endocannabinoid system on cancer patients is warranted.

BREAST CANCER

Recent research has revealed that the endocannabinoid system plays a role in breast cancer by inducing apoptosis, regulating tumor growth and angiogenesis (growth of new blood vessels from pre-existing ones). Though the mechanism of action is not fully understood, cannabidiol was shown to increase apoptosis, reduce migration and inhibit cell proliferation in different cancer cell lines. Additionally, CBD reduced tumor size and decreased the number of lung metastases (spread of cancer cells) in mice injected with breast cancer cell lines. Studies have also shown that delta-9- THC and cannabinol are instrumental in the latter though others have reported that delta-9- THC failed in this respect as well as in inducing apopotosis. It can therefore be theorized that a combination of phytocannabinoids offer great potential for the treatment of breast cancer.

PROSTATE CANCER

Prostate cancer being the second most frequently diagnosed malignancy in men has also stimulated the scientific community and the utilization of cannabinoids in its treatment is at the forefront of research interests. In vitro studies which assess the effects of cannabinoids such as CBD, cannabigerol, cannabichromene, cannabidiol acid and THC acid have been conducted in different cell lines and all were found to inhibit cell proliferation. Putative endocannabinoids such as arvanil and noladin ether have also been evaluated and this effect is maintained. The mechanism of action of cannabinoids in prostate cancer cells has also been recently described. Through a specific signaling pathway following receptor binding, cell proliferation is inhibited and cell cycle arrest followed by apoptosis induced. Other signaling pathways were theorized to possibly be involved.

BONE CANCER

Bone cancer, which is also known as sarcoma, is also a very important form of cancer. In vitro studies in different bone sarcoma cell lines showed a reduction in bone resorption and induction of apoptosis with the administration of multiple cannabinoids or compounds derived from cannabinoids. Pain associated with bone tumors was also found to be reduced by endocannabinoids and the endocannabinoid system.

GLIOMAS

Gliomas (tumours in the brain] are especially aggressive malignant forms of cancer, often resulting in the death of affected patients within one to two years following diagnosis. There is no cure for gliomas and most available treatments provide only minor symptomatic relief.

Numerous preclinical studies and one pilot clinical study have demonstrated that cannabinoids have the ability to act as antineoplastic agents, particularly on glioma cell lines.

Through investigations in 2000, a report was done that the administration of both THC and the synthetic cannabinoid agonist WIN-55, 212, 2 "induced a considerable regression of malignant gliomas" in animals. Researchers again, in 2003, confirmed cannabinoids' ability to inhibit tumour growth in animals.

Recent colleagues reports that THC administration decreases recurrent glioblastoma multiforme (GBM) tumour growth in patients diagnosed with recurrent glioblastoma multiforme (GBM). In the first ever pilot clinical trial assessing the use of cannabinoids and GBM, investigators found that the intratumoral administration of THC was associated with reduced tumour cell proliferation in two of nine subjects. "The fair safety profile of THC, together with its possible anti-proliferative action on tumour cells reported here and in other studies, may set the basis for future trials aimed at evaluating the potential antitumoral activity of cannabinoids".

In addition to cannabinoids' ability to moderate glioma cells, separate studies demonstrate that cannabinoids and endocannabinoids can also inhibit the proliferation of other various cancer cell lines, including breast carcinoma, prostate carcinoma, colorectal carcinoma, gastric adenocarcinoma, skin carcinoma, leukaemia cells, neuroblastoma, lung carcinoma, uterus carcinoma, thyroid epithelioma, pancreatic adenocarcinoma, cervical carcinoma and lymphoma. Studies also indicate that the administration of cannabinoids, in conjunction with conventional anti-cancer therapies, can enhance the effectiveness of standard cancer treatments.

Consequently, many experts now believe that cannabinoids may represent a new class of anticancer drugs that retard cancer growth, inhibit angiogenesis and the metastatic spreading of cancer cells, and have recommended that at least one cannabinoid, cannabidiol, now be utilized in cancer therapy.

Anti-cancer effects have also been found in skin and lung cancers and though some studies have concluded there has been no evidence of lung cancer, chronic obstructive pulmonary disease or respiratory symptoms associated with smoking cannabis, other more recent ones have suggested there are adverse pulmonary effects associated with marijuana inhalation. These include: impaired lung function, damaged large airway mucosa, possible contribution to bullous disease, pneumothorax and respiratory infections.

There was however an association found between frequent marijuana use and testicular germ cell tumors by Trabert et al. in 2011. Further studies are however necessary to evaluate the role of cannabinoid receptors and endocannabinoid signaling in the disease.

HEPATITIS C

Hepatitis C is a viral disease of the liver that afflicts an estimated four million people in the States alone. Chronic Hepatits C is typically associated with fatigue, depression, joint pain and liver impairment, including cirrhosis and liver cancer.

Patients diagnosed with Hepatitis C frequently report using cannabis to treat both symptoms of the disease as well as the nausea associated with antiviral therapy. An observational study by the University of California at San Francisco (UCSF) found that Hepatitis C patients who used cannabis were significantly more likely to adhere to their treatment regimen than patients who didn't use it. Nevertheless, no clinical trial assessing the use of cannabinoids for this indication is available in the scientific literature.

Preclinical data indicates that the endocannabinoid system may moderate aspects of chronic liver disease and that cannabinoids may reduce inflammation in experimental models of hepatitis. However, other clinical reviews have reported a positive association between daily cannabis use and the progression of liver fibrosis (excessive tissue build up) and steatosis (excessive fat build up) in selected hepatitis C patients.

As a result, experts hold divergent opinions regarding the therapeutic use of cannabinoids for Hepatitis C treatment. In conclusion, investigators from Canada and Germany wrote that cannabis' "potential benefits of a higher likelihood of treatment success (for hepatitis C patients) appear to outweigh its risks." By contrast, other experts discourage the use of cannabis in patients with chronic hepatitis until further studies are performed.

HYPERTENSION

High Blood Pressure, or hypertension, afflicts an estimated 1 in 4 adults. This condition puts a strain on the heart and blood vessels and greatly increases the risk of stroke and heart disease.

Emerging research indicates that the endogenous cannabinoid system plays a role in regulating blood pressure, though its mechanism of action is not well understood. Animal studies demonstrate that anandamide and other endocannabinoids profoundly suppress cardiac contractility in hypertension and can normalize blood pressure leading some experts to speculate that the manipulation of the endocannabinoid system "may offer novel therapeutic approaches in a variety of cardiovascular disorders."

A review by Cuhna et al. in 2011 highlighted new pharmacotherapeutic opportunities for cardiovascular disorders through the endocannabinoid system. Not only has it been implicated in effects on heart rate, blood pressure, vasoactivity but also said to possibly play an important role in reducing cardiovascular risk in obese and dyslipidemic patients.

Research on the effects of cannabis on hypertension and other cardiovascular disorders has heightened over the last few years, but though in its early stages, the manipulation of the endocannabinoid system for therapy of the cardiovascular system is a promising area of study.

The administration of natural cannabinoids has yielded conflicting cardiovascular effects on humans and laboratory animals. The vascular response in humans administered cannabis in experimental conditions is typically characterized by a mild increase in heart rate and blood pressure. However, complete tolerance to these effects develops quickly and potential health risks appear minimal.

At this time, research assessing the clinical use of cannabinoids for hypertension is in its infant stage, though further investigation appears warranted.

NAUSEA AND VOMITING

Nausea and vomiting (emesis) occur under a variety of conditions, such as acute viral illnesses, cancer, radiation exposure, chemotherapy treatment, and post-operative recovery, during pregnancy, motion sickness, and poisoning. Both are produced by excitation of one of or a combination of the triggers located in the gastrointestinal tract, brain stem and higher brain centres. There are many cannabinoid receptors in the nucleus of the solitary tract, a part of the brain that is important in the control of emesis. Although the same mechanisms appear to be involved in triggering both nausea and vomiting, one can occur without the other.

Much more is known about the neural mechanisms that produce vomiting than those that produce nausea. This is because the act of vomiting is a complex behaviour involving coordinated changes in the activity of the gastrointestinal tract, respiratory muscles and posture; whereas nausea is a sensation primarily involving higher brain centres and lacks a discrete observable action. Most reports on the antiemetic effects of marijuana or cannabinoids on nausea and vomiting are based on chemotherapy-induced emesis.

CHEMOTHERAPY-INDUCED NAUSEA AND VOMITING

The use of effective chemotherapeutic drugs has produced cures in some cancer-related malignancies and retarded the growth of others. Unfortunately, nausea and vomiting are frequent side effects of these drugs. Nausea ranks behind hair loss as a major concern of patients who undergo chemotherapy, and many rank it as the worst side effect of chemotherapy. The side effects can be so devastating that patients often abandon therapy and suffer a diminished quality of life. As a result, the development of effective strategies to control the emesis induced by many chemotherapeutic agents is a major goal in the supportive care of patients with malignancies.

The mechanism by which chemotherapy induces vomiting is not completely understood. Studies suggest that emesis is caused by the stimulation of receptors in the central nervous system or in the gastrointestinal tract. This stimulation appears to be caused by the drug itself, a metabolite of the drug, or a neurotransmitter. In contrast with an emetic like apomorphine, there is a delay between the administration of chemotherapy and the onset of emesis. This delay depends on the chemotherapy agent; emesis can begin anywhere from a few minutes after the administration of an agent like mustine to an hour for cisplatin.

The most desirable effect of an antiemetic is to completely control emesis, which is currently the primary standard in testing new antiemetic agents. Patients accurately recall the number of emetic episodes, even with antiemetics that are sedating or affect memory. Thus complete control from the onset to the endpoint of an emetic episode is also a highly reliable method of evaluation.

It should also be noted that the frequency of emesis varies depending on the chemotherapeutic agent being used and this factor should be considered when choosing an antiemetic drug. Lastly, control of factors such as the influence of prior chemotherapy and balancing predisposing factors (i.e., gender, age, and prior heavy alcohol usage) among study groups is vital for reliability. Additionally, reliable randomization of patients and blinding techniques (easier when there are no psychoactive effects) are necessary to evaluate how to control vomiting and nausea.

Vomiting and nausea have been found in numerous studies to be regulated by manipulation of the endocannabinoid system both in humans and animals. Nausea associated with chemotherapy is more difficult to control and conventional pharmaceutical agents are not always as effective as patients would like them to be. Recent studies have re-explored that cannabinoids may be useful in controlling these symptoms.

THC/MARIJUANA THERAPY FOR CHEMOTHERAPY-INDUCED NAUSEA AND VOMITING

Cannabinoids are mildly effective in preventing emesis in some patients receiving cancer chemotherapy. Several cannabinoids have been tested as antiemetics, including THC and two synthetic cannabinoids, nabilone and levonantrodol. In addition, smoked marijuana has also been examined.

ANTIEMETIC PROPERTIES OF THC

The quality and usefulness of antiemetic studies depend on adherence to the methodological considerations outlined above. Many of the cannabinoid clinical experiences reported are not based on definitive experimental methods. In studies where THC was compared to placebo, THC was usually found to possess antiemetic properties. However, the chemotherapy drug used varied in most of the trials, and some of the studies consisted of small numbers of patients.

ANTIEMETIC PROPERTIES OF SYNTHETIC THC ANALOGUES

Nabilone (Cestamet) and levonantrodol were tested in a variety of settings, and had results similar to those of THC. While effectiveness was observed in several trials, no significant advantage emerged for these agents. As with the THC trials, nabilone and levonantrodol reduced emesis but not as well as other available agents in moderately to highly emetogenic settings.

ANTIEMETIC PROPERTIES OF CANNABIS

Marijuana has antiemetic effectiveness but its relative value has been difficult to determine.

Studies so far have not shown a clear advantage for smoked marijuana over oral THC, but neither reported data on the time course of antiemetic control, possible advantages of self-titration with the smoked marijuana, or the degree to which patients were able to swallow the pills.

It has been further reported that patients with severe vomiting would experience difficulty in swallowing or keeping down the pills long enough for them to take effect. The onset of the drug effect is much faster when THC is inhaled or injected rather than when it is administered orally. Although many marijuana users have claimed that smoked marijuana is a more effective antiemetic than oral THC, no controlled studies have yet been published that analyze this in sufficient detail to evaluate the extent to which this is the case.

SIDE EFFECTS ASSOCIATED WITH THC/MARIJUANA IN ANTIEMETIC THERAPY

Frequent side effects associated with THC and marijuana includes dizziness, dry mouth, hypertension, moderate sedation, and euphoria or dysphoria. The side effects of smoking marijuana include dizziness, dry mouth, confusion and anxiety. Dry mouth and sedation are the least troubling side effects to patients. Perhaps the most troubling side effects are orthostatic hypotension and dizziness, which could complicate or aggravate existing conditions

On the one hand, there is some amount of disagreement as to whether the psychoactive effects of THC are related to its antiemetic activity. On the other, some investigators believe that such psychoactive effects (euphoria and dysphoria) are often associated with improved antiemetic control. Nevertheless, consensus exists among most investigators that dysphoric effects are more common among patients who have not had prior experience with cannabinoids. This intolerance could be due to inexperience with smoking marijuana and should be an important consideration.

THERAPY FOR CHEMOTHERAPY-INDUCED NAUSEA AND VOMITING

| PRESENT THERAPY |

New types of antiemetics have emerged over the last ten years. They have drastically reduced the nausea and vomiting associated with cancer chemotherapy and literally transformed the acceptance of the drug, cisplatin, by cancer patients. These new antiemetics have few side effects when given on a short-term basis and are convenient in a variety of clinical settings.

Side effects of these antiemetic agents include headache, constipation and alterations in liver function. However, they are generally well tolerated by most patients.

ALTERATIONS OF ONCOLOGISTS TOWARD PRESCRIBING MARIJUANA

As with cannabinoids, smoked marijuana has proven to be effective but the degree to which it was effective was no better than that seen with the available antiemetic agents that are now considered to be marginally satisfactory.

| FUTURE THERAPY |

If improvements are to be made in therapy for chemotherapy-induced nausea and vomiting, it will require the discovery of agents that work through different mechanisms from existing antiemetics, including the serotonin antagonists.

It is theoretically possible that if THC is added to more effective regimens, it might significantly control emesis. Such combinations should aim to be as convenient as possible, especially as it relates to administration and at the same time producing very little side effects. The critical issue is not whether marijuana or cannabinoid drugs might be superior to the new drugs, but rather if there is a group of patients who might obtain additional or better relief from marijuana or cannabinoid drugs.

Finally, the control of nausea and vomiting that begins or persists 24 hours after chemotherapy remains ineffective even with the best antiemetic drug. The pathophysiology appears different from that of acute emesis and it is more likely to occur with a strong emetic agent. However, it varies with each patient. Treatment to prevent this emesis requires dosing after chemotherapy as well as before.

CHEMOTHERAPY-INDUCED NAUSEA

The goal of antiemetic medications is to prevent nausea and vomiting. Hence, antiemetics are typically given before chemotherapy, in which case, a pill is an effective form of drug administration. However, in patients already experiencing nausea and vomiting, pills are generally ineffective, because of the difficulty in swallowing or keeping it down, and the slow onset of the drug effect. This inhalation of a cannabinoid drug (preferably not smoking) would be best for treating chemotherapy-induced nausea.

However, most chemotherapy patients might be reluctant to use marijuana or THC as an antiemetic, as the psychoactive effect sought by those who use marijuana socially are unwanted effects in patients who use the drug therapeutically. In 1998, there were more effective antiemetic agents available than were available earlier and by comparison, cannabinoids are only modest antiemetics. However, when compared in terms of efficacy, marijuana taken either orally as THC or as smoked marijuana, is as effective in the control of nausea and vomiting associated with cancer chemotherapy as those antiemetics that are now being used.

Furthermore, since modern antiemetics likely act through different mechanisms, cannabinoids might be effective for people who respond poorly to currently used antiemetic drugs, or cannabinoids might be more effective in combination with the new drugs than either one alone.

For both reasons, studies of the effects of adjunctive cannabinoids on chemotherapy-induced emesis are worth pursuing for patients whose emesis is not optimally controlled with other agents.

Overall, the effects of oral THC and smoked marijuana are similar, but there are some differences. Such differences might be due to the methods of administration of THC, as well as the mixture of cannabinoids found in the marijuana plant.

Until the development of rapid onset antiemetic drug delivery systems, there will be some patients who suffer from acute emesis for whom standard antiemetic therapy is ineffective. For these patients, it is possible that any harmful effects of smoking marijuana for a limited period of time might be outweighed by its antiemetic benefits. Such patients should be evaluated on a case-by-case basis and treated under close medical supervision.

NEUROLOGICAL DISORDERS

Neurological disorders affect the brain, spinal cord, or peripheral nerves and muscles in the body. On many occasions marijuana has been proposed to offer a source of relief for three general types of neurological disorders. These are muscles spasticity, particularly for multiple sclerosis patients and spinal cord injury victims; movement disorders, such as Parkinson's disease, Huntington's disease, Tourette's syndrome and epilepsy. It is important to note that marijuana is not proposed as a cure for such disorders, but that it might help in the relief of certain associated symptoms.

MUSCLE SPASTICITY

Spasticity is the increased resistance to passive stretch of muscles and increased deep tendon reflexes. Muscles may also contract involuntarily. In some cases these contractions are debilitating and very painful, and require therapy to relieve the spasms and associated pain.

Marijuana's therapeutic uses are well-documented in modern scientific literature. Studies have indicated that marijuana provides symptomatic relief for a number of medical conditions, including nausea and vomiting, stimulating appetite, promoting weight gain, and diminishing intraocular pressure from glaucoma. There is also evidence that smoked marijuana and/or THC reduces muscle spasticity from spinal cord injuries and multiple sclerosis, and diminishes tremors in multiple sclerosis patients. Patients and physicians have also reported that smoked marijuana provides relief from migraine headaches, depression, seizures, insomnia and chronic pain, among other conditions. Clinical studies have also indicated some cannabis derived drugs such as Dronabinol and Sativex are effective in the treatment of muscle spasticity.

There are many reports that state that marijuana can relieve the spasticity associated with multiple sclerosis or spinal cord injury. Animal studies have also shown that cannabinoids affect motor areas in the brain that could influence spasticity.

MULTIPLE SCLEROSIS

Multiple Sclerosis(MS) is a chronic degenerative disease of the central nervous system (CNS) that causes inflammation, muscular weakness and a loss of motor coordination. Some nerve fibres become demyelinated (deinsulated with fibre) while others are destroyed. Scars are then formed (scleroses) resulting in plaques scattered throughout the white matter of the CNS. An increase in MS appears to be caused by abnormal immune activity. Overtime, MS patients typically become permanently disabled, and in some cases the disease can be fatal.

Clinical and anecdotal reports of cannabinoids' ability to reduce MS-related symptoms such as pain, spasticity, depression, fatigue, and incontinence are plentiful in the scientific literature – leading many MS-associated patient organizations, including the Multiple Sclerosis Societies of Britain and Canada, to take positions in favour of the drug's prescription use. Patients with multiple sclerosis typically report engaging in cannabis therapy, with one survey indicating that nearly one in two MS patients use the drug therapeutically.

Clinical data reports (2006), from an extended open-label study of 167 MS patients, found that use of whole plant cannabinoid extracts relieved symptoms of pain, spasticity, and bladder incontinence for an extended period of treatment without requiring subjects to increase their dose. Results in 2007, reported that the administration of cannabis extracts was associated with long-term reductions in neuropathic pain in selected MS patients. On average, patients in the study required fewer daily doses of the drug and reported lower median pain scores the longer they took it. These results would be unlikely in patients suffering from a progressive disease like MS unless the cannabinoids therapy was halting its progression, investigators have suggested.

It has been frequently reported by patients who use marijuana that it reduces muscle spasticity associated with MS. The subjective improvement, while intriguing, does not constitute unequivocal evidence that marijuana relieves spasticity. Survey data does not measure the degree of placebo effect, estimated to be as great as 30 per cent in the treatment of pain. Furthermore, surveys do not separate the effects of marijuana or cannabinoids on mood and anxiety from spasticity.

In general, these descriptive reports are not well supported by clinical data; but this is more due to the limitation of the studies than to negative results. There are no supporting animal data to encourage clinical research in this area, largely due to the lack of good animal models for spasticity as it relates to MS. Without an appropriate model, studies to determine how marijuana or THC might relieve spasticity cannot be conducted. Nonetheless, the survey results suggest that it would be useful to investigate the potential therapeutic value of cannabinoids in relieving symptoms associated with MS. Since THC is mildly sedating, it would be important to distinguish this effect from anti-spasticity in any such investigations. Mild sedatives such as Benadryl or benzodiazepines would be useful control medications for studies on the ability of cannabinoids to relieve muscle spasticity. The regular use of smoked marijuana, however, would be contraindicated in chronic conditions such as MS.

There is an increasing amount of reports to support the improvement of specific MS symptoms in patients treated with cannabinoids. These symptoms include: bladder disturbance, muscle stiffness, muscle spasms, neuropathic pain and sleep. Though no serious safety concerns have surfaced, the associated risks for cognitive damage and other deleterious effects still exist. More recent research has provided evidence to support that cannabinoids may play a more fundamental role in treatment of the disease, as it may have anti-inflammatory effects as well as encourage remyelination (regeneration of the nerve's myelin sheath) and neuroprotection. Currently, there are trials being conducted to evaluate the long term role cannabinoids may have in reducing disability and MS progression.

Cannabis extracts have been implicated in the treatment of bladder dysfunction resulting from multiple sclerosis. It has been found that cannabinoid receptors are located in the lower urinary tract and centers which controls it. As such, systemic cannabinnoids have the potential of becoming clinically significant based on their effect on the lower urinary tract. Patients with MS often experience incontinence (involuntary leakage of urine), urinary urgency and nocturia (the need to urinate at night). Cannabis-based medicines have been shown to reduce these symptoms. The effect of a cannabis extract enriched in CBD on bladder contractility was recently tested by Capasso et al. in vitro. It was found to reduce contractions and this study provides some optimism for patients with MS who suffer from incontinence.

WASTING SYNDROME AND APPETITE STIMULATION

The Wasting Syndrome that occurs in patients with Acquired Immune Deficiency Syndrome (AIDS) is defined as the involuntary loss of more than 10 per cent of baseline average body weight, accompanied by diarrhoea or fever (that is not attributed to other diseases) of more than 30 days. Anorexia, which is a loss of appetite, can accelerate wasting due to limited intake of the necessary nutrients. Both wasting (cachexia) and anorexia are common end-stage features of certain fatal diseases such as AIDS, as well as metastatic cancers. In AIDS, weight loss of as little as 5 per cent is associated with decreased survival and a body weight about one-third below ideal body weight results in death.

Extreme forms of malnutrition are starvation and cachexia. Starvation is the deprivation of essential nutrients to the body and results from famine or poverty, non-absorption, and eating disorders. Starvation results in metabolic adaptations that deplete body fat before losses in lean tissue. Cachexia, in contrast, results when there is tissue injury such as trauma, infection, or tumour, and is characterized by a disproportionate loss of lean body mass, such as skeletal muscle.

The key distinguishing factor between starvation and cachexia is that the provision of food can usually reverse the effects of starvation. However, the effects of cachexia can be reversed only through control of the underlying disease and, at least for some patients, the use of drugs that stimulate metabolism, such as growth hormones or androgenic-anabolic hormones.

MALNUTRITION IN HIV-INFECTED PATIENTS

In 1997, there were more than 30 million people worldwide infected with Human Immunodeficiency Virus (HIV). Malnutrition is common among AIDS patients and plays a significant role in morbidity and mortality.

However, before malnutrition can be treated in HIV patients, the cause (whether starvation or cachexia) and the effects of HIV infection on the metabolic processes have to be determined. The answer depends on the clinical situation and can be a result of either starvation or cachexia or both.

The development of malnutrition in HIV infection is multi-faceted. It results in a disproportionate depletion of body cell mass, total body nitrogen, and skeletal muscle mass which is consistent with cachexia. Body composition studies show that the depletion of body cell (fat-free cellular) mass precedes the progression to cachexia, suggesting that malnutrition can be a consequence of the inflammatory response to the underlying viral infection, rather than a general complication of AIDS. In contrast, weight loss is often episodic and related to acute complications such as febrile opportunistic infections. The mechanisms underlying wasting in HIV-infected patients vary depending on the stage of HIV infection and on specific associated complications.

There are many reasons for decreased food intake among AIDS patients. These include mouth, throat, or oesophageal infections or ulcers, adverse effects of medications, diarrhoea, and enteric infection.

MARIJUANA, THC, AND HIV-INFECTED PATIENTS

Despite their frequency of use, there is little published data on the effectiveness of marijuana or cannabinoids for the treatment of malnutrition and wasting syndrome in HIV-infected patients.

The only cannabinoid evaluated in controlled clinical studies is THC, or dronabinol. HIV/AIDS patients are the largest group who use dronabinol. However, some rejected dronabinol because of the intensity of neuropsychological effects, an inability to easily titrate the oral dose, and the delayed onset together with the prolonged duration of its action. There is evidence to suggest that cannabinoids modulate the immune system, which might be a problem in immunologically-compromised patients. No published studies have formally evaluated the use of any of the other cannabinoids in AIDS wasting or as an appetite stimulant.

There are claims that smoked marijuana is useful for the treatment of HIV associated anorexia and weight loss. Some individuals report a preference for smoked marijuana over oral THC because it gives them the ability to titrate the effects, depending on how much they inhale. In controlled laboratory studies on normal, healthy adults, smoked marijuana was shown to increase body weight, appetite, and food intake. Unfortunately, there have been no controlled studies of the effect of smoked marijuana on appetite, weight gain and body composition in AIDS patients. Donald Abrams at the University of California in San Francisco (UCSF) who conducted the first clinical trial to test the safety of smoked marijuana in AIDS patients, concluded that there is measurable medical benefits to smoking cannabis for HIV related foot pain known as peripheral neuropathy. The study which involved 50 subjects was the first of its kind to include a comparison group which is a hallmark in scientific research. Though many of the individuals involved in the trial exclaimed the treatment is safe and worked in the relief of their symptoms, many critics argued that the test may have not been statistically relevant, and whether marijuana is a treatment one would want to prescribe to an individual whose immune system is compromised.

A major concern that HIV-infected patients have with smoking marijuana is that they might become more vulnerable than other marijuana users to the immunosuppressive effects of marijuana or to the exposure of infectious organisms associated with the marijuana plant material.

THERAPY FOR WASTING SYNDROME IN HIV-INFECTED PATIENTS

| PRESENT THERAPY |

Generally, therapy for wasting in HIV-infected individuals have focused on appetite stimulation.

Few therapies have proven effective in the treatment of AIDS wasting syndrome. The stimulant studied most is megestrol acetate, and it has been shown to increase food intake by about 30 percent over baseline for reasons that remain unknown. Its effect as it relates to the production of significant weight gain is dose-dependent, but the majority of the weight gain is in the fat tissues and not lean body mass.

Although the findings are still preliminary, anabolic compounds, such as testosterone or growth hormone, might be useful in preventing the loss of, or help in restoring lean body mass in AIDS patients. Additionally, enteral and parenteral nutrition have been evaluated and shown to increase weight, but again, the increase is due mainly to body fat than to lean body mass.

The advances in the antiviral treatment of HIV infection coupled with developments in the prophylaxis and therapy of opportunistic infections are encouraging and have recently changed the outlook for the long-term health of HIV-infected individuals. Death rates have been cut in half, and the frequency of serious complications, including malnutrition, has fallen significantly.

| FUTURE THERAPY |

The primary focus of future therapies for wasting in HIV-infected patients is to increase lean body mass and appetite. Active systemic infections are associated with profound anorexia, which is believed to be mediated by cytokines that stimulate inflammation through their actions within and outside the brain. Cytokine inhibitors such as thalidomide have been under investigation as potential treatments to increase lean body mass and reduce malnutrition.

Even though cannabinoids do not appear to restore lean body mass, they might be useful as adjunctive therapy. For example, cannabinoids could be used as an appetite stimulant in patients with diminished appetite who are undergoing resistance exercises or anabolic therapy to increase lean body mass. Additionally, cannabinoids could be beneficial for the provision of a variety of effects, such as increased appetite, while reducing the nausea and vomiting caused by protease inhibitors, as well as the pain and anxiety associated with AIDS.

As it relates to the current knowledge about malnutrition in HIV infected patients, cannabinoids by themselves will not likely be a primary therapy for this condition, but might be useful in combination with other therapies. Specifically, the proposed mechanism of action of increased food intake would most likely be effective in the promotion of increase in skeletal muscle and functional capacity, which is the primary goal in the treatment of cachexia in AIDS patients.

MALNUTRITION IN CANCER PATIENTS

Malnutrition in cancer patients compromises their quality of life and contributes to the progression of their disease. Approximately 30 percent of Americans will develop cancer in their lifetime, of which two-thirds will die as a result of this disease. Depending on the type of cancer, fifty to eighty per cent (50%-80%) of patients will develop cachexia, and up to 50 per cent of these patients will die as a result of cachexia. The cachexia appears to result from the tumour itself and cytokines (proteins secreted by the host during an immune response to tumours) are likely important factors that contribute to the development of this condition. Cachexia does not occur in all cancer patients, but it generally occurs at the late stages of advanced pancreas, lung, and prostate cancers.

The only cannabinoid evaluated for treating cachexia in cancer patients is dronabinol, which has been shown to improve appetite and promote weight gain. Present treatments for cachexia associated with cancer are similar to that for cachexia in AIDS patients. These treatments are usually used at late stages of the disease.

Cannabinoids have also been shown to modulate the immune system, which could be contraindicated for certain cancer patients (both the chemotherapy and cancer can be immuno-suppressive).

Future treatments will probably depend on the development of methods that block cytokine action, and the use of selective B_2-adrenergic receptor agonists to increase muscle masses. Additionally, it is important to identify the patients' individual needs when treating cancer-related cachexia. This is necessary, as some patients might need only a cytokine inhibitor, while others could benefit from combined approaches, such as an appetite stimulant and B_2-adrenergic receptor agonists. In this respect, cannabinoids such as THC might prove useful as part of a combination therapy, particularly as an appetite stimulant, antiemetic, analgesic, anxiolytic and especially for patients in the late stages of disease.

ANOREXIA NERVOSA

Anorexia nervosa is a psychiatric disorder characterized by distorted body image and self-starvation. It affects an estimated 0.6 per cent of the population in the United States, and a greater proportion of girls than boys. The mortality rate is high, and response to standard treatments is poor.

THC appears to be ineffective in treating this disease. One possible explanation for the dysphoria is that THC increases appetite and thus intensifies the mental conflict between hunger and food refusal malnutrition. Furthermore, such patients may have underlying psychiatric disorders (schizophrenia, depression) and the use of cannabinoids might complicate these situations.

RECOMMENDATIONS

The profile of cannabinoid drug effects suggests that they are promising for treating wasting syndrome in AIDS patients. Nausea, appetite loss, pain, and anxiety are symptoms of wasting and can be controlled by marijuana. Although there are medications that are more effective than marijuana for these problems, they are not equally effective for all patients. Thus the development and clinical testing of a rapid onset form of THC for such patients is recommended. Smoking should not be an option as the long-term damage from smoking makes it a poor drug delivery system, particularly for patients with chronic illnesses.

However, terminally ill patients raise another issue. For these patients, the medical harms of smoking are of little consequence. These patients suffer debilitating pain and nausea and the medications identified have failed to provide relief. For them the positive medicinal benefits of smoked marijuana might outweigh the negatives.

In conclusion, it is clear that the therapeutic uses of marijuana discussed in this section have enough evidence not only to support its medicinal uses, but also to justify further clinical studies in each specific case.

There is much support for the use of orally administered THC in the control of nausea and vomiting associated with chemotherapy treatment of cancer, a use which has been further legalized because of the current placement of synthetic oral THC such as Marinol and Dronabinol in Schedule III of the Controlled Substances Act. In fact, Marinol or Dronabinol (in capsule form), which contains THC dissolved in oil, has been marketed for this purpose. Other potential medicinal uses such as in the treatment of glaucoma, asthma, seizures, and insomnia have also had much experimental support.

The possible uses of marijuana as an appetite stimulant is worthy of consideration as the current drugs on the market are not effective. Most if not all of the studies have recommended oral THC, which would seem to be the most appropriate route of delivery, as the slow onset of action (associated with this form of administration) is consistent with the objective of treatment.

The evidence as it relates to the use of marijuana to relieve or improve muscle spasticity is somewhat disappointing and even questionable. It is the general view that the uncoordinating effects of the drug might aggravate underlying neurological conditions.

The development and use of cannabinoids as an analgesic is good. However, an appropriate route of administration needs to be identified as oral THC or smoked marijuana does not seem to be the best method of delivery. Additionally, synthetic cannabinoids that retain the analgesic action but minimize the mental effects should be developed, as this seems to be the more promising indication.

It should be noted that although more controversy surrounds the comparison between orally administered THC and smoked marijuana, there is the belief that smoked marijuana may have other active ingredients, including THC, as 400 or more chemicals are present in the plant or in the smoke. However, this argument cannot be substantiated. Despite the presence of much of smaller amounts (and in less potency) of THC-like substances, no other active ingredients has ever been found or even studied. One advantage of smoking though is that its immediate effect is desirable in conditions where rapid onset action is preferable.

Finally, with the evolution in clinical pharmacology, there needs to be more studies that test the potential therapeutic uses of the drug. After all, it has been more than 35 years since the synthesis of THC.

CANNABIDIOL

The clinical future of numerous amounts of cannabinoids is limited due to their psychoactive properties. Cannabidiol, one of the major non-psychoactive compounds of the Cannabis sativa plant, now presents a potentially safe alternative which may be effective in alleviating neurodegeneration and neuroinflammation associated with CNS degenerative diseases and was recently shown to improve multiple sclerosis-like disease in mice in a study done at Tel Aviv University published in 2011. However, another study by Honarmand et al. in 2011 provided empirical evidence to support the fact that though the use of cannabis alleviates pain and spasticity in MS, it has a negative effect on cognitive function with prolonged use. Cannabidiol was also found by Bergamaschi et al. in 2011 to reduce anxiety and demonstrates anxiolytic effects both in humans and animals. In addition it was said to have possible neuroprotective properties from results of a study done by Demirakca et al. in 2011, which also highlighted the neurotoxic effects of THC in chronic users. This creates the need for further research on individual compounds found in the cannabis plant which may be effective in treating symptoms of specific diseases without having related psychotrophic (affecting the central nervous system) effects.

Hepatic encephalopathy is a neuropsychiatric disorder caused by chronic or acute liver failure. The effects of cannabidiol on brain and liver functions in a model of the disorder were evaluated by Avraham and associates and published in the British Journal of Pharmacology in 2011 and it was found to restore liver function and improve brain pathology. This presents evidence that cannabidiol may not only be active in the brain but also in the liver. There is also recent evidence in the literature highlighting the neurobiological properties of CBD on sleep modulation. The administration of CBD in rats enhanced alertness and suppressed sleep.

Researchers at the University of São Paulo in Brazil concluded that cannabidiol may be useful in the treatment of spinal cord lesions, as improved locomotor recovery and reduced injury extent was observed in rats that were subjected to spinal cord injury.

CROHN'S DISEASE

Researchers at the Tel Aviv University in Israel concluded for the first time that cannabis may have a positive effect on disease activity in Crohn's disease, a chronic inflammatory bowel disease. The study concluded that it may have a positive effect on disease activity as observed from reduction in disease activity index and the need for other drugs and surgery.

METHODS
OF APPLYING CANNABIS AS A MEDICINE

"....A spoonful of sugar, makes the medicine go down
The medicine go down ...in a most delightful way."
- MARY POPPINS

SMOKING AND EATING

Cannabis can either be smoked or ingested. The method used has its own advantage and disadvantages.

SMOKING

This is the most common method of marijuana use. It has a rapid onset action as, within a few minutes of inhalation,

THC reaches the alveoli in the lungs and is absorbed into the blood stream. In less than a minute it reaches the receptors in the brain and organs and has an immediate effect. When the effect begins, the feeling of 'high' continues to grow rapidly for about 15 minutes and peaks in 20 to 30 minutes. After it peaks, the 'high' begins to fade and dissipate after one to three hours. This method of application also relieves symptoms more quickly and is especially advantageous when there is a problem associated with nausea or lack of appetite.

The effect of less potent and lower quality type marijuana is felt as quickly as high quality; however, the feeling of 'high' peaks more quickly and lasts a shorter period of time. It should be noted too that one's tolerance will also affect the 'high'.

INGESTING

The ingestion or eating of marijuana produces a different effect from smoking as the material that is eaten is processed by the liver before it reaches the brain. The material is converted to 11-hydroxy-THC (a metabolite that is four to five times more psychoactively potent than ordinary THC) in the liver. The fact that 11-hydroxy-THC is not produced when marijuana is smoked; ingesting and smoking produce different pharmacological effects.

When marijuana is ingested, the effects take longer to be felt but are of longer duration. This can be helpful as some people can regulate their condition by eating very small amounts at a time. In doing so they do not feel the effects of the drug but the symptoms of their ailment are relieved.

The major disadvantage of eating marijuana is that it is somewhat difficult to predict the level of dosage that is required for the desired effect. This is so because the oral dose may be absorbed more or less easily/quickly depending on the state of the digestive system, the contents of the stomach at the time of ingestion and other hard to predict factors. In some it might take several hours while in others it might take only minutes to take full effect. This makes it difficult to determine the exact dose to be taken.

OINTMENTS AND POULTICES

Some patients apply marijuana externally or topically to the skin in the form of ointments, lotion, or poultices, for the treatment of swollen joints and other ailments.

Cannabis was used as a topical ingredient at the turn of the century either as an anaesthetic or as an antiviral agent for the treatments of foot corns. Topical cannabis applications have also been used in folk medicine in India and Latin America. A popular treatment for arthritis in the Mexican American community is to wrap the joints in a poultice or bandage of cannabis leaves.

It is not clear how well the topical treatments work, if at all. However, some patients claim that they benefited from direct application.

CANNABIS–
DERIVED DRUGS IN
FORMAL MEDICINE

"I will lift mine eyes unto the hills
From whence cometh my help..."
- PSALM 121:1

The debate concerning the medicinal use of herbal cannabis (marijuana) is still swirling, with governments, scientists, members of the legal system and laymen across the
continents having very strong views on both sides of the
argument. However, in the midst of this controversy, there
are cannabis-based medicines that have already been
approved by the United States Food and Drug Administration (USFDA) as human medicines for patients on both
sides of the Atlantic.

There are synthetic cannabinoids known as dronabinol
(Marinol) and nabilone (Cestamet). The medicinal use of
these two drugs (although they are not very popular), unlike
herbal cannabis, is fully supported by a substantial body
of scientific evidence from clinical trials. They have also
satisfied the strict requirements of the United States Food
and Drug Administration (USFDA).

"Of course his appetite has improved...
it's the medical marijuana."

DRONABINOL (MARINOL)

Dronabinol is tetrahydrocannabinol (THC), which occurs naturally and can be extracted from *Cannabis sativa* L (marijuana). It is the generic name given to THC, and is marketed as the medical product known as Marinol.

"MARINOL is a medicine containing the active ingredient dronabinol. Dronabinol is synthetic delta-9-tetrahydrocannabinol, or delta-9-THC (as it is commonly known). Delta-9-tetrahydrocannabinol is also a naturally occurring component of Cannabis sativa L. (marijuana). MARINOL, a standardized product marketed by Unimed Pharmaceuticals, Inc., is dronabinol solution in sesame oil in soft gelatin capsules. Unlike MARINOL, however, marijuana (the plant material) does not provide standardized THC content and often contains impurities (including leaves, mold spores, and bacteria).

In its pure form, THC is a viscous pale yellow resin which is practically insoluble in water. This makes it hard to prepare as a tablet or for use as intravenous injection. Hence, Marinol is prepared by dissolving dronabinol in a small amount of harmless sesame oil and made into a soft gelatin capsule which is easy to swallow and dissolves more readily in the stomach. Each capsule contains 2.5, 5, or 10 milligram of dronabinol.

Marinol is a Schedule II drug, the most tightly controlled prescription drug in the USA. In 1986 dronabinol was approved for treatment of nausea and vomiting associated with cancer chemotherapy in those who failed to respond to conventional treatment. In 1993 it was further approved for use as an appetite suppressant and for treatment of anorexia associated with weight loss in the AIDS wasting syndrome. Eighty per cent of prescriptions are for HIV/AIDS patients. There are no reports of increased immunosuppression.

Marinol has standards set by the USFDA. The Unimed Corporation markets Marinol and its sales gross approximately $20 million annually. Fortunately, dronabinol as a 'street drug' has little value. It has proven to be a poor and flawed substitute for natural marijuana since the effect is slow.

Dronabinol is contraindicated in any patient who has a history of hypersensitivity to any cannabinoid or to sesame oil. They should therefore advise their doctors if they have heart disease; current or past drug or alcohol abuse; mental health problems, including mania, depression, schizophrenia, and allergies to drugs. Women who become pregnant while on dronabinol should stop taking the drug immediately and advise their doctor. It is also a medication with a potential for abuse and physicians and pharmacists should use the same care in prescribing and accounting for dronabinol as they would with morphine or other drugs controlled under Schedule II of the Controlled Substances Acts (USA).

Patients receiving treatments containing dronabinol should be specifically advised not to drive, operate machinery or engage in any hazardous activity until it is established that they are able to tolerate the drug and to perform such tasks safely. They should also be alerted to the potential for addictive central nervous system (CNS) depression, especially if the drug is used concomitantly with alcohol or other CNS depressants such as barbiturates.

Dronabinol also demonstrates reversible effects on mood, cognition, memory and perception. These phenomena appear to be dose related and increase in frequency with higher dosages and subject to great interpatient variability. That is, its effect on patients might differ from one to another. Therefore patients should remain under the supervision of a responsible adult during initial use of dronabinol and following dosage adjustments.

Marinol has a number of limitations which include the following:

- It contains a single medically active cannabinoid, THC, and lacks other potentially active cannabinoids such as cannabidiol (CBD) that is found in natural marijuana,

- It is distributed only in oral doses. Some patients (especially chemotherapy patients) benefit from inhaling the smoke of natural marijuana as inhaling sometimes provides faster relief and easier regulation of dosage,

- Although it comes in well-defined doses, it may not all be absorbed in the digestive system. This results in the common problem of incorrect dosage.

- Marinol is expensive because it is chemically synthesized.

The following are the advantages of Marinol:

- It is medically pure thus eliminating the risk of contamination,

- It does not result in the respiratory hazards of smoking. (Neither does oral preparations of natural cannabis),

- It is legal although its use is tightly restricted.

NABILONE (CESAMET)

Nabilone belongs to a group of medicines known as cannabinoids (due to the similarity of their chemical structure with cannabis).

Nabilone has been found to be effective in the treatment of sickness (an anti-emetic), although the exact method by which it carries out this function is not fully understood. It is used to treat nausea and vomiting caused by medicines used in the treatment of cancer (chemotherapeutic agents).

Nabilone is a potent synthetic analogue of THC, and is the result of research on a wide range of THC analogues, influenced by the need to produce a drug that is not only effective, but lacks the often severe, central side effects of THC. Unlike dronabinol, it is stable crystalline solid. For human use, it is prepared in solid form in capsules containing 1 milligram of nabilone. Capsules are taken by mouth and the dose is usually two milligrams twice per day.

Nabilone is reserved for use in individuals who do not respond to the more commonly used anti-emetics. This is mainly because cannabinoids have potential adverse effects similar to that of cannabis and may cause changes in mood and behaviour. Nabilone is in a class of medications called cannabinoids. It works by affecting the area of the brain that controls nausea and vomiting. This medicine is licensed in the United Kingdom and other countries for use in treatment of nausea and vomiting in cancer chemotherapy, but preliminary clinical studies are now being conducted for its use as a treatment for anxiety.

Nabilone, like THC, seems to have a significant amount of antiemetic activity and has been shown to be very superior to most of the antiemetic drugs currently available in both man and animals. Studies have reported that it was judged to be extremely effective from the first day of treatment in severe nausea and vomiting cases.

SIDE EFFECTS

Medicines and their possible side effects can affect individual people in different ways. The following are some of the side effects that are known to be associated with this medicine. Because a side effect is stated here, it does not mean that all people using this medicine will experience that or any side effect:-

- Drowsiness
- Dry mouth
- Disordered co-ordination
- Blurred vision
- Postural hypertension
- Dizziness

- Euphoria
- Sleepiness
- Disorientation
- Decreased appetite
- Hallucinations
- Psychosis

- Headaches
- Abdominal Pain
- Depression
- Confusion
- Shaking, usually of the Hands (tremor)

- A drop in blood pressure that occurs when going from lying down to sitting or standing, which results in dizziness and lightheadedness (postural hypotension)

Reports of other central nervous system effects were also noted, including feelings of 'highs', which is described as euphoric or dysphoric. It is not clear whether the 'high' is an essential component of its antiemetic activity.

Other areas where nabilone has shown to be effective are in control of nausea and vomiting associated with radiotherapy, total abdominal hysterectomy and in patients experiencing nausea and vomiting as a result of an AIDS related c *Cryptosporidium* infection. However these uses are unlicensed.Treatment with nabilone should begin 1-3 hours before the first dose of chemotherapy and may be continued for up to

48 hours after the end of the chemotherapy cycle. The medicine should be taken at around the same time every day. Ensure that the administration of the drug is done properly. Take nabilone exactly as directed. Do not take more or less of it or take it more often than prescribed.

Nabilone has also proven effective in the lowering of intraocular pressure in animal models and in man, where an oral dose of 1-2 mg produced an average drop of 34 per cent (range 10-54%), in 9 patients with open angle glaucoma. However, failure to find a suitable vehicle for an eye drop formulation of nabilone has thwarted studies of topical preparation.

There is little data available on which the assessment of the use of nabilone in the treatment of multiple sclerosis (MS) can be made. They tend to be sparse, of poor quality, subjective, anecdotal and have taken little account of confounding factors such as duration or severity of the illness and concurrent medication. However in a report of a case study done in 1995, one MS patient was given the drug (1 mg every other day for four weeks), followed by a placebo administered in the same fashion for the same period of time. General feelings of well-being were improved during the period of administration, but rapidly disappeared when the placebo was given.

SATIVEX
GW PHARMACEUTICALS

> "My professional view of cannabis as a substance is that it appears to be a remarkably safe substance in comparison to most medicines prescribed today. The more I learn about this plant the more fascinated I become. It has through its various constituents multiple effects of therapeutic interest, many of which are now being validated by the enormous growth in basic cannabinoid research."
>
> Dr Geoffrey Guy, Chairman of GW Pharmaceuticals."

On June 11, 1998 GW Pharmaceuticals became the first and only company in the United Kingdom licensed to provide raw cannabis materials for trials. The company was adamant about the beneficial uses of cannabis on certain medical symptoms, and this propelled them to apply to the Home office to conduct clinical trials on cannabis. They received two license , a "cultivation" licence which allowed them to grow cannabis plants from seed or through cloning, and a " Possession and Supply for Medical Research" licence which allowed them to store cannabis in specified secure conditions and supply such cannabis for solely research purposes.

GW Pharmaceutical collaborated with Hortapharm a Dutch plant-breeding company. This allowed GW Pharmaceuticals to use any variety of cannabis from Hortapharm's storage, and providing assistance in the cultivation of their own. In return they received the development of devices that would allow for safe administration of the cannabis derived medication to patients.

By November 1998 GW Pharmaceuticals had 5000 cannabis crops growing, the first harvest was taken in January 1999. In June of that said year they made an application to establish a partner company in Canada to further continue their investigations. By November of that said year clinical trials had begun. Humans were given different extracts of cannabis through various devices and monitored during such process. The results of this allowed them to choose the best extracts for further testing .

TABLE 1 | SUMMARY OF GENERAL MEDICAL TRIAL PROCEDURE

PHASE	PHASE OBJECTIVE
Phase 1	Establish safety of drug.
Phase 2	Establish efficacy the drug has on patients.
Phase 3	Large scale trials involving several patients to asses different aspects of drugs, active compounds, target patient groups etc.

In April 2000, the company initiated Phase 2 having received a clinical trial exemption certificate from the Medicines Control Agency. Phase 2 involved patients who had multiple sclerosis, severe pain, spasticity and other related conditions. The trials were done to establish how effective it was to use a cannabis-based sublingual spray to relieve pain. These trials were done in several locations. After successfully completing this phase, Phase 3 trials began.

Phase 3 trials began in May 2001. This phase involved multiple patients who were living in diverse locations, and the company was hoping that by 2003 they would produce their first authorized prescription medicine. This medicine would target persons who suffer from Multiple sclerosis, arthritis, cancer pain and spinal cord injuries amongst others. The company's objective was also to provide a more efficient way of delivery of the drug in a manner where the patients can adjust their doses individually avoiding certain side effects that come along with smoking.

The company successfully produced Sativex, which is their lead product. This product is now approved and recommended in 21 countries 18 of which are in Europe. The drug is used by patients with moderate to severe spasticity due to multiple sclerosis. The drug is also in Phase 3 for the treatment of cancer pain. GW is continuing to expand their market.

FIGURE 1 | SATIVEX

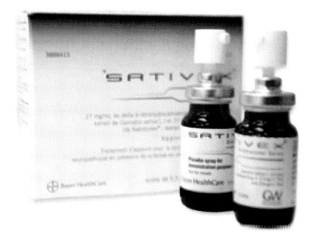

Having been announced on April 19, 2005. Sativex is the world's first prescription medicine derived from the cannabis plant. This marijuana-derived drug is for pain management and has been approved for treatment of Multiple Sclerosis in Canada. It is administered as an oral spray which the patient sprays into his/her mouth from where it is absorbed. This drug consists of a 1:1 ratio of the Cannabinoids, Cannabidiol (CBD) and delta-9-tetrahydrocannabinol (THC). The oral spray prevents the THC from entering the blood too rapidly minimizing the unwanted psychotropic effects. Sativex works by interacting with the cannabinoid receptors that occur throughout the body inclusive of the brain. It imposes an effect on the cell and the nerve impulses it produces which subsequently minimise the symptoms of spasticity.

"Health Canada has approved Sativex (*Cannabis sativa L. extract*); a new drug developed as adjunctive treatment for the symptomatic relief of neuropathic pain in adults with multiple sclerosis (MS). Canada becomes the first country in the world to approve Sativex, a novel prescription pharmaceutical product derived from components of the cannabis plant shown to have therapeutic properties.

Health Canada has approved Sativex with conditions, under the Notice of Compliance with Conditions (NOC/c) policy. Products approved under Health Canada's NOC/c policy, have demonstrated promising benefit, are of high quality and possess an acceptable safety profile based on a benefit/risk assessment for the approved use.

Sativex is the first product indicated in Canada as adjunctive treatment for the symptomatic relief of neuropathic pain in MS. A product resulting from the pioneering research efforts of UK-based GW Pharmaceuticals plc and marketed in Canada by Bayer HealthCare, Pharmaceuticals Division, Sativex is the first product indicated in Canada as adjunctive treatment for the symptomatic relief of neuropathic pain in MS.

Sativex is now licensed as an add-on treatment for MS related moderate to severe spasticity in patients who have either had significant improvement in an initial Sativex trial or whose symptoms are not adequately relieved by one or more oral medications and have had intolerable side effects."

The company is also continuing trials on Sativex to address other medicals problems:

- Sativex Cancer Pain Trials for patients with advanced cancer who experience moderate to severe pain. The company got approved in August 2007 and currently is in Phase 3 of clinical trials.

- Sativex Neuropathic Pain Trials for the symptomatic relief of neuropathic pain in adults suffering from multiple Sclerosis. The company got approved in April 2005 and the drug is currently in Phase 2 of clinical trials.

- Sativex Rheumatoid Arthritis Trials: The Company is the first to do a controlled trial of a cannabis based medicine to treat Rheumatoid Arthritis with favourable results.

- Sativex Bladder Dysfunction Trials for treating individuals with multiple sclerosis who suffer bladder dysfunctions.

CANNADOR

Cannador is an oral capsule developed by the Society for Clinical Research in Germany which contains the entire plant extract. The THC content is fixed while CBD is controlled within a 2:1 ratio of THC: CBD.

The drug has been administered in numerous clinical trials and has been assessed for post-operative pain management, cachexia in cancer patients and spasms, muscle stiffness and pain associated with Multiple Sclerosis.

PHARMACEUTICAL DRUGS BASED ON CANNABIS

Pharmaceutical drugs have been developed which either contain or have similar chemicals as those found in the marijuana (cannabis) plant. Some researchers have used their understanding of how the brain processes cannabinoids to develop drugs which follow the same pathways but work differently than marijuana. Pharmaceutical drugs based on marijuana are divided into four categories and listed below with the names, trade names, manufacturers, approval status, suggested medical use and cannabis-related properties. All drugs referenced are in pill form unless otherwise noted.

Below are tables outlining these chemicals similar to those found in the cannabis plant:

I. Drugs that contain chemicals taken directly from the marijuana plant					
	Name/Trade Name	Manufacturer	Approval Status	Suggested Medical Use	Cannabis-Related Properties
1.	Sativex	GW Pharmaceuticals	U.S. Phase III clinical trials started in late 2006 Approved for use in Canada (2005) and Catalonia, Spain (2005); Licensed to Bayer in the UK and to Almirall in Europe Ongoing Phase III MS (Multiple Sclerosis) study in the UK due to report results in the first quarter (Q1) of 2009 and regulatory submission scheduled by the end of the second quarter (H1) in 2009.	Treatment of neuropathic pain and spasticity in patients with Multiple Sclerosis (MS); Analgesic treatment in adult patients with advanced cancer who experience moderate to severe pain.	Mouth spray whose chemical compound is derived from natural extracts of the cannabis plant

II. Drugs that contain synthetic versions of chemicals naturally found in marijuana					
	Name/Trade Name	Manufacturer	Approval Status	Suggested Medical Use	Cannabis-Related Properties
1.	Dronabinol/ Marinol	Unimed Pharmaceuticals, a subsidiary of Solvay Pharmaceuticals	FDA approved in United States as an appetite stimulant (1992) and for nausea (1985) Approved in Denmark for multiple sclerosis (Sep. 2003)	Treatment of nausea and vomiting for patients in cancer treatment; Appetite stimulant for AIDS patients; Analgesic to ease neuropathic pain in multiple sclerosis patients	Synthetic Delta-9 THC

http://medicalmarijuana.procon.org/viewresource.asp?resourceID=000883

9

RECREATIONAL
USE OF CANNABIS

"Q: Who was the first drug addict in the Bible?
A: Nebuchadnezzar. He was on grass for seven years!
- ANONYMOUS

According to Leslie L. Iversen in his book entitled, *The Science of Marijuana* (2000), "The use of cannabis as a recreational drug was almost unknown in the West until the 1950s and only became widespread during the 1960s." It is important to note, too, that it was used in Jamaica by the Indian indentured labourers in the latter part of the nineteenth century, but it was the Rastafarian movement that popularized its use in modern Jamaica and the rest of the world .It is now a widely used recreational drug.

Initially' it was called 'the rebellious drug' as many young people used it as a symbol of rebellion. Similarly, it would not be surprising that the generation of the 1960s and 1970s, many of whom are against the use and legalization of this drug, were once marijuana smokers.

PERCENTAGE OF RECREATIONAL USAGE OF CANNABIS

According to a report published by the World Health Organization (WHO), cannabis ranks overall as the third most commonly used recreational drug after alcohol and tobacco. The National Council on Drug Abuse (NCDA) in Jamaica reported that the recreational use of cannabis accounts for 29 per cent in the age group 15-50 years in 1994. It has even been immortalized in a song entitled 'Kaya', written by the great reggae legend late Bob Marley in 1978 in which he sang openly:

Got to have Kaya now,

Got to have Kaya now,

Got to have Kaya now,

For the rain is falling'.

Recreational use of marijuana in the same age group also accounted for 32 per cent in the United States in 1996, 37 per cent in Denmark in 1994, 75 per cent in India in 1991 and 20 per cent in the United Kingdom in 1994.

HOW IS CANNABIS CONSUMED?

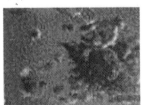

Different methods of consumption are employed by different persons when they are using marijuana. The method of application is also determined by the effect that is desired.

Recreational users of ganja generally smoke it by making spliffs or joints- a home-made cigarette. These are made in a variety of ways. The most popular is by rolling finely chopped ganja in paper. A fine grade paper called rizzler has been used but more recently hemp paper has become the preferred paper. Tobacco leaves are also used to make the joints. Another variation, which also serves as an excellent disguise is the blunt. This is made by removing the tobacco from a regular cigarette and replacing it with ganja. Religious smokers use a pipe.

REASONS FOR RECREATIONAL USE

The reasons for the recreational use of cannabis are wide and varied. It ranges from curiosity and social pressure, to the enhancement of pleasure, enjoyment, relaxation, increased sociability, and because it is a cheaper and more harmless alternative to alcohol and other drugs.

PATTERNS FOR RECREATIONAL USE

| CASUAL |

Irregular use, in amounts of up to 1 g resin at a time to an annual total of no more than 28g (1 ounce).

| REGULAR |

Regular use, typically 3-4 smokes of a joint per day, equivalent to about 14g (1/2 ounce) of cannabis resin per month.

| HEAVY |

Only about 5% of total users, but they are more or less 'permanently stoned', using more than 3-5g of resin per day and 28g (1 ounce) or more per week.

THE EFFECTS OF THE RECREATIONAL USE OF CANNABIS

The effects of the recreational use of ganja are mixed. There is some evidence that it impacts negatively on school performance and social/family relationships. There have been reports of physical illness, symptoms of nausea, vomiting, and sickness.

These symptoms occur shortly after taking the drug, but dissipate over a period of time. Other symptoms include headaches, dizziness, exhaustion, paranoia, fear, depression or hallucinations. Reports even include instances of unpleasant mental experiences, or out of body experiences.

SOURCE: NARCOTIC ENVIRONMENT, USA

RESPONSIBLE DRUG USE

The concept of responsible drug use is that a person can use recreational drugs with reduced or eliminated risk of negatively affecting other parts of one's life or other people's lives. Advocates of this philosophy point to the many well-known artists and intellectuals who have used drugs, experimentally or otherwise, with few detrimental effects on their lives. Critics argue that the drugs are escapist and dangerous, unpredictable and sometimes addictive, and have negative and profound effects in geographic areas well beyond the location of the consumer. It should be noted that these criticisms can apply to a number of non drug related addictions and behavioral abuse disorders. According to medical literature, responsible drug use only becomes drug abuse when the use of the substance significantly interferes with the user's daily life.

IS CANNABIS A GATEWAY DRUG?

As to whether the recreational or even medicinal use of marijuana is a stepping-stone to the use of other illicit drugs, has not been sufficiently proven. However, there is evidence, which suggests that 9 per cent of those who use cannabis may become dependent. But when compared to tobacco (32%), heroin (23%), cocaine (17%) and alcohol (15%), this figure is relatively low.

Young cannabis users are said to be at increased risk for later nicotine addiction. The mixing of tobacco with cannabis (mulling) was found by researchers at the Institute for Social and Preventative Medicine in Switzerland in 2011, to be frequent among young cannabis users which has addiction implications.

IN THE JOURNAL: INSIDE THE GATE: INSIDERS' PERSPECTIVES ON MARI-JUANA AS A GATEWAY DRUG BY RASHI K. SHUKLA

"While the gateway hypothesis is useful for describing possible linkages between early substances that are used and later ones, it is problematic for a number of reasons. Variations in patterns of initiation and progression, and changes in drug involvement in later stages of the drug use career are likely to be overlooked by those promoting the validity of the gateway hypothesis. In the present study, the majority of individuals tried illicit drugs other than marijuana. While some continued to use other illicit substances in adulthood (i.e., at the time of the interview), a number of them only continued to use legal drugs (i.e., alcohol and/or tobacco) and marijuana. More research on the role of marijuana in the later stages of the drug career is needed. Future studies need to continue to examine the relationship between different forms of illicit drug use. Drug research can only be strengthened by continuing to take into account the experiences and perspectives of those involved. Given that marijuana policy is changing, continues to capture national attention, and remains controversial internationally, it is clear that more research is needed."

In support of this Table 1 shows statitistics of the mean age initiation of varied abuse substances.

TABLE 1 MEAN AGE OF DRUG USE INITIATION

DRUG TYPE	MEAN AGE OF INITIATION
Alcohol	13.61
Tobacco	13.80
Marijuana	15.24
Inhalants	16.08
Hallucinogens	18.40
Other Illicit Drugs	19.73
Non-Medical Use of Prescription Pills	18.11

Note: This table has been reprinted from the dissertation (Shukla, 2003).

In conclusion, the recreational use of marijuana will continue into perpetuity. Individuals need to be educated on the associated risks and take the necessary steps to protect themselves. After all, there is a genuine concern that one can develop dependency on this drug.

10
CANNABIS
AND SOME LEGAL CONSIDERATIONS

""Heroes are the people who do what has to be done when it needs to be done, regardless of the consequences!"
- ANONYMOUS

There has been suitably structured legislation sanctioned by national administrations to allow for clinical examination of cannabis for the development of natural or synthetic products. As a result, one of the lawful reasons for possession includes use of the drug in scientific research or laboratory testing. In these countries where medicinal use is authorized, the preparation, dispensing, and administration of therapeutic presentations of cannabis may be lawful, as well as the corresponding possession by a patient for whom such a preparation has been properly prescribed.

Most discussions about medicine are often from a political or social perspective, leaving science and humanitarian concerns as less important. Scientists and medical researchers compete for funding from governmental agencies and private businesses. If the government has strong anti-marijuana policies, then the studies they fund will seek further incriminating evidence concerning the effectiveness of marijuana. To this end, therefore, the main policy issue that should be considered is not whether marijuana is the best medicine, but rather, whether people who use it medicinally should be treated as criminals.

Since 1996 steps has been taken in several states in the US for the usage of marijuana, now 18 states in the United States along with the District of Columbia has laws that allow the medicinal use of Cannabis. 14 of these steps have taken steps to decriminalize the plant. Colorado and Washington DC became the first two states to legalize Marijuana for recreational use and sale.

Most people who use cannabis medicinally risk prosecution if found either possessing or cultivating it. The number of prosecutions for the possession of cannabis arising from medicinal use is not known. Fortunately, most people who are prosecuted for using it medicinally receive a suspended sentence.

MEDICINAL MARIJUANA VERSUS DRONABINOL

Meanwhile, the debate on medicinal marijuana versus Marinol (dronabinol) continues. It is loosely referred to as a legal alternative to smoked marijuana, although very few reports speak of Marinol's numerous side effects or of patient claims that marijuana administers significantly better than synthetic THC.

Marijuana is used in its whole form as a cigarette and Marinolin tablets. The two essential points of greater bodily absorption and greater self-medicating controls, which are possible with medical marijuana use and not Marinol use, cannot be denied even by the well-known anti-marijuana studies. Many drug companies profess the possibility that the cannabinoid inducing psychotropic effects can be avoided by synthesis of analogues which act only on specific sites of the brain (CB2 receptors).

The evidence that marijuana contains more than one active ingredient, thereby implying that Marinol cannot possibly imitate all of marijua-

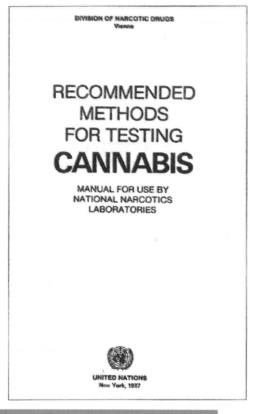

DIVISION OF NARCOTIC DRUGS
Vienna

RECOMMENDED METHODS FOR TESTING
CANNABIS

MANUAL FOR USE BY
NATIONAL NARCOTICS
LABORATORIES

UNITED NATIONS
New York, 1987

SOURCE: UNITED NATIONS BOOKLET ON TESTING FOR CANNABIS

na's medical effects, finds favour among many respected groups that object to the current drug policy. Since marijuana is composed of hundreds of compounds, it seems wrong for medical policy to accept only one of those compounds as medically useful. Although many legislatures are influential, the drug policy disfavours the medicinal uses of marijuana to such an extent that even the recommendations of these organizations are rejected.

Governments typically accept or reject scientific studies based on their impact on the desired policies, so medical issues are doomed if government chooses not to support them.

Having extensively analyzed the Marinol versus marijuana debate from a popular culture perspective, and within a historical and theoretical context, it is now apparent just how differently the two essentially similar substances are treated. Marinol enjoys cultural and medical legitimacy from society, as well as tax breaks and open market privileges from the government. Medical marijuana users still risk imprisonment and social discrimination, while simultaneously suffering from terrible and fatal illnesses.

Despite the abundance of scientific information and organizational support verifying marijuana's numerous medical benefits, the US

Federal government still chooses to validate the inferior Marinol medication, and continues its war on marijuana users. As a result, more research into the synthetic cannabinoids may lead to herbal cannabis becoming obsolete.

The United States Congress (USC) instituted the Controlled Substances Act (CSA) in 1970, which classified drugs and substances in five regulatory schedules, according to legal and scientific criteria, which determines how harmful they are. However, there was a mechanism put in place whereby changes could be made in the schedules. Cannabis was

placed as marijuana in Schedule 1, despite clear evidence that it lacked the dependency status required for either Schedule 1 or Schedule II status. It was said at the time that marijuana might generate severe psychological or physical dependence and enough studies were not done to prove otherwise.

In 1989, more became known about the effects of marijuana and cannabinoid drugs. Marijuana's actions are now said to occur through an endogenous cannabinoid receptor system. This information has subsequently contributed much to the understanding of the action of marijuana.

Schedule 1 drugs are subject to a near complete prohibition and are only legally available for research under the tightest controls. The CSA states that a drug may not be placed in Schedule 1 unless the following three findings are established:

- the drug must have a high potential for abuse relative to other controlled substances.

- it must have no currently accepted medicinal use in the United States.

- it lacks accepted safety for use under medical supervision (21 USC 821 (B) (1)).

Seven factors must be examined for rescheduling:

- the actual or relative potential for abuse,

- other scientific knowledge of effects,

- the history and pattern of abuse,

- the scope and significance of abuse,

- whether there is a risk to public health,

- psychic or psychological dependence liability, and

- whether the substance is a precursor to a controlled substance.

The results of the many reviews as well as new information may require the United States to amend international treaties regarding cannabis, in addition to rescheduling marijuana under the CSA. With respect to the scheduling of THC, the active ingredient in marijuana, the US government could also petition for the amendment of international treaties and international rescheduling.

If cannabis and its cannabinoids were moved from Schedule 1 to Schedule II they could then be manufactured, distributed and prescribed by doctors even before any form of cannabis medication is licensed and distributed, as research licenses would no longer be required. What actually prevents many companies from initiating research is the difficulty of obtaining a license, yet licensing depends on research and clinical trials.

Recently, the American Medical Association (AMA) has changed its policy on medical marijuana, urging the federal government to review the drug's status as a top-tier controlled dangerous substance.

The agency adopted the policy to help facilitate scientific research and the development of cannabinoid-based medicines, Edward Langston, MD, an AMA board member, said in a statement. "Despite more than 30 years of clinical research, only a small number of randomized, controlled trials have been conducted on smoked cannabis."

However, the AMA emphasized that the policy change "should not be viewed as an endorsement of state-based medical cannabis programs, the legalization of marijuana, or that scientific evidence on the therapeutic use of cannabis meets the current standards for a prescription drug product."

The policy also calls for the National Institutes of Health to facilitate grant applications for well-designed trials of medical marijuana. It asks the agency to make funding available and confirm that the National Institute on Drug Abuse will supply the drug to researchers via the Drug Enforcement Agency.

The AMA is not the only physicians' organization to reconsider its stand on medical marijuana. In 2008, the American College of Physicians issued a position statement supporting research into the therapeutic role of the drug. The paper states that while the use of marijuana for some conditions such as HIV wasting and chemotherapy have been well documented, less information is available about other potential medical uses.

Many insist that anecdotal evidence, however large in volume, is not sufficient reason for rescheduling. Others advise that immediate rescheduling would actually threaten proper trials by encouraging patients to use cannabis in an uncontrolled manner rather than enlisting for the trial and risk receiving a placebo. Patients could declare in writing that they knew beforehand of the risks associated with the use of cannabis. Likewise they should be able to make an informed choice about therapeutic agents and this would result from proper trials and research.

Alternatives to rescheduling are (i) allowing commercial cultivation, (ii) the registration of patients who are authorized to cultivate their own,(iii) the formation of co-operatives, (iv) the limitation, as with diamorphine (heroine) and cocaine, (v) giving doctors the authorization to prescribe it.

Morphine is often prescribed for pain, yet it is more dangerous than marijuana. It is derived from the opium poppy (Papaver somniferium), and is related to heroin, which is highly addictive. Nevertheless, there is no attempt by Federal officials to limit the appropriate and legitimate use of morphine. (Source: Knight-Ridder News Service, monitored in Austin American Statesman, June 22, 1991; Dallas Morning News article and CBS 60 Minutes segment, December 1, 1991.)

Allowing the smoking and prescription of marijuana would go against the current attempts to discourage its use. Also, some believe that changing the law is not justified until nabilone and dronabinol may be prescribed on an unlicensed basis for many conditions.

Different users get different benefits from different preparations of marijuana so most patients would rather not use a standardized preparation, although this is better than nothing. The laws could be changed to allow the prescription of cannabinoids to patients with particular medical conditions that are not sufficiently controlled by existing treatments. Yet the stigma of working with cannabis-based substances, and its categorization as Schedule 1 controlled drug, has deterred many pharmacological researchers from developing new cannabis-based medicines for commercial clinical use, which could prove to be superior. The small number of clinical research trials or commercial development in this area is also due to the bureaucratic control which links cannabis to drugs like narcotics.

There is concern that cannabis or its preparations, which are provided for medicinal use, may be used recreationally and also that some doctors might even benefit from fraudulent prescriptions. This simple matter can be addressed by instituting a labelling design, which disguises prescribed drugs such as cannabinoids. Patients could also be cautioned to keep such drugs in a secure place.

Another concern is that many of those requesting the medicinal use of cannabis are in truth promoting the legalization crusade. Accordingly, the potential medicinal uses for cannabis and its derivatives must be considered separately from the debate on prohibition of recreational use.

However, this is going to be a difficult task. Recently, the Supreme Court of the USA seemed unconvinced by arguments that seriously ill patients should be able to use marijuana to ease their suffering without fear of violating federal drug laws. Despite the fact that some justices seemed sympathetic to the plight of patients who say they have no alternative, the majority did not appear ready to effectively override federal law by allowing a 'medical necessity' defence for marijuana use.

The dilemma pits public health groups and civil libertarians against antidrug forces and parents' organizations. The National Organization for Reform of Marijuana Laws (NORML) told the justices that this (case) is not about a right to get 'stoned'...(but) the right of personal choices of the chronically and terminally ill. On the other hand, the Family Research Council argued that legalizing marijuana would change attitudes toward the perceived dangerousness of illicit drug use.

It is interesting to note that in the USA, drug trafficking amounting to approximately US$400 billion is the single largest area of economic activity, despite the large amount of capital that has been invested in rehabilitation, law enforcement and control. This amount even exceeds annual oil sales. Also, new drug cartels are being formed, the international drug trade is expanding and the incidence of drug abuse continues to increase.

The stance of the Government of the United States and the other countries that are signatories to the many treaties that criminalize the use of marijuana is not typical among other governments. In fact, since 1995, countries such as Canada, Great Britain, Poland, Hungary, Korea, among others, have been growing hemp legally.

To date Jamaica is still considering its approach to marijuana, a drug revered by members of the island's large Rastafarian population, who say smoking it is part of their religion.

'The highest court in the land'.

A seven-member government commission was appointed to research possible changes to the Caribbean nation's anti-drug laws, which law enforcement officers complain are clogging courts and jails with marijuana-related cases.

In 2003, a government commission recommended legalizing marijuana in small amounts for personal use. However, lawmakers never acted, saying legalization might entail loss of their country's U.S. anti-drug certification. Countries that lose it face economic sanctions.

Members of the Rastafarian movement, which emerged in Jamaica in the 1930s out of anger over the oppression of blacks, have long lobbied for the legalization of the drug that they say brings them closer to the divine.

In addition, a few other nations have explored other ways to manage cannabis other than prohibition and punishment. For example, Holland practices a de facto legislation that works. That is, although there is prohibitive penal legislation aimed at drug traffickers, the emphasis of the law is on enforcement that is aimed at the reduction in the supply of drugs rather than an incarceration of offenders.

THE JAMAICAN SIDE

The issue in Jamaica is societal rather than medical. Persons who had little medical knowledge of this drug made legal decisions for Jamaica in the past. In 1960, a person found in possession of one 'spliff' was incarcerated for 18 months. In the 1970s, the law was modified leaving Resident Magistrates with the task of deciding on the punishment.

In 1977, according to the Jamaica Information Service, a committee of both Houses of Parliament recommended the decriminalization of ganja for personal use. This committee set out to look at the 'criminality, legislation, uses and abuses and possible medicinal properties of ganja'. They proposed a maximum penalty of J$50 (then US$20) for use of ganja on the street or in public places and a maximum fine of J$10 (then US$4) for the possession of two ounces of the substance in public places. They also recommended that a person caught using more than the prescribed quantity of ganja in public should be arrested or imprisoned or gain a criminal record on conviction for such an offence.

However, the committee finally opposed the legalization of ganja because of Jamaica's treaty obligations. It therefore called for a revision of the terms of the UN 1961 International Convention of Drugs. In the 1980s there was an increase in illicit drug smuggling to the USA mainly from Jamaica, Mexico and Columbia. In 1985, a United States congressman recommended that aid to Jamaica (US$50 million between 1980-1984) be stopped until there was evidence of increased anti-smuggling enforcement.

As a result, most of the enforcement emphasis was placed on reducing cultivation, trade and export activity. In 1999, $13.25 million was spent on the control of illegal drugs. Eleven million dollars was spent on the legal aspects and $2 million spent on demand control. There has been increased international cooperation to curtail the export of ganja. Accordingly, Jamaica, Canada, and the USA are signatories to Latin America and the United Nation protocols.

A National Commission on ganja was set up in the year 2000 to carry out a comprehensive review of the use of the plant, with specific focus on whether the substance could or should be decriminalized for use in defined circumstances and specific conditions.

Chevannes to head ganja commission

DEAN of the Faculty of Social Sciences at the University of the West Indies, Professor Barry Chevannes, is to head the National Commission on Ganja recently announced by Prime Minister P J Patterson.

The Commission will carry out a comprehensive review of the use of the plant, with specific focus on whether the substance could or should be decriminalised for use in defined circumstances and specific conditions.

The other members named to the Commission are Dr Eileen Goldson from the National Council on Drug Abuse as the deputy chairperson; Rev Webster Edwards; Norma Linton, an attorney-at-law; Dimario McDowell, graphic artist/music promoter; Barbara Smith, former principal of Montego Bay High School, and Tony Freckleton, a businessman from Mandeville.

The Commission will:

• receive submissions or memoranda, hear testimony, evaluate research and   studies, engage in dialogue with relevant interest groups, and undertake wide   public consultations with the aim of guiding a national approach;

CHEVANNES...expected to submit report in nine months

• indicate what changes, if any, are required to existing laws or entail new legislation, taking account of the social, cultural, economic and international   factors;

• recommend the diplomatic initiatives, security considerations, educational process and programme of public information which will need to be undertaken in the light of whatever changes may be proposed;

• consider and report on any other matter sufficiently related to the foregoing; and

• make such interim reports as it may deem fit and a final report within a period of nine months from the first sitting.

The commission is expected to finalise its report within a maximum period of nine months, and "...until the final report is received and acted upon, all existing laws on the use of ganja will remain in place and will be enforced", Patterson said in a statement on September 14.

Barry Chevannes (Professor of Anthropology at the University of the West Indies) headed the Commission. It included deputy chairperson Dr. Eileen Goldson (from National Council on Drug Abuse), Reverend Webster Edwards, Norma Linton (Attorney-at-law), Dimario McDowell (graphic artist, musical promoter), Barbara Smith (former principal of Montego Bay High School), and Tony Freckleton (a businessman from Mandeville).

The aim of the Commission was to:

- receive submissions or memoranda, hear testimony, evaluate research and studies, engage in dialogue with relevant interest groups, and undertake wide public consultations with the aim of guiding national approach;

- indicate what changes, if any, are required to the existing laws or entail new legislation, taking account of social, cultural, economic and international factors;

- recommend the diplomatic initiatives, security considerations, educational process and programme of public information which will need to be undertaken in light if whatever changes may be proposed;

- consider and report on any other matter sufficiently related to the foregoing; and to make such interim reports, as it may deem necessary and a final report within a period of nine months from the first sitting.

Since 2001, The Jamaica National Commission slowed down its work to reexamine the island nation's marijuana's policies led by Dr. Chevannes, the government-appointed panel has visited eleven parishes and heard from more than 150 people and institutions.

The Commission, however, turned over to the government in July 2001, a report that gave no direct indication of whether it will recommend any decriminalization of the weed widely used in Jamaica. Chevannes comments, at that time, suggested that decriminalization may well be the commission's final recommendations. He stated further that the commission had deduced so far that most persons and organisations would support the decriminalization of the use of ganja for private purposes and in private spaces. He also added that the minority preferred to maintain the status quo regarding the criminal status of ganja in Jamaica.

The Commission also recognized the broad popularity of ganja among Jamaicans and suggested that decriminalization would merely regularize the status quo. "One opinion," Chevannes said, "is that decriminalization would not significantly increase the use of marijuana." "Right now," he added, "anyone who wants to smoke ganja is virtually at liberty to do so. It is available at large gatherings, and indeed, if police were to arrest everyone who is doing it, tens of thousands would be in jail."

In 2000, Jamaican Police made approximately 5000 arrests for ganja charges, 90 per cent of which were minor offenses. "So arguably," Chevannes said, "the only thing the decriminalization of it would be doing is taking the status of a crime off thousands of people. And most of them are young people. Were the commission to recommend decriminalization, it would not seriously change anything here."

Much of the concern in Jamaica surrounds the increase in the use and abuse of marijuana by young people. It has been shown to be costly medically and it also has negative effects on the quality of family life. However, the Coptics in the parish of St. Thomas are an example of law-abiding citizens who smoke ganja for religious reasons. Many consider the punishment for ganja use too harsh and not in keeping with the extent of the crime.

Research conducted at the Princess Margaret Hospital in St. Thomas on pregnant women using ganja showed normal deliveries and no visible harmful effects for up to five years after. Ganja is less addictive than alcohol, tobacco and caffeine, which are all legal. These have addictive properties while ganja is more of a habituation drug. Smoked ganja has

the same carcinogenic ingredients as tobacco. It also produces similar side effects, such as wheezing.

Some believe that decriminalization might result in intrusion on the rights of individuals. It is also felt that, like cigarettes, the use of ganja in public will become out of control.

ILLEGAL DRUG TRADE

The illegal drug trade is a global black market consisting of the cultivation, manufacture, distribution and sale of illegal controlled drugs. Most jurisdictions prohibit trade, except under license, of many types of drug by drug control laws. Some drugs, notably alcohol and tobacco, are outside the scope of these laws, but may be subject to control under other laws.

The illicit drug trade operates similarly to other underground markets. Various drug cartels specialize in the separate processes along the supply chain, often localized to maximize production efficiency and

PACKAGED GANJA IN A BOX

minimize damages caused by law enforcement. Depending on the profitability of each layer, cartels usually vary in size, consistency, and organization. The chain ranges from low-level street dealers who may be drug users themselves, through street gangs and contractor-like middlemen, up to multinational empires that rival governments in size.

The drugs are grown in wilderness areas, on farms, produced in indoor or outdoor residential gardens or indoor hydroponic grow-ops, or manufactured in drug labs located anywhere from a residential basement to an abandoned facility. The common characteristic binding these production locations is that they are discreet to avoid detection, and thus they may be located in any ordinary setting without raising notice. Much illegal drug cultivation and manufacture takes place in developing nations, although production also occurs in the developed world.

In locales where the drug trade is illegal, police departments as well as courts and prisons may expend significant resources in pursuing drug-related crime. Additionally, through the influence of a number of black market players, corruption is a problem, especially in poorer societies.

Consumption of illegal drugs is widespread globally. While consumers avoid taxation by buying on the black market, the high costs involved in protecting trade routes from law enforcement lead to inflated prices.

Additionally, various laws criminalize certain kinds of *trade* of drugs that are otherwise legal (for example, untaxed cigarettes). In these cases, the drugs are often manufactured and partially distributed by the normal legal channels, and diverted at some point into illegal channels.

Finally, many governments restrict the production and sale of large classes of drugs through prescription systems.

In World Drug Report 2006 UNODC focused on *The New Cannabis*, distribution of stronger marijuana with more THC and its health effects.

Around that time Most of the high grade cannabis sold in the United States was cultivated in hidden grow operations indoors. The number one producer was California with an annual revenue of nearly 14 billion dollars in production, Tennessee was second with nearly 5 billion in production, Kentucky was third with around 4.5 billion, Hawaii was fourth with close to 4 billion, and Washington is fifth with a little over a billion.

LEGALITY OF CANNABIS BY COUNTRY

COUNTRY	LEGAL STATUS	NOTES
ALBANIA	Illegal	Possession is illegal
ARGENTINA	Illegal (Decriminalized)	Decriminalized for personal use in small amounts and for consumption only in private locations. Public consumption is generally accepted among the young adults and overlooked by police in the suburbs. Consumption for medical purposes is accepted but not legislated (only in private locations). Cultivating, selling and transporting large amounts is illegal and punishable by present laws.
ANTIGUA AND BARBUDA	Illegal	Possession is illegal
AUSTRALIA	Illegal (Decriminalized)	Certain states of Australia have decriminalized cannabis possession. In Tasmania, Victoria and Queensland possession of up to 50 grams is a ticketed offense. If cannabis is found to be in possession with intent to sell, criminal convictions apply.

COUNTRY	LEGAL STATUS	NOTES
BAHRAIN	Illegal	Possession is illegal
BANGLADESH	Legal	No cannabis laws
BELGIUM	Illegal (Decriminalized)	For adults in Belgium, consumption in one's home and possession of quantities of up to 3 grams or one female plant is legal.
BERMUDA	Illegal	According to the Misuse of Drugs act 1972, possession and sale of the drug is illegal. Possession of 20 grams or more is considered intent to supply. Increased penalty zones, such as schools, rehab facilities, hospitals, airports and day care centres, are enforced.
BOLIVIA	Illegal	Possession is illegal.
BRAZIL	Illegal	Purchase, use and cultivation is illegal.
BULGARIA	Illegal	Until 2004 a loosely defined "personal dose" existed, since then all quantities are punishable by prison time up to 15 years
CANADA	Illegal (Decriminalized)	Main article: Cannabis legalization in Canada
CHILE	Illegal (Decriminalized)	Cultivation of Cannabis plants other than for personal use is considered illegal without a permit from the Agriculture Ministry. Though consumption and possession in small quantities alone on a private property is legal, consumption by a group of individuals is illegal.
CHINA	Illegal	Cannabis is considered a schedule II substance under Chinese law. Possession of even small quantities can result from as little as a fine up to years of imprisonment, the enforcement and penalties of the law is highly inconsistent throughout the country.

COUNTRY	LEGAL STATUS	NOTES
COLOMBIA	Illegal (Decriminalized)	Since 1994, cannabis has been decriminalized for possession of small amounts up to 20 grams for personal consumption, however sale and cultivation remains illegal.
COSTA RICA	Illegal (Decriminalized)	Possession is illegal
COTE D'IVOIRE	Illegal	Possesion is illegal
CROATIA	Illegal (Decriminalized)	Illegal to possess, buy, or sell any amount of cannabis. Under the law criminal penalties can be up to three years of imprisonment with fines of up to €700. For amounts less than 1 gram the penalty is an infraction fine, mandatory rehabilitation, and probation.[10]
CUBA	illegal	Possession is illegal
CYPRUS	Illegal	
CZECH REPUBLIC	Illegal (Decriminalized)	As of November 2007, sale of marijuana has been criminalized nationally. Though possession of small amount is legal for personal use. In March 2008, the Czech Supreme Court ruled that cultivation of agricultural cannabis is not the same as the production of marijuana.
DENMARK	Legal	Not considered an offense.
DOMINICA	Illegal	Possession is illegal
DOMINICAN REPUBLIC	Illegal	Possession is illegal
EGYPT	Illegal	
ECUADOR	Illegal	Possession illegal. No move to decriminalize.

COUNTRY	LEGAL STATUS	NOTES
ESTONIA	Illegal	Possession illegal. Only seeds legal but not their export/import
FINLAND	Illegal	Medical use decriminalized
FRANCE	Illegal	Cultivating, selling, owning or consuming cannabis is prohibited.
GERMANY	Illegal (Decriminalized)	Possession of small amounts for personal use at home is not prosecuted, but the drug is confiscated. The definition of "small amount" is different in each federal state; the tolerated amount ranges from 3 grams in Brandenburg to 30 grams in Schleswig-Holstein. The sale is illegal. Possession of larger amounts is usually only punished with a fine, unless the intention to sell is evident. Cultivation of cannabis is also illegal, but usually not prosecuted if the plants are not in flower and the amount of plants is rather small (the plants will be confiscated though). Only flowering female plants are treated like the possession of cannabis products; the exact amount of THC in the buds will be lab analyzed and determines the assumed amount of processed marijuana. Possession of small amounts of marijuana/hashish was ruled legal by the German Federal Constitutional Court in 1994.
GHANA	Illegal	
GREECE	Illegal	
GUATEMALA	Illegal	

COUNTRY	LEGAL STATUS	NOTES
HUNGARY	Illegal	There is no distinction in Hungarian law between illicit drugs according to dangers. Heroin use has the same consequences as cannabis use. Hungarian law prohibits the distribution, and any use (including medical use). However, the Penal code distinguishes the punishment between sale and personal use. 283. § (1) paragraph (a) states that "One cannot be punished for drug misuse; if a small, personal amount is produced, acquired, or in possession..." and continues to state that "... provided that before final verdict is determined a verification is provided that continuous 6 month therapy has taken place". The law determines that a "personal quantity" is defined as 1 gram of active substance (i.e. THC), therefore this equates to 12-100 grams of marijuana if calculated that marijuana contains 1-8% THC per unit mass. Possession of larger amounts can lead to a 5 to 10-year prison sentence.
ICELAND	Illegal	Consumption is illegal even in small amounts. Possession, sale, transportation and cultivation could result in jail time. Possession is not strictly enforced. Heavy fines are given.
INDONESIA	Illegal	Personal use in small amounts: Maximum sentence of four (4) years in prison (additional fines may apply) if caught by the police in possession, intoxication or by positive urine test. However, if the user voluntarily reports himself/herself to the police, or is reported by his/her family, the sentence shall be no more than 6 months in prison or a fine of not more than Rp 2.000.000 (two million Indonesian Rupiah/ USD$200-250).

COUNTRY	LEGAL STATUS	NOTES
INDIA	Legal (Regulated by Government)	Used during observance of certain Hind rituals. Government-owned shops in holy cities like Varanasi sell cannabis in the form of bhang.
IRELAND	Illegal	
IRAN	Legal/Illegal	Growing cannabis is legal if planted for food purposes as the seeds are eaten b the Iranian people, and companies ofte draw oil from the seeds which are sold legally. Using cannabis for psychoactive purposes is technically illegal and so smoking it in public is an example of wh can be considered an illegal ingestion, but the enforcement of this is next to nothing since it is usually not possible to tell what a person is smoking and since smoking other herbs is tolerated or lega not much is ever done.
ISRAEL	Illegal	Often unenforced. Very small scale of legal usage of medicinal cannabis.
ITALY	Legal	
JAMAICA	Illegal	Cultivation, retail and consumption are illegal. However this is often overlooked and cannabis is sold openly.
JAPAN	Illegal	Possession is punishable by up to five years in prison with forced labour
KENYA	Illegal	Decriminalized although possession of large quantities can lead to prosecution with a maximum of 6 months in prison. [citation needed]
SOUTH KOREA	Illegal	Not tolerated. Hair tests can be taken upon suspicion. Jail time minimum 6 months.[citation needed]
KUWAIT	Illegal	
LATVIA	Illegal	

COUNTRY	LEGAL STATUS	NOTES
LIBERIA	Illegal	
LITHUANIA	Illegal	
LUXEMBOURG	Illegal	Possession, transportation and consumption are illegal. Prosecution depends on the amount of cannabis one possesses. Since 2001, prison penalty has been substituted by a monetary fine ranging from 250 to 2500 Euros.
REPUBLIC OF MACEDONIA	Illegal (Decriminalized)	Possessors of small quantities (usually about 5 grams) of cannabis are usually not prosecuted. However, if one possesses a larger amount, a jail sentence of anywhere from three months to five years could possibly be given.
MALAYSIA	Illegal	Malaysian legislation provides for a mandatory death penalty for convicted drug traffickers. Individuals arrested in possession of 15 grams (1/2 ounce) of heroin or 200 grams (seven ounces) of marijuana are presumed by law to be trafficking in drugs.
MALTA	Illegal	
MAURITIUS	Illegal	
MEXICO	Illegal	Main article: Mexican Drug War
MOLDOVA	Illegal	
MOROCCO	Illegal	Cultivating, selling, owning or consuming cannabis is prohibited. Though cultivating it has been traditionally tolerated in the Rif region.
NEPAL	Illegal	Though cannabis is illegal, it is consumed openly.
NETHERLANDS	Legal/Illegal	Main article: Drug policy of the Netherlands

COUNTRY	LEGAL STATUS	NOTES
NEW ZEALAND	Illegal	Cannabis is scheduled as a Class C substance. Cultivation, possession or sale of cannabis is illegal.
NORWAY	Illegal	Up to 15 grams is considered an amount for personal use, and is punished with a fine of 1500-5000 kroner in the case of first-time offenders; possessing more is considered dealing and punished more harshly. Repeat offenders or dealers face prison charges.
PAKISTAN	Legal/Illegal	Although laws exist against its usage, marijuana and hash are generally tolerated in Pakistan, and laws against usage are rarely, if ever, enforced. Traditionally smoked in Hujra (Guest houses) and used in cultural circles for social reasons for some 1500 years. Various forms available such as Garda, the purer, safer and historic form used in the country and in recent years the Chars form which is adulterated and sold in the big cities for profit and exported to South Asia (India, Bangladesh etc...)Cannabis Indica grows widely throughout India, from whence it derives its etymology, as well as other areas like Afghanistan and the rest of Central Asia due to the favourable climate. It grows wildly and isn't usually controlled. Most people just remove this weed from their farming zones to make space for other crops.
PARAGUAY	Illegal	
PERU	Illegal (Decriminalized)	Possession of up to 8 grams (0.28 oz) of marijuana is legal as long as one is not in possession of another drug.

COUNTRY	LEGAL STATUS	NOTES
PHILIPPINES	Illegal	A fine of PHP 500,000 - 10,000 and life imprisonment for possession of more than 10 grams. A fine and 20 years imprisonment to life imprisonment for possession of more than 5 grams but less than 10 grams. A fine and imprisonment of at least 12 years and a maximum of 20 years for possession of less than 5 grams.
POLAND	Illegal	Possession leads to criminal prosecution even for very small quantities (<0.001). The Polish government in June 2005 began offering rehabilitation services in place of jail time.
PORTUGAL	Illegal (decriminalized)	
PUERTO RICO	Illegal	
ROMANIA	Illegal	Illegal but not very hard to find at certain events or in special, sometimes secret, places. Unenforced. Possession of small quantities is punishable by a small fine of about $150-200 USD. Possession of large amounts may result in 3-6 years of jail time, and sale may result in more than 6 years jail time.
RUSSIA	Illegal (Decriminalized)	In 2003, possession of up to 20g of marijuana, as well as small quantities of many other drugs, ceased to be a criminal offence. Since 2006, this "legal" amount was lowered to 6 g.
SAUDI ARABIA	Illegal	Use and possession for personal use of any kind of drugs is punishable by imprisonment if caught. Imprisonment for personal use could go up to 6 months jail time or more. Dealing and smuggling of high amounts of drugs usually result in harsher prison time or even execution, although recently executions are rare. Foreigners who use drugs might be deported.

COUNTRY	LEGAL STATUS	NOTES
SERBIA	Illegal	
SLOVENIA	Illegal	
SOUTH AFRICA	Illegal	
SPAIN	Decriminalized	Cannabis was introduced to Spain in the Middle Ages by the Moors. It is tolerated in private although its sale is illegal.
SIERRA LEONE	Illegal	
SINGAPORE	Illegal	Cannabis is a Class A drug under the Misuse of Drugs Act, making it illegal to cultivate, sell, or possess. Trafficking in more than 250 grams of Cannabis is punishable by death.
SWEDEN	Illegal	No distinction is made towards other drugs: Possession of all quantities as well as use is illegal. The maximum penalty of six months imprisonment for minor offenses (such as personal use) makes the police eligible to arrest and take drug test upon suspicion. Fines are the most common sanction. The maximum sentence for aggravated drug offenses (and smuggling, which is regulated in a separate law) is ten years imprisonment.
SWITZERLAND	Illegal	Although tolerated in small amounts for personal use at home.
TAIWAN	Illegal	Cannabis is a Schedule 2 narcotic in Taiwan, and possession can result in up to 3 years imprisonment.
TANZANIA	Illegal	
THAILAND	Illegal	
TURKEY	Illegal	

COUNTRY	LEGAL STATUS	NOTES
UNITED ARAB EMIRATES	Illegal	Even the smallest amounts of the drug can lead to a mandatory four-year prison sentence.
UNITED KINGDOM	Illegal	Main article: Cannabis reclassification in the United Kingdom Cannabis is an illegal, Class B drug in the UK.
USA	Illegal	Main article: Legal history of marijuana in the United States Laws vary by state, though state law is superseded by federal law which classifies cannabis as a Schedule I substance, the same classification as heroin and LSD. Now decriminalized in MA as well as parts of CA. Marijuana was recently made legal in Colorado and Washington DC
URUGUAY		Almost legal , process is underway
VENEZUELA	Illegal (Decriminalized)	Possession of up to 20 grams results in a mandatory drug treatment program.
VIETNAM	Illegal	Possession of large quantities is enforced.

SOCIOECONOMIC IMPACT OF CANNABIS

The legalization of cannabis for medicinal purposes is becoming more prominent globally. The fact that the drug will become readily available presents an increased risk for the passive and/or active ingestion by children. There are reported cases of unexplained comas being found later to be associated with cannabis ingestion and as such, it is imperative that with the advent of the legalization of marijuana, public education highlighting its risks in children is implemented.

Marijuana use may also impact behavioral decisions. For example, increased sexual risk taking in a study among young women was shown to be associated with marijuana use in a study done by Anderson and

Stein in 2011. These risks include the non-use of condoms with casual sexual partners and increased sexual activity.

For the first time however, a model was developed by Schwilke et al to differentiate new cannabis use from residual urinary cannabinoid excretion in chronic, daily cannabis users. This is extremely important in drug-testing programs such as those for military and criminal justice, clinicians, staff and toxicologists.

With the advent of synthetic cannabinoids, legal problems associated with cannabis are increasing. These compounds which were developed solely for experimental purposes are now finding its way to herbal smoking mixtures. The compounds are more potent than traditional cannabis and are widely manufactured despite authoritative efforts to control them. Safety concerns have stemmed from this issue in many countries.

While scientific research continues to reveal the numerous medicinal properties of cannabis, justification for its legalization in many countries is becoming more evident. Jamaica and many countries around the world are still trying to weigh the benefits of utilizing the plant against its negative effects and socioeconomic implications. There is great economic potential for Jamaica should cannabis be legalized as it opens doors for commercial applications whether as pharmaceutical agents or otherwise and more valuable scientific research may evolve from it. There are other legal products such as tobacco which are known to have a plethora of negative effects both medically and socially when compared with marijuana. The negative impacts as it relates to abuse of the drug and health concerns cannot be ignored and as such the legalization of marijuana will continue to be a controversial issue in many societies.

11

SUMMARY
AND THE WAY FORWARD

"Things which matter most must never be at the mercy of things which matter least!"
- GOETHE 1749-1832

The purpose of this book is not to persuade or encourage the reader to join either side of the debate on cannabis. Rather, it seeks to educate the reader. The fact is, advances in cannabinoid science have given rise to many new opportunities for the development of medicinally useful cannabinoid based drugs. The accumulated data suggest a variety of uses, particularly for pain relief, antiemesis, glaucoma and appetite stimulation.

For patients such as those with AIDS or those undergoing chemotherapy who suffer simultaneously from severe pain, nausea, and appetite loss, cannabinoid drugs might offer a broad spectrum of relief not found in any other single medication. The data is weaker for muscle spasticity, but somewhat promising. The least promising categories are movement disorders and epilepsy. Animal data are fairly supportive of a potential for cannabinoids in the treatment of movement disorders and might eventually yield stronger results. The therapeutic effects of cannabinoids were mainly established for THC, which is the primary psychoactive ingredient of marijuana. However, it does not follow that smoking marijuana is good medicine. Canasol is a departure from smoking in terms of its therapeutic and social acceptance.

Although marijuana smoke delivers THC and other cannabinoids to the body, it also delivers harmful substances, including most of those found in tobacco smoke. In addition, plants contain a variable mixture of biologically-active compounds and cannot be expected to provide a precisely defined drug effect. For those reasons, there seems to be little future in smoked marijuana as a medicinally approved medication. However the increasing ability to provide marijuana extracts with controlled preparation of THC (mood influence) to CBD (neuromuscular influence) could lead to enhanced medical appraisals in a variety of disease states.

If there is any future in cannabinoid drugs, it lies with agents of more certain composition. While clinical trials are the route to the development of approved medication, they are also valuable for other reasons. For example, the personal medicinal use of smoked marijuana to treat certain symptoms is reason enough to advocate clinical trials, whether or not it is approved. These trials would assess the degree to which the symptoms or the course of the diseases are affected.

Controlled studies that test the safety and efficacy of marijuana use are an important component to the understanding of the course of any disease, particularly such as AIDS, where the use of marijuana is prevalent. The argument against the future of smoked marijuana for treating any condition lies not in its effectiveness, but in the associated risks. These risks could be overcome by the development of a non-smoking, rapid onset delivery system for cannabinoid drugs.

Two factors should be taken into consideration when following the traditional path of drug development for cannabinoids. The first is timing. Patients who are currently suffering from debilitating conditions unrelieved by legally available drugs, and who might find relief with smoked marijuana, will find little comfort in a promise of a better drug ten years from now.

HEMP, HEMP, HURRAH!

YOU COULD SAY that hemp is where soy was 15 years ago, an offbeat product with an exotic, even illicit reputation and an overlooked nutritional reservoir. Hemp is rich in protein (a higher concentration than in beef, fish or poultry), and hempseed oil contains lots of omega-3 and omega-6 essential fatty acids, including gamma linoleic acid (GLA), the same substance people pay big money for in supplement form. GLA helps lower LDL, the "bad" cholesterol.

Like soy, hemp is a staple in Asian diets, having been cultivated as a food for 5,000 years. And should you find its link to marijuana troubling, take heart; hemp is legal under U.S. federal law and is used in the production of many foods and products, although it is illegal for U.S. farmers to grow without a permit. To reap its benefits, sprinkle toasted hempseed on cereal, salad, soups and pasta.

MEN'S FITNESS JUNE 2001 WWW.MENSFITNESS.COM

In terms of good medicine, marijuana should rarely be recommended unless all reasonable options have been eliminated. It is conceivable that the medical and scientific opinion might find itself in conflict with drug regulations. This presents a policy issue that must balance, at least temporarily, the needs of individual patients with broader social issues. Our assessment of the scientific data on the medical value of marijuana and its constituent cannabinoids is one such component in the attainment of that balance.

The second is a practical one. Although most scientists who study cannabinoids would agree that the scientific pathways to cannabinoid drug development are clearly marked, there is no guarantee that the benefits yielded from scientific research will be made available to the public. Cannabinoid-based drugs will only become generally available if there is enough incentive for private enterprise to develop and market such drugs, and if there is a sustained public investment in cannabinoid drug research and development.

Although many abuse cannabis, the focus of the research should be on the therapeutic value of the cannabinoid-based drugs and its use in the treatment of specific symptoms or diseases. This is not substance abuse. Scientific data indicate the potential therapeutic value of cannabinoid drugs, primarily THC, for pain relief, control of nausea and vomiting, glaucoma and appetite stimulation. Smoked marijuana, however, is a crude THC delivery system that also delivers harmful substances.

Clinical trials of cannabinoid drugs for symptom management should be conducted with the goal of developing rapid onset, reliable, and safe delivery systems.

EUROPE
GOES TO POT

Technically, it is still illegal, but so many cannabis users flout the law that governments opt to go easy

LIGHTING UP ON THE CONTINENT

PORTUGAL	BELGIUM	BRITAIN	FRANCE
The law: Europe's newest, most liberal policy decriminalizes all drugs, from marijuana to heroin The impact: Community service and blacklisting at clubs substitute for prison; "patients" are sent to rehab	The law: Medical use of cannabis allowed; new statute being debated to permit growth and use of small amounts for pleasure The impact: Arrest only those who harm selves, or others, like minors, by example	The law: Police in one area of London try a new plan to caution users and confiscate their dope, rather than prosecute The impact: Frees police time for handling serious crime	The law: Pot use can trigger a year in jail or a $3,500 fine, but local police can decide what to tolerate The impact: Agreeing to therapy eliminates a sentence, and judges can exercise wide latitude

TIME, AUGUST 20, 2001

Clinical trials of marijuana use for medicinal purposes should be conducted when and if institutional review boards approve trials. It should involve only short-term marijuana use (less than 6 months), and conducted in patients with conditions for which there is reasonable expectation of effectiveness. The data relating to its effectiveness should be collected and analyzed.

Short-term use of smoked marijuana (less than six months) for patients with incapacitating symptoms (such as persistent pain or vomiting) must meet the following conditions:

- documented evidence that all approved medications failed to provide relief;

- the symptoms can reasonably be expected to be relieved by rapid onset cannabinoid drugs;

- the treatment is administered under medical supervision in a manner that allows for assessment of the effectiveness of the treatment;

- a physician who gives marijuana to a patient for a specified use should do it in a controlled environment, one that is comparable to an institutional review board that could provide guidance within 24 hours of a submission.

Until a non-smoking, rapid onset cannabinoid drug delivery system becomes available, there is no clear alternative for people suffering from chronic conditions that might be relieved by smoking marijuana, such as pain or AIDS wasting. One possible approach is to perform clinical trials in which patients are fully informed of their status as experimental subjects who are using a possibly harmful drug delivery system. Their condition should be closely monitored and documented under medical supervision, thereby increasing the knowledge base of the risks and benefits of marijuana use under such conditions.

These clinical trials are recommended using the same control mechanism as that proposed in the above recommendations.

Public opinion on the medicinal value of marijuana has been sharply divided. Some dismiss medicinal marijuana as a hoax that exploits our natural compassion for the sick; others claim it is a uniquely soothing medicine that has been withheld from patients through regulations based on false claims. Proponents of both views cite 'scientific evidence' to support their views.

NEW DYNAMICS IN MARIJUANA LEGALIZATION

The International Scene

With little more than a side-note the legalization of Marijuana has now emerged into a "movement", a subject that main Government bodies are now paying attention to. Instead of succumbing to years of discrimination, scoffing, ridicule and consistent objection, Cannabis on its own has shown that it is indeed worthy of acknowledgment.

Science has shown that Marijuana has extensive therapeutic applications. Before this, Marijuana's "good" was only word-of-mouth given, deemed unsubstantiated and unimportant. However now, several individuals and selected groups are now expressing what would be termed a "balanced view" on Marijuana, one of these individuals being Dr. Sanjay Gupta.

Sanjay Gupta is a practicing neurosurgeon, who is also CNN's Chief Medical Correspondent. After spending one year around the world researching Cannabis he released a controversial article entitled "Why I changed my mind on Weed". In this article he systematically presented his findings which challenged the current perception of weed by the mass. His article can be spearheaded by his statement *"We have been terribly and systematically misled for nearly 70 years in the United States, and I apologize for my own role in that."*

In the article he acknowledges that he due to lack of proper research, he skipped out marijuana research done in smaller countries and came to the conclusion that marijuana was not beneficial. He argued accurately that the Drug Enforcement Agency has wrongly placed marijuana as a schedule 1 substance, a category characterized by no accepted medicinal use and a high potential for abuse. An impeccable point was drawn when he stated that in 1944 the New York Academy of science found that marijuana did not lead to significant addiction, and it wasn't a gateway drug to morphine, heroin or cocaine addiction. In addition in his one year journey he found that there existed hundreds of journals documented between 1840 and 1930. These papers discussed medical marijuana to treat neuralgia, convulsive disorders, and emaciation among others. Similarly, the U.S. National Library of Medicine recently pulled 20,000 recent papers, however these describe the adverse effects of Marijuana, he subsequently stated "I calculated about 6% of the current U.S. marijuana studies investigate the benefits of medical marijuana. The rest are designed to investigate harm. That imbalance paints a highly distorted picture."

He briefly addressed the issue that researchers have in doing experiments with marijuana which mainly constitutes the availability of marijuana and the tedious process of getting approval to use such. Marijuana usage by the scientists also needs approval from NIDA. He pointed that the National Institute on Drug Abuse (NIDA) core mission is studying abuse rather than benefits. And he therefore suggested it is unmerited in being a part of the approval process. Conclusively he stated that "As much as I searched, I could not find a documented case of death from marijuana overdose .It is perhaps no surprise then that 76% of physicians recently surveyed said they would approve the use of marijuana to help ease a woman's pain from breast cancer". Some light was shown on countries such as Spain and Israel that are researching the anti-cancer effects of marijuana and its components along with other research looking at marijuana therapeutic usage in alleviating symptoms of Post Traumatic Stress Disorder (PTSD) and neuro-protection.

Dr. Gupta's Article was also heavily supplemented by a 43 minute documentary entitled "Weed" shown on CNN. In his documentary Dr. Gupta uses real life stories to debunk some of the negative notions on marijuana. While maintaining a balanced view by looking at ways marijuana affects individuals cognitively and socially.

In his first presentation he presented the case of Charlotte Figi a 5 year old girl who suffers from Dravet Syndrome, a severe intractable form of epilepsy. Charlotte lives in Colorado, a state that allows for Marijuana to be used medicinally and recreationally. She started having seizures at 3 months old despite being born healthy and was developing in like manner. She was declining cognitively, showing attention deficit amongst other traits. Children who suffer from Dravet syndrome normally die at a young age. Her parents had tried everything for two years which included diets and risky prescriptions. In 2011 at 5 years old her father was deployed to Afghanistan, Charlotte's father in his state did some research and found out that Marijuana could assist her after seeing it being used on another child. Being a man of military Mr. Figi has never been associated with marijuana as this was taboo and could affect his career, though he lived in a state that avidly uses it. Marijuana was the last option for their daughter who was at the time having 300 seizures for the week which was becoming dangerous and life threating. Within this time her options for getting better included using veterinary drugs used in dogs or placed in a state of induced coma so her body could rest; both being unfavorable and distasteful. Desperate and fragile her parents agreed to try the marijuana subsequently.

Initially it took a while to get Charlotte approved since she was too young to be on the plant, and doctors wouldn't prescribe marijuana to a child. After eventually getting approved they needed to get a plant that was low in THC but high in CBD so to prevent the child from experiencing a 'high" at such a tender age . This was not a popular type of weed and proved challenging to source. Her mother eventually found a strain in a Denver Dispensary. She then found a way to extract the medicine from the marijuana, measure it with a syringe and squirted it under the tongue. The results were astounding; she didn't have a seizure that day. After trying it a year later she was having only one seizure a week, she was eating on her own after two years on a feeding tube, talking and walking. Despite such breakthrough, there still exist some opposition including the Miami Children's Hospital which stated that "At present, there is no evidence that cannabidiol is effective for the treatment of epilepsy", The American Academy of Pediatrics and National Institute on Drug Abuse

In another case, Chaz Moore, 19 years of age suffers from diaphragmatic myoclonus, which causes him to speak in hiccups, one syllable at a time. Pharmaceuticals did not work for him and similarly to Charlotte marijuana was the last option. In speaking with Dr. Gupta, Moore showed how marijuana high in CBD has been effective in treating his condition. After Convulsing for 7 minutes in his presence he smoked the marijuana and began speaking fluently in less than a minute. He would before using marijuana have these attacks at times 40 times a day.

WHAT IT DOES TO THE BRAIN?

Dr. *Staci Gruber* is Director of the Cognitive and Clinical Neuroimaging Core at McLean Hospital's Brain Imaging Center. In her discussion with Dr. Gupta says, in summary, when an individual takes that first smoke, receptors throughout the brain respond. These areas are responsible for things such as pleasure, learning, memory, sensation; sense of time and space, coordination and movement, appetite, thus the first smoke has an all-around impact. Therefore the marijuana severely enhances the emotional state of a person. The Documentary also supported this with claims that artists make saying marijuana helps them to be more creative. He used the example of a painter Amir who smokes to facilitate his painting. He says it makes him more relaxed, less critical, and less worrying and enhances his creativity. He also described how important it is for him to keep a balance by explaining that too much marijuana makes him paranoid, apprehensive, too analytical among other attributes. Dr. Gruber commented that smoking marijuana allows the brain to perceive things differently; there is a reduction in inhibitory function which helps the subject to be more creative.

Cart Hart, a Neuroscientist at Columbian University is now studying the cognitive effects of Marijuana. It is now being revealed that the section of the brain that becomes mostly affected is the prefrontal cortex. This section contains more marijuana receptors and is involved in planning, thinking, coordinating. Therefore marijuana can impact these functions.

An Experiment done by CNN affiliates K.I.R.O in Washington State revealed the following:

The experiment consisted of a habitual smoker and a novice smoker (Infrequent, weekend smoker). The novice was allowed to smoke and drive at the same time; the more the subject smoked the more trouble he had driving. Similarly the habitual smoker smoked while driving and didn't experience the same. This was again confirmed by Dr. Gupta as he drove with Chaz Moore and saw that his driving ability wasn't affected by his marijuana usage. It's seen where you don't see as much cognitive disturbances in habitual smokers versus novices.

The documentary further discussed the impact of marijuana smoking on younger individuals. The smoking is said to impair the brain in sections that the brain uses to communicate. It becomes disrupted since the brain is at a delicate time in development. Individuals, who smoke young exhibit slowness, lower IQs and psychotic disorder. This however is not conclusive.

Dr. Alan Shackelford Charlotte Figi's doctor is committed to marijuana research which has somehow outcasted him in the medical committee through criticism. This has propelled him to travel the world for more answers which led him to the medical marijuana research capital Israel. Research of Cannabis in epilepsy started in Israel by using rats, presently aiming to do clinical tests in humans. The Ministry of Health in Israel is currently Studying a variety of illnesses such as PTSD, Crohn's disease, pain and cancer. It was quite relevant to discuss Dr. Gupta's Journey, as this will definitely affect the dynamics of marijuana legalization in countries around the world.

The international Narcotics Control Board (INCB) president Raymond Yans in the board's 2012 report cautioned that legalizing marijuana for recreational use could be an advantage for criminals in the criminal underworld. He stated that "organized criminal groups would get even more deeply involved, for instance by creating a black market for the illicit supply of newly legalized drugs to young people". In responding to the recent legalization of recreational marijuana in some states, the INCB reports says these states are being operated in a manner that is "completely inappropriate and outside of the conventions". He further argued that some declarations and initiatives are inclusive of proposals that would allow for the cultivation and consumption of cannabis for non-medical purposes. Consequently he says this will violate international drug control conventions. Additionally he added that persons in favor of the legalization of marijuana "ignore the commitment that all governments have made to promote the health and well-being of their communities." A month prior, Marine General John Kelly, head of the United States Southern Command, said the decision to legalize marijuana for medical marijuana is "dumb". He states "A lot of people are fooled to think that drug use can be recreational. This is one of the biggest issues with which the country (US) has to contend,"

WORLD HEALTH ORGANIZATION & CANNABIS LEGALIZATION

After 15 years, in 1997 The World Health Organization published a report on cannabis entitled, "Cannabis: A health perspective and research agenda". This report was scrutinized in the media which said the WHO suppressed information on important findings on cannabis. The finding stated that even if marijuana was consumed on the same scales as alcohol or tobacco it is still safer than both. The suppressed passage said its findings were "not to promote one drug over another but rather to minimise double standards that have operated in appraising the health effects of cannabis." WHO in response said it didn't include this comparison with other drug "the reliability and public health significance of such comparisons are doubtful."

UNITED NATIONS & CANNABIS LEGALISATION

The United Nation's International Narcotic Control Board (INCB) is an independent body of experts established by the United Nations to monitor countries' compliance with international drug treaties. The United Nation's International Narcotic Control Board currently says no to the Legalisation of Marijuana. With the recent legalization of the non-medical use of Marijuana in Washington and Colorado, the INCB had several remarks in opposition to such move. In its annual report, Raymond Yans, INCB president said such legalization in these states violates the international drug convention and that it is "a great threat to public health and the well-being of society far beyond those states." He further stated that "They also undermine the humanitarian aims of the drug control system and are a threat to public health and wellbeing". The INCB's annual report also warns of what is described as "unprecedented surge" in the growth of legal highs which is a new psychoactive drug largely synthesised by chemists in South-East Asia and which are not under international controls. He said the supply of these drugs are increasing dramatically- "The total number of such substances on the market has been estimated to be in the order of thousands, posing a significant challenge to public health systems in preventing and dealing with their abuse," says the UN drugs annual report. Yans also commented on Britain's defence against these legal high. They have introduced a banning system which temporarily bans 'legal high' as soon as they appear on the market. He also commented that other countries have been taking other steps such as using early warning systems, tightening control on retailers among other steps.

Uruguay draft Marijuana bill has also heavily scrutinized by the INCB. The INCB stated that the law would "be in complete contravention to the provisions of the international drug treaties to which Uruguay is party" referring to Single Convention on Narcotic Drugs of 1961, which bans the sale of cannabis for non-medical use. INCB said that if IT happened it "might have serious consequences for the health and welfare of the population and for the prevention of cannabis abuse among the youth". The Uruguayan government argues that by bringing the sale of cannabis under state control, it will remove profits from drug dealers and divert users from harder drugs.

THE EMERGING DISCUSSION IN JAMAICA AND THE CARIBBEAN

Marijuana came to Jamaica in the 1800s by East Indian Indentured workers. Similar to other countries Jamaica also has the issue of legalization of Marijuana on their Hands. Recently there has been traction in this movement as more countries are saying yes to the legalization of Cannabis, more recently Uruguay along with Colorado and Washington in the United States. The view on the legalization of marijuana in Jamaica is a mixture of yes and no.

In light of the recent ban on the smoking of cigarettes in public spaces, Health Minister Dr. Fenton Ferguson remains oblivious to the view he will adopt as it pertains to the legalization of Marijuana. When asked he said "That is not on my agenda at this time. What is on my agenda in terms of tobacco is Article 13 of the Framework Convention on Tobacco Control, which speaks to advertising, promotion and sponsorship. That is on my mind," furthermore he added, "What is on my mind (is) Article 15 of the Framework Convention as it relates to illicit sale of tobacco,"

On the other side of the spectrum, Paul Chang chairman of the Ganja Law Reform Coalition (GLRC) has called for the legalization of Marijuana that follows the Uruguayan draft bill for Marijuana Legalization. In short, in this model growers, sellers and consumers of the plant will need license and must be on a consensual age at least 18 years, persons won't also be able to buy more than 40 grams a month at pharmacies. Paul Chang therefore advocates for such a model to be implemented. His argument followed the basis that the drug could be a guide for Jamaica's Legislators to use medicinal cannabis to generate tax revenue. This would be done through giving permits to tourist visiting the island to use the cannabis for medicinal reasons, and this would lead to what was described as a "renaissance in Jamaica's agriculture".

Jamaica's parliament has once again looked to the United States legislature prior to determining their stance on a crucial topic - decriminalization of ganja - which can have serious socio-economic consequences for the island and its citizens. The National Ganja Commission has long recommended that marijuana be decriminalized for private, personal use by adults as well as for sacramental religious purposes

- the latter speaks directly to the island's Rastafarian population who continue to fight for this right.

Parliament has recently signalled that it is seriously reconsidering its stance and will debate the proposed changes to current cannabis laws which will see an ease on restrictions on the plant, the high grade variety of which has been linked to Jamaica for decades through song and other accolades. Mark Golding, Jamaica's current Justice Minister, recently told one of the island's leading daily newspapers that revisions to laws in Colorado and Washington and the seeming change of attitude towards the issue by the federal government are positive signs in the global review of the use of cannabis. This point is made noting that Jamaica's refusal to review ganja laws over the past 50 years has mainly been at the insistence of the United States – a major source of funding.

As the world intensifies its review of cannabis especially for medicinal and therapeutic use, Jamaica's Ministry of Justice is feverishly working to formally present its position and a proposal for the way forward. This latest move is drawing mixed reactions, more positive than negative, as some citizens view the frequent arrests and criminalization of Jamaican youth in particular as an exercise in futility and a waste of the country's already limited financial resources and distracts the security forces from focusing on hard core drugs such as cocaine and related criminal activities.

The ever evolving geopolitics of the region has also forced other member states of the Caribbean Community to rethink their position on the decriminalization of cannabis. Most Caribbean states share a history of economic dependence of foreign aid, grants and other forms of financial assistance. Advocates such as the vocal and controversial Prime Minister of St Vincent and the Grenadines, Ralph Gonsalves, sees the move to decriminalize as a possible economic stimulus which presents major opportunities for growth among the 15 member states in areas such as agriculture and processing. He formally presented this position in a letter to CARICOM's Chair on September 2, 2013 calling for preliminary talks on the issue.

In spite of Gonsalves and other supporting member states call for an objective and focused review, other islands such as St Kitts and Nevis continue to be in total opposition of any move to decriminalize marijuana regardless of its proven medicinal and therapeutic purposes in addition to other potentially beneficial uses which are currently being researched. Trinidad and Tobago has commissioned a study on the pros and cons of the legalization of ganja under the directive of Prime Minister and current Chairwoman of CARICOM, Kamla Persad-Bissessar. These findings are scheduled for presentation at the heads of government meeting to be held in February 2014.

Gonsalves and others such as the authors of this book, continue to press for a sense of urgency in the collective review of ganja as the region is perilously positioned to lose the research and development race globally which could see us importing medicine, nutraceuticals and cosmoceuticals derived from ganja legally grown and processed in places such as the United States which currently sees the plant being legal in 20 of 50 states. This figure could shift drastically and in key areas within the next 5 years at a minimum.

Jamaica has an existing and developing body of research and qualified professionals with an interest in the plant and can aggressively take a clear leadership role in positioning ganja for medicinal and therapeutic use and marketing for the economic development of not only the island but the region.

AND FINALLY, . . . WHAT DO WE THE AUTHORS SAY?

Marijuana appears to have some potential as a medicine for certain conditions. These conditions need to be carefully studied and appraised medically and scientifically with respect to the response to marijuana in large scale, double blind, cross over, multicentre clinical trials, much as has been and is being done in chronic disease drug trials. In particular the type and mode of administration have to be assessed for reproducibility and timing of efficacy.

New and novel methods of delivery systems which could separate the psychoactive from the specific action required, ought to be investigated as we do agree that smoking for medical purposes provides too much of an indeterminate and unpredictable dosage of the active principle (s), as well as presenting the undesired fallout from smoking per se.

It is long term measures such as these that will be required to influence governmental decisions as to how best to manage cannabis, the plant, and its extracts and preparations.

There seems to be enough evidence also to support the view that certain individuals are predisposed to develop mental illness after prolonged use but this may be no greater a social problem than that of the other well known and commonly used 'social drugs' such as in alcohol and tobacco preparations.

The authors are of the view that adult possession for personal and private use ought not to attract criminal sanctions.

The present state of knowledge does not justify criminalization for its possession and/or use and governmental funds used in pursuit of private personal use ought to be diverted elsewhere. *Nevertheless the current status of 'anxiety' about marijuana does support a need for controlling its production for research and medicinal application. Marketing and trafficking, however, must be subject to the full measure of the law.*

UK police relax ganja laws

BY HUNTLEY MEDLEY
Observer correspondent

ONDON — Increasing public support for after laws on the possession and use of annabis in Britain has forced Scotland Yard to athorise a controversial pilot project in south ondon which will see people caught with small mounts of the drug being let off with only an n-the-spot warning and the weed being onfiscated.

The project, which is set to run from July 2 to e end of December this year, is the brainchild of ambeth borough police commander, Brian addick, and will be operational in south London ommunities, including Brixton, home to large umbers of persons of Jamaican and other West dian origin.

A Scotland Yard spokesperson told the *bserver* last week that the move does not epresent a change of official government policy n marijuana possession and use, which remain legal, but is an initiative falling within iscretionary powers granted the police by the Home Office.

Paddick told journalists that the move is aimed at giving his limited number of police officers more time to tackle hard drugs and crimes associated particularly with crack cocaine. Met police commissioner, Sir John Stevens, has described the plan as "sensible and progressive".

It is said that it takes two officers up to five hours to process someone caught with cannabis, while the new policy could see a possession case being disposed of in 10 minutes. Not only is the new measure expected to free up London police to concentrate on more serious crimes — a central issue in the recent general election campaign — but it is also expected to result in significant savings in administrative legal costs.

Unlike a caution or arrest, which becomes part of permanent police records, a warning under the new plan is only noted by local police and does not have to be declared by someone applying for a job.

Last October, a national survey conducted by the reputable polling organisation, Mori, showed that 64 per cent of respondents felt that the police spend too much time prosecuting cannabis users instead of dealing with more serious crimes. Police figures show that in 1999 more than 19,000 people were warned, fined or tried and found guilty of cannabis-related offences compared to just over 600 for crack.

The British government continues to resist calls to follow in the footsteps of some other European states and relax laws governing the possession and use of cannabis. A Police Federation-sponsored report earlier this year called for a review of the country's 30 year-old drug laws, and a House of Lords science and technology committee recently recommended amending the laws to authorise medical prescription of cannabis derivatives.

While the Labour government is keen to maintain a policy of being tough on crime and the causes of crime — a regular refrain in the election campaign — and is known to be wary of taking any official move to soften cannabis laws, police officials are optimistic that the south London experiment will bring visible results.

Based on its results in Lambeth, the scheme could be extended to other parts of the capital by next year.

THE OBSERVER, TUESDAY JUNE 26, 2001

CANADA

New regulations broaden use of medical marijuana

TORONTO (AP):

CANADIANS SUFFERING from terminal illnesses and chronic conditions such as arthritis can legally grow and smoke marijuana, or designate someone else to grow it for them, under regulations that took effect yesterday.

The new rules are part of the first system in the world that includes a government-approved and paid-for supply of marijuana, now being grown in a former mine in northern Manitoba.

The rules will expand the number of people beyond the 292 in the country currently exempted from federal drug laws that make it a criminal offence to grow and use marijuana.

While some in Canada complain the new regulations create bureaucratic hurdles and put doctors in the unsettling role of prescribing something they know little about, the Canadian system looks wonderful to medical marijuana advocates across the world.

"We're kind of envious of Canadians having the luxury of complaining about the minutiae of the programme," said Chuck Thomas of the Washington-based Marijuana Policy Project. "It seems like a reasonable system."

Eight US states have taken some kind of step toward permitting the medicinal use of marijuana. The US Supreme Court, however, ruled earlier this year that there is no exception in federal law for people to use marijuana, so even people with state medical-exemptions could face arrest if they do.

In Canada, attitudes are different.

The new health regulations were drawn up after a court ruling last year that gave the government until July 31 to create a way for people requiring marijuana for medicinal purposes to legally obtain it.

The new rules permit drug possession for the terminally ill with a prognosis of death within one year; those with symptoms associated with specific serious medical conditions; and those with other medical conditions who have statements from two doctors saying conventional treatments have not worked. Eligible patients include those with severe arthritis, cancer, HIV/AIDS and multiple sclerosis.

More than 500 new applications are pending, and more are expected, according to the federal health ministry.

The Canadian Medical Association, which represents tens of thousands of doctors, opposes the new regulations because they make physicians responsible for prescribing a substance that lacks significant clinical research on its effects. Without the cooperation of doctors, patients cannot get medical marijuana exemptions.

Under the regulations, people can grow and possess marijuana for medical needs, or name someone to grow it for them, including the government.

In Flin Flon, Manitoba, a mining town hundreds of kilometers (miles) north of the US border, Prairie Plant Systems is growing marijuana in a former copper mine under a government contract worth more than US$3.5 million.

Company head Brent Zettl expects the first harvest of marijuana that will be supplied by the government to eligible patients and used for research on therapeutic effects. Company head Brent Zettl uses the same techniques that were used to grow berries and roses in the tapped-out mine beneath Trout Lake.

In town, a novelty store has sold 6,000 T-shirts bearing a new slogan for Flin Flon — Marijuana Growing Capital of Canada.

THE DAILY GLEANER, TUESDAY JULY 31, 2001

APPENDIX 1

THE JAMAICAN LEGAL POSITION

BY MRS. VELMA BROWN–HAMILTON

"Countries all over the world are being forced to give consideration to the complex but delicate issues of social, economic, cultural and security policies which relate to the issue of ganja;- Jamaica can be no exception." (Prime Minister P.J. Patterson, The Daily Gleaner, September 14, 2000).

The Prime Minister further went on to state that all the evidence of the herb's potency would be revisited. The National Commission on Ganja has been established to review the ganja debate regarding decriminalization or non-decriminalization of ganja in well-defined circumstances and under specific conditions.

One of the Terms of Reference of the National Commission is: "to indicate what changes, if any are required to existing laws or enact new legislation, taking into account the social, cultural, economic and international factors."

To evaluate the legal considerations of ganja in Jamaica it is necessary to start with the present law that governs ganja. The relevant legislation includes:

First at the Shanghai Convention in 1909 and the Hague International Opium Convention in 1912, some of the world's most influential countries including Britain, had decided to prohibit the use of opium (Richard Lord: 1984).

- · The Dangerous Drugs Act 1948

- · The Drugs Offences (Forfeiture of Proceeds) Act 1994

- · Mutual Assistance (Criminal Matters) Act 1995

- · Money Laundering Act 1998

- · The Drug Court (Treatment and Rehabilitation of Offenders) Act 1999

DANGEROUS DRUGS ACT (1948) OF JAMAICA: THE BACKGROUND

Cannabis, which was known as Hemp at the first Opium Conference, was not mentioned in the text of the agenda for the Conference, but during its proceedings a resolution was included to the effect that the Conference should consider it desirable to study the question of Indian Hemp from the statistical and scientific point of view, with the objective of regulating its abuses (Fraser: 1974).

As a result of the Conference, the Dangerous Drugs Act was enacted in Britain, which was the first of a series of statutes that placed an 'increasing number of substances under increasingly strict control.' After the 1920 Act, subsequent legislation was enacted that was either an extension or modification of the existing restrictions. The number of controlled drugs steadily increased, as did the number of controls and the penalties for their contravention.

The 1923 Dangerous Drugs act gave the police officers investigating drug offences the power to obtain search warrants. The 1925 Drugs Act extended the controls to include Cannabis after it was denounced as harmful by the Egyptian delegates at the Second Open Conference and Geneva Convention in 1925 (Richard Lord: 1984).

The legislation in the British colonies, including Jamaica, conformed in pattern and concept to the 1925 Dangerous Drugs Act. Jamaica enacted the Dangerous Drugs Law, (Cap 78) of the 1938 Edition of the Laws of Jamaica, which was repealed by the Dangerous Drugs Act on April 15, 1948. This Act, (Cap 90) is in effect and is now subjected to the amendments made over time. (28 of 1954, 1 of 1961, 31 of 1961; Acts 10 of 1964, 9 of 1972; Sch. 16 of 1974: 12 of 1985; Sch. 17 of 1987, 21 of 1987 and 30 of 1994).

The Dangerous Drugs Act and its antecedent legislation, dating back to 1924 and which was aimed at the promotion of public health and safety, have been settled by the highest court of the land. The purpose or intention of the Act may be ascertained from Lord Diplock's speech in *Director of Public Prosecutions v. Wishart Brooks* [1974 12 All E.R. 840] in which he stated that the provisions of the Dangerous Drugs Act were legislated in the interest of public health.

In this case ganja was characterized as a dangerous drug, the possession of which the legislature intended to prohibit, in that someone ought not to knowingly have that drug in his or her physical custody or control. Section 2 of the Act exempts from its penal provisions medicinal preparations made from the ganja plant. It is evident for this purpose, that the Act has a lot to do with issues concerning health and safety, as it is more or less secular in nature and as it renders any person liable to criminal prosecution and conviction for contraveningits penal provisions.

SUMMARY OF THE LEGISLATION - PART III A GANJA
| EXPORT AND IMPORT OF GANJA |
(Section 7A(3) s. 12)

"Export" (with its grammatical variations and cognate expressions) in relation to Jamaica, means to take or cause to be taken out of the island by land, air, or water, otherwise than in transit.

"Import" (with its grammatical variations and cognate expressions) in relation to Jamaica, means to bring or cause to be brought into the island by land, air, or water, otherwise than in transit.

The penalties for drug trafficking appear to be rather harsh and draconian, especially as they relate to the confiscation of the assets of convicted drug traffickers. Colin Bobb-Semple, who wrote on issues relating to the prosecution and sentencing of drug-traffickers in England and Wales, alluded to the fact that there are several ethical concerns that cannot be readily ignored. For example, the provisions concerning the confiscation of assets of convicted drug traffickers are draconian.

The courts seemed to be enabled to make assumptions that an offender has benefited from drug trafficking in respect of offences for which there have been no convictions. There are many instances where countries are actually exploited, but this is not very easily proven and as a result the rigors of the sentencing provisions may be justifiably tempered according to the nature of the case, especially where there are vulnerable couriers involved.

Another concern in this regard, is whether the courts are totally justified in all cases where they give minimal or no consideration to alleviating factors, which may be involved in the relevant case. The fact is, there are some factors that lessen the punishment handed out in criminal cases, and these should probably be considered. It is not clear why such factors (especially as they relate to the offender) which are normally factors worthy of consideration in criminal cases (other than those involving drug trafficking) are excluded from the contemplation of the courts in these cases.

These factors include:

1. previous good character;

2. a pillar of the community; and

3. caring for young children.

There are those who believe that these factors should be given less weight in drug trafficking cases as those who organize drug trafficking normally tend to select persons who fall into those categories in the expectation that they would receive a lenient sentence if caught. However, it is not proven that the severe sentencing policy is a deterrent. It is clear from observation that organizers do not appear to be deterred by the sentences, as they take calculated risks with the couriers in the hope that detection would be avoided.

It also appears that there is very little difference between the sentencing of simple couriers and major organizers, because sentencing is governed by the weight of the drug imported. What is also noticeable is that the sentencing of couriers appear to be higher than that relating to dealers. Dealers are sometimes treated very leniently, depending on the amount of the drug supplied, whether the supply was for gain, or their role within the chain of supply.

Another issue of interest and concern is whether it is proper for the courts to assume that assets have been obtained as a result of drug trafficking by a person convicted of a drug trafficking offence. In most cases, it has not been proven that the people obtained those assets as a result of drug trafficking. Therefore, it is not necessarily a fair assumption to say that any property held by the offender was received by the offender as a payment or reward in connection with drug trafficking carried out by that offender. Especially the property owned since conviction, or property transferred to him within a certain number of years immediately preceding the institution of proceedings. This is particularly so when viewed in terms of the treatment of that property, when the assumption is made.

METHODS OF TRANSPORTING GANJA

DRUG OFFENCES (FORFEITURE OF PROCEEDS) ACT 1994

Essentially, the problems related to the trafficking of dangerous drugs would be better dealt with if a properly organized system were put in place and the problem attacked at the source. Searches for the sources of supply could be conducted as well as for the areas where the substance is being grown illegally. The relaxation of sentencing should be considered, and discretion used in the matter, as severe sentencing does not appear to act as a deterrent.

Cultivation, Selling, Production and Dealing in Ganja Under s.7B (a)- (c) of this Act. Every person who:

• cultivates, gathers, produces, sells or otherwise deals in ganja;

METHODS OF TRANSPORTING GANJA

- or being the owner or occupier of any premises, uses such premises for the cultivation or storage of ganja or selling or otherwise dealing in ganja;

- or uses any conveyance for carrying ganja;

- or for the purpose of selling;

- or otherwise dealing in ganja;

- or being the owner or person in charge of any conveyance knowingly permits it to be so used, shall be guilty of an offence.

On conviction before a Circuit Court, the offender shall be:

- Sentenced to a fine of not less than ($200) two hundred dollars for each ounce of ganja which the court is satisfied is the subject of the offence; or

- Sentenced to imprisonment for a term not exceeding thirty five (35) years; or to both such fine and imprisonment.

In summary, conviction before a Resident Magistrate, notwithstanding s. 44 of the Interpretation Act, makes the offender liable in a court of law:

- To a fine, not less than one hundred dollars ($100) and no more than two hundred dollars ($200) for each ounce of ganja which the Resident Magistrate is satisfied is the subject matter of the offence

- However no such fine should exceed five hundred thousand dollars ($500,000)

- To imprisonment for a term not exceeding three (3) years; or both such fine and imprisonment under Section s. 7B (d) - (e) of the Act.

Every person who has in his possession any ganja shall be guilty of an offence under s. 7C (a) of the Act. On conviction before a Circuit Court shall be sentenced to a fine; or to imprisonment for a term not exceeding five (5) years; or to both such fine and imprisonment. In summary, conviction before a Resident Magistrate shall be liable:

- To a fine not exceeding one ($100) hundred dollars for each ounce of ganja which the Resident Magistrate is satisfied is the subject matter of the offence,

- However any such fines shall not exceed fifteen ($15,000) thousand dollars; or

- Imprisonment for not more than three (3) years; or

- To both such fine and imprisonment under Section s. 7C (b) of the Act.

INTERPRETATION OF THE COURTS

It was submitted in the case of *R v Cecil Taylor* (1940) 3 J. L.R. 228, that the word ganja (as used in the Dangerous Drugs Law, Cap 78 of the Revised Laws of Jamaica, 1938 Edition) did not include 'ganja sticks' because it is not from the leaves of the plant that the dangerous drug is derived. The Court strongly disagreed with this submission:

> We are unable to accept this contention. The word ganja is not defined in the Dangerous Drugs Law although the botanical name of the plant is given. It is clear, however, from the enactment itself that is used in its most comprehensive sense and intended to include not only the plant itself but also its component parts. The law makes it unlawful to import ganja, to cultivate, sell or otherwise deal in it, or to be in possession of it. From these provisions the intention of the Legislature is clear.

> The very existence of ganja in Jamaica is totally prohibited: it does not matter whether it is the sticks, seeds, leaves or the plants themselves; they are equally prohibited- *Per Seton J. at p. 229.*

It is clear from the interpretation of the court in *R. v Cecil Taylor*, which a general strong prohibitive stance was taken with regards to ganja, in that the Dangerous Drugs Law included all its components, and not just that component deemed to be harmful at the time.

The Dangerous Drugs Act 1948 defines ganja in Part 1, Section 2:

"Ganja" includes all parts of the plant known as *Cannabis sativa* from which the resin has not been extracted and includes any resin obtained from the plant, but does not include medicinal preparations made from the plant.

In the case of *R. v George Green (1969) 14 WIR 204*; the Court of Appeal of Jamaica discussed the meaning of ganja for the purposes of the Act. It was held that the term ganja as defined by Section s. 2 of the Dangerous Drugs Law, (Cap 90) is referable only to the pistillate plant known as *Cannabis sativa* and does not include any part of the staminate plant. In this case, it was argued that there was no distinction made between the pistillate plant and the staminate plant.

However,*R. v George Green* has established that the Dangerous Drugs Act (Cap 90) has interpreted the Act plainly and it is referable to the pistillate plant known as *Cannabis sativa*. The significance of this is that in comparing the two cases 1940 and 1969, the law has changed from a total prohibition, to one where proof is required by a judge or jury as the case may be, that the illegal substance is *Cannabis sativa*. This is made possible by the statutory provision, which requires a government analyst certificate to verify that the substance is ganja as defined under s. 27 of the Dangerous Drugs Act.

In any proceedings against any person for an offence against this Act, the production of a certificate signed by a Government Chemist or any Analyst (designated under the provisions of section 17 of the Food and Drugs Act) shall be sufficient evidence of facts therein stated. This is unless the person charged requires that the Government Chemist or any Analyst be summoned as a witness. In such case the Court shall cause him to attend and give evidence in the same way as any other witness.

The Court allowed the appeal on the ground that the "state of the evidence in this case was such that no reasonable jury could have been satisfied beyond reasonable doubt that any of the plants which the defendant cultivated was the pistillate plant known as *Cannabis sativa*. In those circumstances the learned trial judge ought to have withdrawn the case from the jury." Per Shelley J.A. at p. 214.

This position was upheld by the Court of Appeal in *R. v McLeod* on April 13, 1973, in which *R. v George Green* was followed. The Court held that the prosecution must prove beyond reasonable doubt that the substance was pistillate.

This is one of the elements that have to be proven to obtain a conviction. In terms of possession of ganja, the Court of Appeal established in *R. v Livingston* (I 1952) 6 J.L.R. 95 held that to ground a conviction for being 'in possession of ganja' the Court must be satisfied that:

a. not only did the accused person have knowledge that he had the thing in question, but also

b. that he had knowledge that the thing possessed was ganja.

Furthermore, that knowledge, sufficient to established means, may be actual knowledge, which may be inferred from the act of possession, or from the nature of the acts done, or from both, or if it falls short of actual knowledge. It may be inferred if the defendant deliberately shut his eyes to an obvious means of knowledge by refraining from making inquiries, the result of which he may not care to have (Aubrey Fraser: 1973).

These principles are evident in the case of *R. v. Maragh (1964)* 8 J.L.R. 342, which relied on the authority of *R. v. Cavendish (1961)*, 2 All ER 856 where Lord Parker CJ said:

> "Certain propositions are quite clear. It is quite clear, without referring to the authority that for a man to have possession, actual or constructive, of goods, something more must be proved, than that the goods have been found on his premises. It must be shown if he was either absent and that on his return he has become aware of them and exercised control over them, or that the goods had come albeit in his absence, at his invitation or by arrangement. The latter was the case sought to be made".

In applying this to the facts of *R. v. Maragh,* the Resident Magistrate had to decide whether:

- the appellant was in possession or control of the shop,

- he was aware of the existence of the tin containing 24 packets of ganja,

- he had knowledge of the contents of the tin.

If on any of these questions there was doubt, then the appellant would have been entitled to an acquittal. The judgment acknowledges that the case of *R. v. Cavendish,* shows how slight the evidence is which is necessary to support the conclusion that the owner or possessor of premises, has possession or has assumed control of something found upon his premises. In that case the Court of Appeal rejected the submission of no case and was able to infer from the facts the necessary elements of possession.

Therefore in *R. v. Maragh*, the issue of whether knowledge could be attributed to the appellant was inferred from the manner in which these packages were made up and from the place where they were found.

The Courts have emphasized the fact that mere knowledge is insufficient ground for conviction of a charge of possession. In *R. v. Hopeton Morgan* (1986) 23 J.L.R. 484, the appellant was convicted for having ganja in his possession and taking steps preparatory to exporting ganja. The appellant's case in the court below and on appeal was that there was no real evidence of his involvement to support the charges. J.A. Carberry stated that, "there was clearly knowledge on the part of the appellant as to what was going on, and it was clearly guilty knowledge. While knowledge alone is not sufficient ground for a charge of possession, in all the circumstances of this case there was sufficient evidence to support the conviction on Count I as regards the possession of ganja."

However due to the substances of the case of *R. v. Alphonso Lawrence* (1969) 11 J.L.R 384 it was argued that although the appellant was in the room with the illegal substance, he would not necessarily have had any guilty knowledge of the existence of the ganja. On appeal against conviction it was held that on the evidence deduced particularly (i) the quantity of the ganja found in the room was so minimal, (ii) the search took place at 2a.m. (iii) another occupant of the room was seen to act in a manner that suggested that she had hidden the ganja, and not the appellant.

DUTY OF THE JUDGE

In drug offences, the case law has shown that the judge who is guided by the law and evidence may infer from the circumstances and the conduct of the accused the necessary elements for conviction if they are not readily identifiable.

"If you ask me then what is the responsibility of a...Magistrate in the adjudication of drug offences...I would unhesitatingly reply to afford the accused person a fair trial in accordance with the evidence and the law and to impose an appropriate sentence if the accused is found guilty in all circumstances"(Mr. Justice Rattray:1999).

The case of *R. v Hopeton Morgan* confers on the judge a duty not to act on their private or personal knowledge of facts even where it is based on evidence given before them in a previous case. Therefore, where the judge at first instance in his reason for judgment said:

"On the question of taking steps to export, there was no direct evidence from this. However, drawing on my experience I was able to say that where ganja is being transported for local use, this is not the method of packaging. The method used in this case was similar to these used in Portland and St. James where persons attempt to go on board the cruise ships or air crafts, and I have worked in Portland and St. James."

The Magistrate had relied on the doctrine of Judicial Notice. The Court of Appeal found that this use of the doctrine seems to have been wrong and to involve an unwarranted extension of the doctrine (Carberry J.A at p.486).

The judgment discussed relevant rules:

"The general rule is that neither judge nor a juror may act on his personal knowledge of the facts" and "that the basic essential element is that the fact judicially noticed should be of a class that is so generally known as to give rise to the presumption that all persons are aware of it." (p. 487).

Therefore the Magistrate was not justified in extending the use of Judicial Notice to the extent that he did, or in importing into the case his personal experience from Portland and St. James.

MEDICINAL PREPARATIONS

In the case of *R. v. Sutton (1967)* 10 J.L.R 278, it was argued on behalf of the appellant that the ganja was being used by him to cure his asthma. Section 2 of the Act defines ganja as not including medicinal preparations made from the plant. Therefore Counsel for the Defense argued that the Crown had failed to negate the defence that the substance found in the appellant's possession was a medicinal preparation. The Court held that "the question whether what the appellant had in his possession was a medicinal preparation was a matter of exception or defence within the terms of Section 25 of the Dangerous Drugs Law, which would have been peculiarly within the knowledge of the defendant." The legal burden of proving this was placed on the appellant by Section 25 and he had failed to do so.

MUTUAL ASSISTANCE (CRIMINAL MATTERS) ACT 1995

This Act allows the Minister of National Security and Justice or someone deriving authority from him to request assistance of a foreign state 'in respect of investigations and proceedings in relation to a criminal matter. The law is applicable to offences committed under the Drug Offences (Forfeiture of Proceeds) Act of 1994. Jamaica has entered into mutual assistance treaties with some forty-eight (48) designated commonwealth countries and the United States (US Department of State March 1997).

THE DRUG COURT (TREATMENT AND REHABILITATION OF OFFENDERS) ACT 1999

The aim of this Act is to:

- reduce the incidence of drug use and dependence by criminals whose drug use is related to their criminal activity;

- reduce the level of criminal activity that results from drug abuse;

- provide assistance to those persons that will enable them to function as law-abiding citizens.

Section 3 of the Act: "Drug" for the purposes of this Act includes alcohol and any dangerous drugs falling within Parts TH, IIIA and IV of the Dangerous Drugs Act. Part IIIA is the section of the Act on Ganja.

INTERNATIONAL OBLIGATIONS

Jamaica ratified the 1988 UN Drug Convention in December 1995. Under Article 3 of the Convention which deals with Offences and Sanctions, each party shall adopt such measures as may be necessary to establish as criminal offence under its domestic law when committed intentionally:

1. the production, manufacture, extraction, preparation, offering, offering for sale, distribution, sale, delivery on any terms whatsoever, brokerage, dispatch, dispatch 'in transit, transport, importation or exportation of any narcotic drug or any psychotropic substance;

2. the cultivation of opium poppy, coca bush or cannabis plant for the purpose of production of narcotic drugs;

3. the possession or purchase of any narcotic drug for the purpose of any of the activities enumerated in (1) above.

MONEY LAUNDERING ACT 1998

A person shall be guilty of the offence of money laundering if he knows at the time that he is:

·   engaging in a transaction that involves property that is derived from the commission of a specified offence; or

·   acquiring, possessing, using, concealing, disguising, disposing of or bringing into Jamaica, any such property; or

·   converting or transferring that property or removing it from Jamaica- Section 3 of the Act.

"Specified offence" under Section 2 of the Act means an offence listed in the Schedule. The Schedule includes the cultivation of Cannabis plant for the purpose of the production of narcotic drugs contrary to the provisions of the Dangerous Drugs Act. It only criminalizes the laundering of proceeds of drug-related crime.

APPENDIX 2

MARIHUANA-HASHISH EPIDEMIC AND ITS IMPACT ON UNITED STATES SECURITY

Dr John A.S. Hall, Friday, May 17, 1974 U.S. SENATE,

Subcommittee To Investigate The Administration Of the Internal Security Act And Other Internal Security Laws Of The Committee On The Judiciary, Washington, D.C.

The subcommittee met, pursuant to recess, at 10 a.m., in room 2228, Dirksen Senate Office Building, Senate Edward J. Gurney presiding. Also present: J.G. Sourwine, chief counsel; David Martin, senior analyst.

SENATOR GURNEY: The subcommittee will come to order, please. I wish we could come to order because we are wasting time.

Would you gentlemen rise, please? Will you all raise your right hand?

Do you swear to tell the truth, the whole truth, and nothing but the truth, so help you God?

(All witnesses replied "I do.")

SENATOR GURNEY: Thank you. We have a long series of witnesses here today, as we know, and I have obligations that require me to leave for Florida early in the afternoon so I would hope we could be speedy and as brief as we can, and, in no way underestimating the extreme importance of this testimony, but, as I say, try to get the facts out as quickly as we can.

The first witness will be Dr. Hall.

Dr. Hall, will you identify yourself for the record, please? You don't have to stand up, just state who you are, you know, your name, where you reside.

TESTIMONY OF DR. JOHN A.S. HALL, JAMAICA

DR. HALL: I am Chairman of the Department of Medicine at the Kingston Hospital in Jamaica.

SENATOR GURNEY: And I will ask a few questions, Dr. Hall, to establish your qualifications here. As I understand it, you received your medical degree from the University of London, King's College, in 1951.

DR. HALL: That is correct.

SENATOR GURNEY: And you went on to take a Diploma in Neurology from the London Medical School in 1958?

DR. HALL: That is correct.

SENATOR GURNEY: Subsequently you had Observation Fellowships in Neurology at the Neurological Institute in New York, at the Department of Neurology in Pennsylvania Hospital, and at the Beaumont Hospital, University of Lausanne, in Switzerland?

DR. HALL: That is correct.

SENATOR GURNEY: And you served as medical officer in the Ministry of Health in Jamaica from 1952 to 1960.

DR. HALL: Correct.

SENATOR GURNEY: And you are currently Associate Lecturer in Medicine at the University of the West Indies and visiting Assistant Professor of Neurology at Columbia University?

DR. HALL: Correct.

SENATOR GURNEY: And you have been senior physician and elected Chairman of the Department of Medicine of the Kingston Hospital in Kingston, Jamaica, since 1965?

DR. HALL: Correct

SENATOR GURNEY: Would you proceed with your statement, Dr. Hall?

MR. SOURWINE: Mr. Chairman, may I venture a suggestion?

SENATOR GURNEY: Yes, indeed.

MR. SOURWINE: The Chair might wish to order that all of the prepared statements go into the record as though read at the beginning of each witness' presentation, leaving him free to repeat the statement or ad lib or, make emphasis and instruct integration of the two when the record is corrected for printing so that nothing will be lost and time might be saved.

SENATOR GURNEY: That is a good suggestion, Mr. Counsel, and that is so ordered.

DR. HALL: Mr. Chairman, may I thank you and your staff for giving me this opportunity to appear on this distinguished panel.

In a previous publication I pointed to the fortuitous introduction of ganja or marihuana into Jamaica in the 18th century as a possible source of fibre plant, by the English plantation owner Matthew Walker at his Botanical Gardens in Gordon Town, near Kingston.

The Indian connection following the arrival of indentured labourers at the end of the last century is established historical fact.

SENATOR GURNEY: Doctor, I wonder if you could point that microphone directly into your mouth so that it will pick up your voice just a little better.

DR. HALL: Quiet acceptance and public indifference to the use of ganja continued until 1954 when the village, Pinnacle, in the hills of St. Catherine some 20 miles from Kingston, was destroyed by a police raiding party. The village becomes notorious as the home of praedial larceny, a centre for the propagation and use of ganja, and the headquarters of the Rastafari cult.

The resulting dispersal of the Rastafari cultists into the urban slums of Kingston, and into rural areas, was to have far-reaching consequences, as has been published in data elsewhere.

I became interested in cannabis as a clinical problem because of:

1. its ready availability in Jamaica; it grows in any backyard and in the wooded forests;

2. ill-defined and undocumented clinical manifestations;

3. bizarre, sometimes short-lived confusional states seen in urban and rural practice;

4. folklore; and,

5. the impact of American culture mores on our island community.

With these factors in mind, I have over the years inquired routinely of all patients at initial interview whether they smoke ganja or drink ganja tea. The Department of Medicine at the Kingston Public Hospital sees 12,000 outpatients at its clinic annually.

My team sees approximately 5,000 of these patients, who represent a spectrum ranging from the unemployed ghetto dwellers to the upper middle class.

It has been possible therefore:

1. to arrive at a relative incidence of ganja usage,

2. to study the motivation for its use,

3. to identify clinical pictures with which its use is associated more often than coincidence will allow,

4. to do certain laboratory studies,

5. to gain some insight into its psychocultural effects.

Ours is an adult clinic. Males are almost exclusively smokers of ganja although urbanization and fashion are causing other trends. These males come from the social spectrum indicated above. The age range was 15- 65 years.

Ganja tea is used about equally among working class men and women. In the first 4 months of this year, for example, there were just over 35 self-confessed ganja users among just over 1,000 clinic patients. This incidence of 3 per cent contrasts with other reports of widespread use, and is in line with the incidence say of Parkinsonism with constitutes 2.5 per cent of my clinic population, and is uncommon condition in Jamaica. It is accepted that the clinic population is not all embracing; but if this figure were even tripled, we arrive at 9 per cent.

Motivation for the use of ganja is summarized as follows:

1. curiosity,

2. conformity with the group; social, religious, political,

3. relief of tension,

4. stimulation of thought and physical activity,

5. folk medicine.

In our observation, dosage depends on:

1. manner and frequency of use,

2. variations in dosage per se,

3. potency of preparation smoked or brewed,

4. unreliable retrospective recall of frequency of use,

5. technique of smoking,

6. personal and intragroup variations,

7. limitations of costs,

8. legal strictures against possession and use of ganja.

It is noteworthy that a joint, or marihuana cigarette costs in our situation 40 to 50 cents, while a bottle of beer costs 25 cents and a quart of rum costs $1.80. A chillum pipe full of dried leaves is equivalent to about five cigarettes. To reach the same "high" using alcohol or ganja, the cost would be more with ganja. This challenges a point made by others that ganja is poor man's substitute for alcohol.

Significantly, none of these patients has been exposed to amphetamines, LSD, heroin, or other hallucinogens. Those interviewed could do without ganja for long periods of months at a time. Ritual smokers also knew when they had had enough.

My findings were essentially nonclinical and clinical.

The nonclinical findings related mainly to:

1. educational level,

2. occupational status,

3. marital status,

4. criminal record, on which I have commented on in a previous publication.

The levels that are quoted were quite low but certainly are not universally applicable as broader observation at the clinic, community or national level could indicate. The same observations would apply to criminal record.

Clinical findings were certainly more significant and were divided into immediate and long-term findings.

The immediate findings have been fully corroborated by other people who have found autonomic over activity as shown by papillary dilation, conjunctival suffusion, profuse diaphoresis, tachycardia, and mild hypotension. Shortly after these some of my cases showed hypothalamic over activity, that is mild euphoria; others showed medullary stimulation by way of sedation or acute vomiting.

The long-term effects were also quite remarkable. These were as follows:

1. RESPIRATORY COMPLICATIONS

An emphysema-bronchitis syndrome, common among Indian labourers of a past generation, who were well known for their ganja smoking habits, is now a well recognized present day finding among black male labourers. Indeed, one of our cases died from acute pulmonary embolism and at autopsy demonstrated spontaneous thrombosis of the pulmonary artery. In the autopsy room in general, the barrel-shaped, emphysematous chest, is a common finding in Rastafarian cultists. This raises questions of their smoking habits and the possible action of toxic metabolites from ganja acting on the pulmonary parenchyma, a point which was substantiated by one of yesterday's speakers, Dr. Leuchtenberger.

2. G-I TRACT INVOLVEMENT

In a small sample series two cases previously published had radiologically proven duodenal ulcers also raising the question of toxic metabolites, vagal stimulation, or a parallel to the excretion of morphine in the stomach.

Further observation suggests a greater association between duodenal ulcers and ganja smokers, attending the clinic, than coincidence would allow. Detailed studies of gastric fluid and gastroscopic studies are clearly indicated.

Among chronic ganja smokers obesity is never seen. The Rastafari cultists fully substantiate this point of the slim body build. Constant craving for sugar cane, highly sweetened beverages, or sweets is noted in many habitual smokers and cultists after smoking ganja. Many smokers also allege an increase of appetite. Persistent observation on our part of the absence of obesity suggests some interference with the metabolic pathways for depositing body fat. The PBI studied in a small series to date has not indicated thyroid hyperactivity and comment was made yesterday by one of the speakers on this interference with fatty metabolism.

3. CNC CHANGES

Ganja has long been regarded both by the laity and the profession as a cause of psychosis in Jamaica. The unrivalled, accumulated, experience of Cooke, Royes, and Williams, who were in recent years senior medical offers at the Bellevue Hospital, in Kingston, Jamaica, fully substantiates this. The observations also of Prince, Greenfield, and others corroborate this view. There is also the Moroccan report of Benabud. It is a common experience in my wards, three to six cases per year of ganja psychosis being referred to the psychiatry clinic;this was noted in my preliminary report on ganja smoking in Jamaica. My experience can be readily duplicated in hospitals around Jamaica.

It is noteworthy that a survey in a village of relatively well peasant farmers, for instance, might be misleading.

An incidence of 20 per cent impotence as a presenting feature among males who have smoked ganja for 5 or more years, was reported by me earlier. Several colleagues in private practice have been alerted to this and tend to corroborate my view of this problem. The difficulties of assessing this symptom are self-evident. The likely involvement of the autonomic pathways awaits neuropathological studies.

Personality changes among ganja smokers and members of the Rasta-fari cult are a matter of common observation in Jamaica. The apathy, retreat from reality, the incapacity or unwillingness for sustained concentration, and the lifetime of drifting are best summed up in the "amotivational syndrome" of McGlothin and West.

Many smokers come to no grief, as it were, after several years of ganja use. On this basis some workers and the media make a fashionable virtue of its use; they recommend it as a panacea for poverty, or a benev-olent alternative to alcohol.

This view is, at best, half-truth. Common observation in Jamaica is that ganja smoking can be a catalyst for cataclysmic change for ill in the life of a ganja smoker. The Rastafarians to whom I have referred earlier in particular typify this picture. Those interested can refer to the work of Smith, Augier and others, and Kitzinger, previously published.

Mr. Chairman, I have documented some laboratory data which I shall ask to be incorporated in the record, but I draw particular attention to hypoglycaemia, that is to say, a fall in the normal blood sugar which was seen in three of eight cases, 1 hour after smoking 25 grams of dried leaf in a standard pipe.

MR. MARTIN: Is this a major drop in blood sugar level?

DR. HALL: Below the normal accepted level.

MR. MARTIN: But a substantial drop?

DR. HALL: Yes, of, say from 120 before smoking to levels of 50 or less within an hour of smoking 25 grams of dried leaf.

MR. MARTIN: Within an hour of smoking?

DR. HALL: Precisely. May I continue?

MR. MARTIN: Please.

DR. HALL: This raises the question of the relevance of repeated hypoglycaemia to personality changes and psychosis well documented by others. Mr. Chairman, the dilemma facing most societies regarding the legalized or uninhibited use of ganja is created, in my view, by vested interests and the media. In my country, Jamaica, many people do smoke ganja. I repeat, without apparent ill effects. There is, however, a growing number of young adults especially who are being pushed over the edge of the abyss, and are hanging in there in a world of chemically-induced, drug-induced, fantasy and non-productively.

One can visualize at the national level ganja smoking changing the lifestyle of a society, undermining economic productivity, and impairing a country's military effectiveness.

One can visualize too, a totalitarian regime promoting it as an emotional escape valve, rather like institutionalized festivities.

In Jamaica the vast silent majority recognize all these points and are not confused. They recognize the liaison and involvement with crime both local and international.

In my view they are determined to preserve the Judeo-Christian ethic of pleasurable reward for hard work and the competitive, achievement, oriented value system.

Thank you, Mr. Chairman.

SENATOR GURNEY: Thank you, Dr. Hall, for your remarks.

MR. MARTIN: Dr. Hall, as you know, there is a widespread impression in our country that almost the entire Jamaican population is caught up in an endemic marihuana binge-that all Jamaicans are on ganja.

Your statement suggests this to be very much exaggerated. If I understood you correctly, you estimate the percentage of the population on ganja to be somewhere between 3 per cent and 9 per cent, based on your continuing study of the hospital population.

DR. HALL: That is correct, sir.

The impression of widespread use is created mainly by the publicity given to visitors from North America who have found Jamaica a *locus classicus* for obtaining and smoking ganja.

MR. MARTIN: The tourists have no trouble getting ganja and marihuana in Jamaica?

DR. HALL: None whatever, and frequently get into trouble with the law.

MR. MARTIN: And ganja has no serious trouble getting from Jamaica into the United States? As you know, there is an increasing amount coming into our country?

DR. HALL: There is well-established traffic.

SENATOR GURNEY: Incidentally, on that question, Dr. Hall, my State is the State of Florida. One of the principal sources of flow into Florida is Jamaica, this is a well known fact. Is your government doing anything to interdict this flow of marihuana into Florida?

DR. HALL: Yes, I am in a position to speak of that. The government is taking the most stringent measures to intercept international shipments coming by private aircraft and presently there are some very serious cases before the courts at this moment.

SENATOR GURNEY: They are making a good effort to try to stop this?

DR. HALL: Very much so, Mr. Chairman.

SENATOR GURNEY: Thank you.

MR. MARTIN: Jamaican marihuana is pretty good stuff, as they say. It is supposed to be substantially stronger than Mexican marihuana, is that correct?

DR. HALL: That has generally been said, but I have myself no figure as to the quantum of THC in our ganja.

MR. MARTIN: The fact that Jamaica has a relatively large population of chronic smokers, perhaps not as an overall percentage but you have a population of chronic smokers going back many years, this affords certain advantages in studying the long-term impact of chronic marihuana smoking?

DR. HALL: Decidedly so.

MR. MARTIN: You may be aware, Dr. Hall, of a recent study which has been reported on in America press, a study done in Jamaica funded by the National Institute for Mental Health. This study, as you know, came up with the nearest thing to a clean bill of health that has yet been published-no change in functional ability, no change in respiratory function, no changes in chromosomes- the nonsmokers suffered more chromosomes damage than the smokers- no change in brainwave patterns, nothing at all. Do you know anything about this study?

DR. HALL: Yes, I am familiar with it.

MR. MARTIN: Do the implications of this study- well, from what you have said here, the implications certainly do not conform to your experience with thousands of marihuana smokers?

DR. HALL: That is correct. The study to which you refer does not have the general support of experienced clinicians and other workers in the field. We believe that the selection with which the study was done was faulty and that in regard to the reported absence of any change in the chromosome the statement that there was no respiratory effect, it is unfounded.

MR. MARTIN: From your experience and contacts you believe that the great majority of doctors in Jamaica who have had actual experience with marihuana smokers-ganja smokers are convinced that it has a substantial negative effect?

DR. HALL: That is correct.

MR. MARTIN: Thank you very much. I have no further questions.

SENATOR GURNEY: Mr. Sourwine.

MR. SOURWINE: I have no questions, Mr. Chairman, but I respectfully suggest that the study which was the subject of the last question has not been identified for the record. It is not the usual thing, as the Chair knows, for the committee to shoot arrows into the air. If the witness credits a study, the record ought to show what this study is.

SENATOR GURNEY: Could you identify the study, Dr. Hall?

DR. HALL: The study about which I was speaking was a study mounted by Professor Beaubrun, Vera Rubin and Comitas. I believe they were funded by one of your national agencies.

SENATOR GURNEY: When was the study made?

DR. HALL: It was reported in 1972 and serialized in our national press.

SENATOR GURNEY: Do you know how long they spent on this study?

DR. HALL: Some months in 1971.

SENATOR GURNEY: Thank you, Dr. Hall.

DR. HALL: Thank you.

APPENDIX 3

THE MENTAL HEALTH PERSPECTIVE OF CANNABIS USE IN JAMAICA

Frederick W. Hickling, BSc, MB.BS, DM., MRCPsych, FRSM, Professor of Psychiatry, Department of Community Health and Psychiatry, University of the West Indies, Mona, Kingston 7, JAMAICA.

The controversy concerning the clinical effects of Cannabis on the mind has raged for decades. Chopra & Smith [1], Ghodse [2], and Tunving [3] have argued that cannabis in sufficient dosage can cause psychosis, a syndrome consisting of sudden onset of confusion, delusions, hallucinations, emotional instability, temporary amnesia, disorientation, depersonalization and paranoia.

However, even these authors admit that the clinical evidence that is available does not prove causality, and that the evidence of Cannabis causing a functional psychosis is even less convincing. In the context of Jamaica, the birthplace of the Rastafari Movement, it can easily be understood how a hostile world view of a movement which challenges orthodox Christianity and the capitalist system would be tempted to link Rastafari and the associated Cannabis use with madness and psychosis.

In a paper presented to the joint American Psychiatric Association- Caribbean Psychiatric Association meeting held in Ocho Rios Jamaica in 1969, Prince [4] described Rastafarianism as a status of group delusions. He was vigorously challenged by representatives of the movement who were present at the meeting who thought he was being racist and not only did he misunderstand the movement, but he also misrepresented its tenets. Professor Ari Kiev [5], the discussant of the paper, also challenged Prince's views. Kiev concluded:

"Is there such a thing as a group delusion? I think not, for such a concept is a contradiction in terms...Delusions, in contrast to beliefs, are generally over-inclusive, and the patient's life is so disorganized that diagnosis is not difficult...the diagnosis of psychiatric disturbance cannot be based on social behavior. It must be based on examination of the mental state which is important if you do transcultural work, and if you train people from different cultures."

Rastafarians, like Christians, Muslims, Communists or any other human group are capable of experiencing mental illness of all forms. As Kiev points out, diagnosis must be based on mental state examination, and not on social behavior. However, the Rastafarian's experience creates situations whereby unusual presentations can be expected. In the last two decades, clinicians in Jamaica and in other countries in which large Afro-Caribbean populations are, have had many experiences in which the social behavior in Rastafari have presented a challenge in diagnosis and management, particularly in young middle-class blacks.

It was in this context in the mid 1970s, while I was the Physician Super-intendent of Jamaica's single mental hospital and the Director of the Mental Health Services for the country, when I decided to challenge the social hostility and prejudice by wearing my hair in dreadlocks. This social issue was affecting the Rastafari movement in Jamaica and in many mentally ill patients. The fact is, I was then also host of a very popular and high profile Radio Psychiatry program [6] that was aired weekly. I created a forum for issues to be challenged publicly and worked through nationally over a period of nearly ten years. Many case studies presented themselves on this forum, and it was possible to confront myths and prejudices at first hand, and to challenge loose theories of causation by practical, real cases that were open to national scrutiny.

In the clinical context the most important controversy has centered on the clinical existence of a clearly delineated entity called cannabis psychosis. Most authors conclude that it is a dubious clinical concept.

It is certainly not recognized nosologically by two popular psychiatric classification systems, DSM IV or ICD 10. Especially in the psychological set of the Rastafari, the differential diagnosis of psychosis with concomitant cannabis use presents difficulty, and the following case studies reflect the four major diagnostic categories, which, in this author's experience the diagnosis is often confused. These are schizophrenia, brief reactive psychosis, borderline personality disorder and adolescent crisis.

CASE STUDY 1

A 28-year-old dreadlocks Rastafari musician of social class III origin presented with classical symptoms of a schizophrenic illness (DSM IV 295.3) with command and third person auditory hallucinations, visual hallucinations, thought disorder, paranoid delusions and passivity feelings of control. There was a very strong family history of schizophrenia, with three brothers of seven suffering from the condition. He reported having used two to three spliffs of cannabis daily for ten years prior to the first onset of his acute illness. His condition has deteriorated to that of chronic schizophrenia, with maintenance depot phenothiazine medication, repeat hospitalizations and rehabilitative care.

In every case of cannabis psychosis identified by other clinicians which has been seen by this author, the diagnosis of schizophrenia can usually be made after follow up, or after careful clinical evaluation. Case study 1 is a classic example. This man was initially identified as having a cannabis psychosis. Within a few years the diagnosis of schizophrenia became clinically self-evident. In a recent study Hickling and Rodgers Johnson, [7] of 291 first contact patients in Jamaica, with a Present State Evaluation [8] diagnosis of schizophrenia, 114 (39%) were cannabis users. Since 40% of the Jamaican population uses cannabis regularly [9], [10], this finding supports the suggestion that cannabis use is not etiologically responsible for schizophrenia.

Similarly in a recent study [11] in which 23 psychotic patients whose urine tested positively for cannabis were compared to 46 psychotic patients with urine which tested negative for cannabis, there was no statistical difference in psychopathology, DSM-III diagnoses, ethnicity, socio-economic class, or marital status. McGuire and his colleagues concluded that psychosis that develops in the context of cannabis use does not have specific psychopathology, and suggested that cannabis psychosis is not a valid diagnostic entity.

CASE STUDY 2

A 32-year-old black middle-class male, who has a brilliant school record in Jamaica, the United States and Canada, with spectacular business accomplishments, and well known media personality began making drastic changes in his life when he began to explore the culture of Rastafari. He rejected his white, North American wife, gave up his successful business and career, became a vegetarian and a heavy user of marijuana, and grew his hair into dreadlocks.

Having spent time in a number of rural Rastafari communes, he developed a number of acute psychotic episodes for which he was seen by other psychiatrists in Jamaica and diagnosed as having schizophrenia, or ganja psychosis. He was eventually admitted to the Jamaican mental hospital, was withdrawn from phenothiazine medication over a period of months, and started individual psychotherapy. He also started socio-drama group psychotherapy [12] at that time.

During these sessions he was able to work through his conflicts about race and class in Jamaica, and diagnosis of borderline personality disorder (DSM IV 301.83) was made. He was discharged from hospital after several months and has lived without a recurrence of psychiatric illness for over 20 years, although he continues to live with Rastafari dreadlocks, and has continued to smoke Cannabis. He has also successfully returned to part-time employment.

This patient caused significant controversy within the psychiatric community in Jamaica, as he was presented at the time when problems of this nature had just started to emerge. He was initially identified as having a Cannabis psychosis by clinicians in Jamaica, and repeated psychotic breaks resulted in the diagnostic reclassification as schizophrenia.

Finally, his response to psychotherapy with a long-term follow up over 20 years without a repeat of the psychosis even in the face of continued habitual heavy use of cannabis, and open espousal of the Rastafari lifestyle, has vindicated the clinical challenge to the diagnosis of cannabis psychosis. No doubt similar diagnostic puzzles are present in North America and elsewhere.

CASE STUDY 3

A 25-year-old middle-class female was admitted to hospital with an acute psychosis, presenting with paranoid delusions, auditory hallucinations, thought disorder and bizarre behavior. She had dropped out of University earlier in the year and went to live in a Rastafari commune with her boyfriend. She had a baby six months prior to admission. She was treated with phenothiazine medication and responded quickly to treatment. She then reported the difficulties that she experienced with her new baby in the Rastafari commune.

She had to live apart from her mate whenever she had menstrual bleeding, and was required to carry out domestic activity for him and other members of the commune at a level which she had not been accustomed to at her own home. She was regarded with suspicion as an outsider in the commune, and found a low level of support from her baby's father. Psychotherapy after hospitalization revealed that she was having significant family conflict, especially with her father, about herself becoming a Rasta and growing dreadlocks. She settled quickly, returned to Kingston and to University, and over twenty years later is running a successful professional business without a recurrence of her illness. She still remains a dreadlock Rastafari. Her diagnosis was that of Brief Reactive Psychosis (DSM IV 298.80)

A number of authors have described "a typical psychosis" in Afro-Caribbean people, particularly in the United Kingdom, which has often been attributed to the abuse of cannabis (13, 14). No doubt this young woman would have been diagnosed similarly, and a casual connection made to her Cannabis use. However, her rapid recovery without recurrence of the psychosis, and her continued use of Cannabis and maintenance of the Rastafari lifestyle tend to suggest alternative diagnostic and etiological conclusions.

The Rastafari movement is essentially a male dominated one, and although the woman is the Queen to her Rastaman, and is allowed to work if she wishes, she is subject to several taboos and rigid restrictions. During menstruation, the woman must stay by herself, and cannot cook for her man or participate in any activities with him. Oral sex is not permitted and there is controversy about polygamy, although monogamy is the norm for most Rastafari families.

Recent participatory research in gender relations in Rastafari concludes that there exists a strong patriarchal emphasis within the 'livity' of Rastafari (15). This is as an attempt by some Rastafari males to subordinate females as a means of making up for their own sense of powerlessness within the present system. Although the tendency for a positive emphasis on male responsibility exists within the brethren, which they perceive to be lacking in other social relationships in society, it is suggested that these factors may be more causally associated with psychosis as presented in this case study.

CASE STUDY 4

A 17- year-old Afro- Chinese male was brought to the clinic in Jamaica by his upper middle class Afro-Chinese father and his Black mother, complaining that their son's behavior had changed over the previous eighteen months, and that he had taken up with "bad company". He had grown his hair in dreadlocks, stopped eating with the family, became a vegetarian, and was preparing his owns meals separately. The young man asserted that there was nothing wrong with him, but that he had become a Rastafarian, a religion that his parents did not understand. He reported that his mother was ashamed of him, as she believed that Rastas were scum of the earth, and they did not want a Rasta in their family as they lived in 'high' society. He smoked one spliff weekly, believed that Selassie was the true and living God, and that his parents did not believe that God could be a living person.

He was well educated and worked as a camera technician in his fathers business. Mental state examination revealed no abnormality, and after a couple of family therapy sessions, parents and son reported that things were better at home, as he had stopped quarrelling, even though they did not accept each other's religious belief systems and ideological world view.

By making the diagnosis on the basis of the mental status examination, the correct therapeutic intervention could be applied. This scenario has become increasingly common in Jamaica in recent years as more and more middle class Jamaican youth have become involved in the transformation to Rastafari, and have come in conflict with their families and communities.

Has cannabis ever been used clinically in the treatment of mental illness in Jamaica? It is well known that the Jamaican people have used Cannabis for self- medication for a wide variety of physical and mental conditions including asthma, dysmenorrhoea, and anxiety. ,there are no recorded cases of the use of Cannabis in the treatment of mental illness in Jamaica by the orthodox medical profession.

CASE STUDY 5

A 26-year-old white male, born in the United Kingdom, had come to Jamaica at age 8 when his father had migrated to Jamaica in the early 1950s as a colonial civil servant. He described his father as being racist, authoritarian and alcoholic, and his mother as a passive, manipulative, over-protective housewife. His younger brother was a homosexual and a cocaine addict.

He received his secondary schooling in Jamaica and his university education in the United Kingdom. He was a civil engineer who worked for a private firm in Jamaica, where his partners were very supportive of him and had made repeated attempts to help him to deal with his 10-year history of alcoholism. He had multiple admissions to hospital for suicidal attempts, delirium tremens, and alcohol detoxification. Over 10-year period, four other psychiatrists who had treated him with a variety of detoxification and deconditioning programs, such as psycho-pharmacology, psychotherapy and behavior modification therapy, had seen him. He was admitted to Bellevue Hospital 1976 when I was the Senior Medical Officer of that institution. He was recruited in a Cannabis replacement psychotherapy program where the negotiated agreement was that he could smoke three spliffs of cannabis per day in place of all alcohol consumption.

Within two weeks he had stopped drinking alcohol altogether and reported that he was smoking 3-4 spliffs per day. His craving for alcohol ceased and we were able to engage in an intense reconstructive psychotherapy process to help him to deal with his underlying personality disorder. During this process he worked through race, class and sexual conflicts in 3 sessions per week for the five weeks he remained in hospital. He continued Cannabis replacement psychotherapy as an outpatient for 1 year. He remained well for 3 years and had a relapse and brief hospitalization.

He again became a teetotaller and we continued to confront his deep-seated racist problems. He has remained well, till present, with no alcohol use and only occasional cannabis use. He continues to pursue a successful managerial career.

I presented this case study in 1980 at a Clinical-Pathological Conference at the Faculty of Medicine at the University of the West Indies in Jamaica. The response of the Faculty was controversial, especially as the patient was present in the audience, and acknowledged publicly the painful personality conflicts, and the value he had received from this therapeutic activity. I presented the case again in 1981 at an international conference on cannabis use in Amsterdam.

The title of the presentation was "Cannabis replacement psychotherapy in a case of resistant alcoholism".

My presentation was reported in newspapers and magazines across Europe. In Britain, *The Times, The Guardian and The Economist* reported on my presentation, and discussed in some detail this particular case study. *The Daily Gleaner* in Jamaica, following my return from the conference noted the reports in the British press as a front-page news item. Within days of the report in the *Gleaner,* I received a letter from the Permanent Secretary in the Ministry of Health-my employer- acknowledging the news report, and expressly forbidding me from conducting therapeutic experiments with cannabis at the Bellevue Hospital. I also presented this case study at a conference on the clinical uses of Cannabis held in 1996 in Berlin[16].

Following my experience of studying the effects of Cannabis, I am of the opinion that the psychoactive properties of Cannabis have a significant psychotherapeutic effect, which has not been systematically studied by the medical profession. It is my hypothesis that the capacity of cannabis to loosen cortical associations creates a powerful platform for psychological conflicts, especially those associated with oppressive cultural penetration (brainwashing), by facilitating the sharpening of internal cultural psychic connections. In my view, explorations along these lines will produce a rich dividend for psychotherapeutic intervention in the future.

1. Chopra G.S. & Smith, J.W. (1974) *Psychotic reactions following Cannabis use in the East Indians.* Archives of General Psychiatry 30: 24-27

2. Tunving, K. (1987) *Psychiatric Aspects of cannabis Use in Adolescents and Young Adults.* Pediatrician 14:83-91

3. Ghodse A.H. (1986) " *Cannabis Psychosis."* British Journal of Addiction 81: 473-478

4. Prince R. *The Rastafari of Jamaica: A study of group beliefs and social stress.* Paper presented at American Psychiatric Association/ Caribbean Psychiatric Association meeting, Ocho Rios, Jamaica, May 1969.

5. Kiev, Ari. Discussant; *The Rastafari of Jamaica.* By Prince, R. Paper presented at American Psychiatric Association/Caribbean Psychiatric Association meeting, Ocho Rios, Jamaica, May 1969.

6. Hickling, F.W. (1992) *"Radio Psychiatry and Community Mental Health."* Hospital and Community Psychiatry 43: 739-741.

7. Hickling F.W. & Rodgers-Johnson, P. (1993) *"A Prospective first contact incidence study of schizophrenia in Jamaica"* In Press.

8. Wing, J.K., Cooper, J.E., Sartorious, N., (1974) *"The Measurement and Classification of Psychiatric Symptoms".* London: Cambridge University Press

9. Rubin, V. & Comitas, L. (1976) *"Ganja in Jamaica-The Effects of Marihuana Use".*

10. Dreher, M.C. (1982) *"Working Men and Ganja-Marijuana Use on Rural Jamaica".* Philadelphia Institute of the Study of Human Issues.

11. McGuire, P., Jones, P., Bebbington, P., et al (1994) *"Acute Psychosis Associated with Cannabis Use: Psychopathology and Socio-demographic Variables".* Schizophrenia Research, In Press

12. Hickling FW. *"Socio-drama in the Rehabilitation of Chronic Mental Illness."* Hospital and Community Psychiatry (1989) 40: 402-406.

13. Hemsi, L.K. (1967) *"Psychiatry morbidity of the West Indian immigrants."* Social Psychiatry 2: 95-100

14. Leff, J. (1988) *"Psychiatry Around the Globe. A Transcultural View."* London: Royal College of Psychiatrists.

15. Tafari-Ama I. *A Historical Analysis of Grassroots Resistance in Jamaica: A Case Study of Participatory Research on Gender Relations in Rastsfari. MSc Thesis.* Institute of Social Studies, The Hague, 1989.

APPENDIX 4A

THE USE OF CERTAIN CANNABIS DERIVATIVES (CANASOL) IN GLAUCOMA

PROFESSOR EMERITUS MANLEY WEST,
Pharmacology Section, Department of Basic Medical Sciences,
University of the West Indies, Mona, Jamaica

INTRODUCTION:

Glaucoma may be defined as a group of ocular conditions characterized by raised intraocular pressure. Approximately 300 persons per 100,000 suffer from glaucoma. The prevalence increases with age and involves about 1 percent of the population over 40. Almost 80,000 Americans have glaucoma of one form or another.

Primary open angle is the most common form; it causes insidious asymptomatic, bilateral visual loss. About 15 per cent of Caucasians with glaucoma have closed angle glaucoma, and this percentage may be seen higher in Asians. Glaucoma is more prevalent, begins earlier in life, and progresses faster among blacks than among other races. Jamaica, in particular, with a population of about 3 million has about 3 per cent of this number suffering from glaucoma.

Normal intraocular pressure is from 10 to 20 mm Hg. Elevated intraocular pressure is usually associated with damage to the optic disk and visual field loss. In spite of a fundamental interest and research in this area, the precise mechanism by which ocular hypertension damages to the optic disk is not clearly understood.

Aqueous humor is the fluid that circulates within the eyes to provide nourishment to the tissues. It is produced by the ciliary processes in the posterior chamber of the eyes and passes from the posterior chamber through the pupil to the anterior chamber of the eyes and exits through the outflow system at the peripheral angle of the anterior chamber. Two factors are really important in the dynamics of aqueous humor:

1. Irregularities in drainage or outflow of the aqueous humor.

2. Irregularities in the inflow.

Inflow should balance outflow to maintain a steady state of intraocular pressure. Reducing aqueous production and hence inflow should be an accepted method of reducing intraocular pressure in all forms of glaucoma. The treatment involves a medical or surgical approach. The surgical approach should be used only after medical attempts have failed.

At present we do not know how either endogenous or exogenous stimulators or inhibitors may alter aqueous humor formation and intraocular pressure. However, the adenylate cyclase complex in the ciliary process acts to reduce flow in a manner that is not known. It is known that the cholera toxin induces a watery diarrhoea by stimulating an intestinal epithelial adenylate cyclase with the result of sodium and water being drawn into the lumen of the intestine. (Wray et al. 1981). This same toxin increases endolymph production in the inner ear.

Stimulation of adenylate cyclase activity will accelerate production of cyclic AMP in epithelial cells and cause movement of fluid from the basal to the apical portions of the cells and hence into the lumen. It is known that cyclic AMP will increase the permeability of luminal membranes. It is also known that adrenaline enhances the intraocular accumulation of cyclic AMP by activating adenylate. The same line of reasoning holds for the ciliary epithelium, but the movement of fluid is reversed due to the invagination of the optical vesicles during the development of the eye. Therefore, it should not be difficult to accept that the receptor complex in the secretory tissues of the eye, the ciliary processes, may be the area where research should be directed to find an acceptable medication for glaucoma.

TREATMENT

The management of glaucoma is best left to the ophthalmologist, but the size and importance of the problem calls for the cooperation of other health professionals. The medical treatment is divided into two major areas:

1. Reduction of aqueous humor production and

2. Facilitation of aqueous humor outflow.

Canasol is a fairly new drug that reduces inflow and has significant advantages when compared to the synthetic drugs.

Current antiglaucoma medications are not always effective and have significant side effects. Pilocarpine and other miotic drugs (which constrict the pupil, thereby increasing the fluid outflow) may cause blurred vision during the day due to ciliary body spasm and impaired vision at night caused by miosis. Furthermore, the miotics may contribute to the development of cataracts and may predispose the patient to uveitis and retinal detachment. The carbonic anhydrase inhibitors, such as Diamox, can produce electrolyte imbalance, fatigue, decreased appetite and weight loss, and kidney stones.

Epinephrine eye drops may cause eye pain or headache because they dilate pupils to inhibit the inflow of fluid. Because they can be absorbed into the circulation, they may also cause heart palpitations and nervousness. The most popular glaucoma medication is Timoptic (generic name, timolol maleate), a beta-blocker, which is believed to decrease eye fluid production. Initial adverse reactions noted were mild ocular irritations and slight reduction in the resting heart rate. Later reports identified problems associated with nerves, digestion, vision, skin, and respiration (Miller 1980: the Harvard Medical School Health Letter 1979).

CANASOL

For many years it was observed in Israel and the United States that the Cannabis plant has ocular hypotensive effects, and vast sums of money were invested in these countries in research to develop therapeutically useful compounds. These ocular hypotensive compounds represent a new class of chemicals that are more potent in reducing intraocular pressure than most of the other accepted drugs used clinically and with none of their side effects.

Canasol is a sterile ophthalmic preparation developed from *Cannabis sativa* specifically for the management of glaucoma. It is the result of ten years of study at the University of the West Indies in the pharmacology and ophthalmology departments and in private ophthalmic clinics. (West and Lockhart 1978, 1980 Figure 1.)

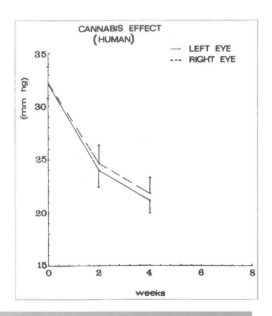

FIGURE 1: EFFECT OF 5% CANNABIS OPHTHALMIC DROPS APPLIED TOPICALLY TO THE HUMAN EYE WITH GLAUCOMA UP TO 4 WEEKS OF TREATMENT.

Whereas international researchers concentrated their efforts on some cannabinoids that are psychoactive, at the University of the West Indies our research efforts were directed at other compounds of this plant since we were looking at long-term therapy. Now that the effectiveness of Canasol in glaucoma has been established in the Caribbean region and, according to private communication, in Australia, New Zealand, Columbia, and England, research is being directed at its mode and mechanism of action (Gutierrez and

Gutierrez, 1995). There is evidence that we may be looking at adrenergic receptor control of aqueous humor dynamics. Here Canasol could make a significant contribution to ophthalmology.

Effect of Canasol ophthalmic solution 0.1 percent w/v applied topically to the human eye with glaucoma. (Standard errors of mean are omitted on this and the following three figures).

For Jamaica the introduction of this drug is timely considering the proportion of the population with glaucoma and the severe foreign exchange problems that now exist. For this reason the treatment of Jamaicans facilitates research in this area.

PHARMACOLOGY

Canasol is unique in that when applied to one eye it does not cross over the contralateral eye. There is now evidence that no appreciable amount passes into the systemic circulation and thus it has a predominantly local effect. This action of Canasol may be a function of its chemical nature. As demonstrated in animals and humans, the onset of action is very rapid and can be detected within minutes after a single topical application to the eye. At 15 minutes there is a decrease of approximately 50% in the original intraocular

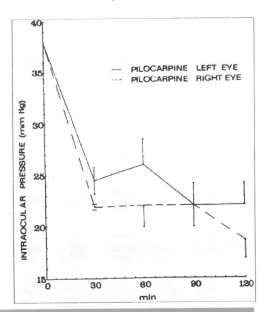

FIGURE 2:EFFECT OF A SINGLE TOPICAL APPLICATION OF 4% PILOCARPINE SULPHATE ON THE INTRAOCULAR PRESSURE IN THE DOG'S EYE.

pressure, and this reaches a maximum at 90 minutes after application. (see Figure 2)

Canasol has no effect on pupil size. Laboratory and clinical studies have shown that Canasol is more effective on a weight basis in lowering intraocular pressure when Canasol is combined with pilocarpine or timolol maleate (see Figures 3 &4). Though there has been no scientific evaluation to verify this claim, recent reports by ophthalmologists in Jamaica indicate that patients on Canasol may have improved vision at night. Canasol lowers the pressure in both the normal eye and the eye with glaucoma; however, the ocular hypotensive effect is most pronounced in the eye with glaucoma.

The mode and mechanism of the action of Canasol is not clear at this time, but this is not unique to Canasol; there are many drugs whose mechanisms of action were not worked out until after they had been in clinical use, for example, Digitalis.

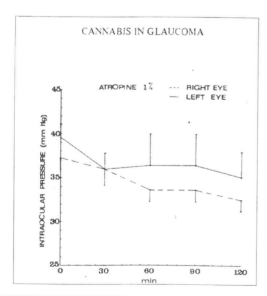

FIGURE 3: EFFECT OF A SINGLE TOPICAL APPLICATION OF 1% ATROPINE SULPHATE ON THE INTRAOCULAR PRESSURE IN DOG'S EYES.

However, the significant fall in intraocular pressure in animals in counteracted by several adrenolytic agents, whether they are applied topically to the eye or injected intravenously. Examples of these agents are tolazoline, azapetine, and phenoxybenzamine. Clinical experience has shown that when patients are already on anti-hypertensive medication, particularly alpha-adrenergic blocking drugs, the frequency of dosing should be increased to produce the desired effect.

Percentage change in ocular hypotension by Canasol 0.1 per cent and Timolol 0.5 per cent (in dogs).

The depletion of catecholamine stores in animals significantly reduces the effectiveness of Canasol. Extensive animal studies show that Canasol has no effect on the outflow mechanism. In animals, if the cervical (sympathetic) nerve is severed, the intraocular pressure is increased and Canasol, which lowers intraocular pressure, may not reduce it. Present knowledge thus indicates that Canasol lowers intraocular pressure by adrenergic stimulation, and the site may be in the ciliary apparatus.

Canasol eye drops may be used for (1) open or closed angle glaucoma or (2) raised intraocular pressure in patients who are at sufficient risk to require the lowering of their intraocular pressure. To date no adverse effects have been reported following the use of over 90,000 phials (or small bottle) of sterile Canasol eye drops.

Summation or potentiation of Timolol in the presence of Canasol. The potentiation is the same irrespective of which drug is instilled first (in dogs).

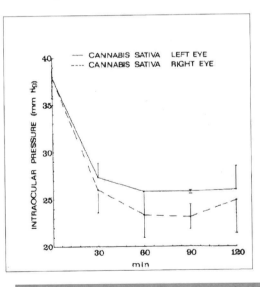

FIGURE 4: EFFECT OF A SINGLE TOPICAL APPLICATION OF 5% CANNABIS ON THE INTRAOCULAR PRESSURE IN DOG'S EYES.

Canasol is supplied in boxes of 25 phials. The solution is sterile and is contained in standard plastic eye-drop bottles (5 ml). Concentration is 0.1% weight/volume. It should be stored in a cool dark place. In Jamaica it is manufactured by Ampec Chemicals Limited and marketed by Medigrace Limited in Kingston.

APPENDIX 4B

THE POTENTIAL USE OF CANNABIS SATIVA IN OPHTHALMOLOGY

A. B. LOCKHART, F.R.C.S.; M. E. WEST, PH.D. AND H.I.C LOWE, PH.D., Departments Ophthalmology and Pharmacology, University of the West Indies, Mona, Jamaica

INTRODUCTION

Interest in the therapeutic potential of cannabis (ganja) has been with us for many years and its early use dates back over one hundred years (Reynolds, 1890; Kabelikm, 1955; Bennet, 1975).

Although there have been several early reports of therapeutic benefits from cannabis, most of them were not characterized by in-depth scientific investigations because of the legal, social and chemical problems encountered. For example, the drug has been used as a hypotensive (Dixon, 1899; Dewey et al, 1970; Forney, 1971), diuretic (Barry et al, 1970), antidepressant (Todd, 1946), analgesic (Chopra and Chopra, 1957) and depressant agent (Layman and Milton, 1971).

In modern clinical practice, the trend has been to use a pure compound of unit dosage, which exhibits specific pharmacological actions. The isolation, chemical stability and the special solvent systems, which are needed to solubilize the active component of cannabis, are some of the factors, which have delayed clinical assessment of this drug.

Despite the drawbacks, there is currently fresh inquiry concerning its social, legal and pharmacological action with a view to establishing sound scientific evidence, where possible, so that a direct clinical use could be made of this drug.

At this point in time, Jamaica seems to be one of the major suppliers of Cannabis to the world. This drug (ganja) has now become of cultural importance to Jamaica. Rubin and Comitas (1975) stated that, "For the better part of the century, ganja has been used by Jamaicans, not for euphoric 'high', but as an energizer among working men, as a prophylactic or therapeutic tea by women and children and as a medicine by nearly everyone, smokers and non-smokers alike. It forms an integral part of the Jamaican cultural tradition and value system."

As a result of clinical observations, controlled studies carried out by us and the work of other researchers (Helper and Frank, 1971), the use of Cannabis in controlling glaucoma was identified. It has now been decided to formulate ophthalmic preparations of tetrahydrocannabinol and its derivatives and to investigate their possible effects on intraocular pressure.

MATERIALS AND METHODS

For this study, a total of 80 patients were selected. Forty patients had raised intraocular tension and were clinically diagnosed as having glaucoma. The second group of forty cases had normal tension. The tension in both eyes for each patient was measured every 15 minutes for two hours and the results for each eye recorded separately in tabular form. For the glaucoma and non-glaucoma groups, the intraocular was measured before and after smoking (a) a regular cigarette and (b) a cannabis cigarette. No attempt was made to quantify the weight of tobacco in the normal cigarette or Cannabis in the Cannabis cigarette.

The results of this study are represented graphically.

RESULTS

The intraocular pressure in the left eye of the glaucoma patient showed a marked fall from just over 33 mm Hg to 18.6 mm Hg in two hours, after smoking a single Cannabis cigarette. In contrast, a single normal tobacco cigarette showed initial rise in intraocular pressure from 23

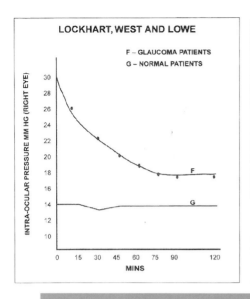

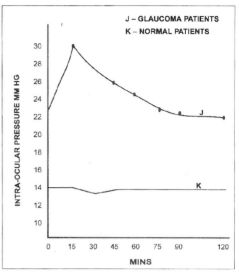

FIGURE 3: EFFECT OF A SINGLE TOPICAL APPLICATION OF 1% ATROPINE SULPHATE ON THE INTRA-OCULAR PRESSURE IN THE DOG'S EYES.

mm Hg to 27.4 mm Hg in 30 minutes and then a gradual fall to 22.8 mm Hg in two hours. In the left eye with a normal intraocular pressure, there was no real change in pressure after smoking Cannabis or tobacco cigarette. In graph F, Figure 2, the Cannabis cigarette produced a similar fall in intraocular pressure in the right eye with glaucoma, while the tobacco cigarette produced the usual rise in pressure (23.0-09.8 mm Hg) (Graph J, Fig. 3) followed by a gradual fall to 22.6 mm Hg. Again, there was little change in the normal pressure in the right eye, whether the patient smoked tobacco or Cannabis cigarette (Graphs G&K).

DISCUSSION

It is reported in the literature that the active component of *Cannabis sativa* lowers intraocular pressure (Helper & Frank, 1971; Goodman and Gilman, 1975). In our experiments, we did not monitor the systematic blood pressure which usually parallels intraocular pressure, and in the literature there is confusion as to whether it is the vehicle used to solubilize the cannabinoids that produce the hypotensive effect or not (Mechoulam, 1973).

The most consistent cardiovascular actions of Cannabis are increase in heart rate and marked reddening of the conjunctivae (Goodman and Gilman, 1975). Our findings showed that whereas tobacco cigarettes produced a rise followed by a fall in intraocular pressure, cannabis cigarettes produced a consistent fall in pressure without prior rise. In the eye without glaucoma, there was no real change in pressure, whether the patient smoked tobacco cigarettes or cannabis cigarettes.

It was interesting to observe that cannabis was only effective in lowering the intraocular pressure in glaucoma patients, and therefore this lowering of pressure may not be as a result of lowering of systemic blood pressure.

At this point in time there are no substantiated indications for the use of cannabis in man (Goodman and Gilman, 1975). Nevertheless, its therapeutic benefit in glaucoma may delay the onset of blindness caused by this condition and may thus become the first substantiated use in man.

At present we are conducting further studies in the use of ophthalmic preparations from *Cannabis sativa* in order to establish the mode and mechanism of its action in glaucoma.

SUMMARY

Forty patients with glaucoma and forty with normal intraocular tension were examined for changes in intraocular pressure before and after smoking tobacco and cannabis cigarettes. Smoking of cannabis cigarettes decreased the intraocular pressure in glaucoma. Smoking of tobacco cigarettes produced an initial rise in pressure followed by a fall. There was no change in the patients with normal intraocular tension.

ACKNOWLEDGMENTS

We wish to thank Dr. Winston Davidson, Permanent Secretary in the Ministry of Health and Environment Control, the Hon. Keble Munn and the Staff of the Ministry of Security and Justice, and the Police Administration for affording us the necessary legal protection in the use of *Cannabis sativa.*

1. Barry, H., Perhach, J. L. and Kubena, R. K. (1970) Pharmacologist, 12, 258.

2. Benet, S. (1975) '*Early Diffusion and Folk Use of Hemp'. In: Cannabis and Culture, Ed.* Vera Rubin, The Hague Mouton.

3. Chopra, I.C. Chopra, R. W. (1957) Bull Narcotics, 9, 4.

4. Dewey, W. L., Peng, T. and Harris, L. S. (1970) Europ. J. Pharmacol., 12, 382.

5. Dixon, W. E. (1899) Brit. Med. J., 2, 1354.

6. Ford, R. D. and McMillan, D. E. (1971) Fed. Proc. Amer. Soc. Exp. Biol., 30, 279.

7. Forney, R. B. (1971) N. Y. Acad. Sci. Conference on Marijuana, abstract 7.

8. Goodman, L. S. and Gilman, A. G. (1975). *The Pharmacological Basis of Therapeutics* (5th Ed,) pp. 306-308

9. Helper, R. s. and Frank, m. (1971) J. Amer. Med. Ass., 217, 1392.

10. Kabelikm, J., Krejci, Z and Santavy, F. (1960). Bull Narcotics, 12, 3 & 5.

11. Layman, J. M. and Milton, A. S. (1971) Brit. J. Pharmacol., 41, 379.

12. Mechoulam, R. (1973) Marijuana: *Chemistry, Pharmacology, Metabolism and clinical Effects,* p.231.

13. Reynolds, J. R (1890) '*Therapeutic Use And Toxic Effects of Cannabis Indica',* Lancet, 637-638.

14. Rubin, V. and Comitas, L. (1975) *'Ganja in Jamaica'*. The Hague Molton Press.

15. Schultz, O. E. and Haffner, G. (1958) arch. Pharm. (Weinheim) 291, 391.

16. Todd, A. R. (1946) Experimentia, 2, 55.

APPENDIX 5

MEDICAL MARIJUANA: THE CONTINUING STORY

BY BRIGID KANE
Annals of Internal Medicine Vol 134 No. 12 19 June 2001, 1159-1162

Marijuana — the common name for the variable combination of substances in the leaves, flower tops, and even small branches of the hemp plant *Cannabis sativa* L. -has been used as a medicinal herb for centuries. According to historical studies of medical practices in numerous ancient cultures, marijuana was believed to have curative properties, delivered through teas, oils and ointments made from the hemp plant and from smoking dried parts of the plant in pipes and as cigarettes.

Modern scientific investigation into the potential therapeutic uses of marijuana essentially began in the 1960s with the isolation and chemical characterization of the cannabinoids, a family of compounds in the hemp plant that is responsible for the psychoactive properties of marijuana. The cannabinoids, primarily delta-9-tetrahydrocannabinol, more commonly called tetrahydrocannabinol (or THC), are also responsible for the antiemetic, analgesic, appetite-stimulating, and anti-anxiety or sedative effects of marijuana. In the 1980s, basic science research provided key evidence that explains the reported therapeutic effects of marijuana: The identification of two types of cannabinoid receptors in humans-in the brain and throughout the body on cells of the immune system- and the identification of natural cannabinoid molecules in the body that bind to and activate these receptors. The discoveries have opened the door to understanding the mechanisms of action of endogenous cannabinoids, as well as plant-derived or synthetic cannabinoids, in humans.

"Certainly not all kinds of the pathways are worked out, and probably not all of the involved molecules have been identified yet," commented Billy Martin, Ph.D of the Pharmacology and Toxicology department of the Commonwealth University in Richmond, Virginia, "But we're on the right track, characterizing the normal physiological pathways use by the cannabinoids to effect pain modulation, control of movement, control of visceral sensations, and other processes."

THE PUBLIC ISSUES

Recently, the biomedical community, patients, patient advocates, and the public have been drawn once again to the ongoing debate about marijuana as medicine with the impending US Supreme Court ruling on the legality of the "medical necessity" defense made by the Oakland (California) Cannabis Buyers' Cooperative. The case stems from a 1998 US Justice Department civil law suit against the Oakland Cannabis Buyers' Cooperative and five other California marijuana "pharmacies" for violation of federal drug laws by growing and distributing marijuana. These buyers clubs have been sanctioned by the state of California as places for patients with such conditions as cancer, multiple sclerosis, AIDS, glaucoma, and chronic intractable pain to purchase marijuana or marijuana plants legally.

Since 1996, when California's Compassionate Use Act (Proposition 215) was adopted, California residents with specific medical conditions for which marijuana provides relief have been permitted to purchase, grow and use marijuana on a physician's recommendation. Seven other states have adopted medical marijuana laws or passed ballot initiatives, indicating that at least a majority of the vomiting public in these states believes in the therapeutic potential of smoking marijuana.

However, the US Congress has taken a very different position- that marijuana is illegal and its use is never appropriate, not even for medical purposes. Although the Supreme Court ruling on the Oakland Cannabis Buyers' Cooperative case will be very specific (addressing a decision of the 9th US Circuit Court Appeals that upheld the medical necessity defense, allowing the operation of marijuana buyers clubs), it will likely have some trickle-down effect on patients, physicians and distributors or brokers of marijuana. The ruling, which is expected to be handed down by July 2001, will not strike any of the state laws.

Other countries, most notably Canada and the United Kingdom, are also examining medical use of marijuana from a legal and drug-policy perspective. In April 2001, the Canadian government proposed rules, effective 31 July 2001 that would allow patients with specific medical conditions to buy, grow, and use marijuana on a physician's recommendation.

THE LAW AND MEDICAL USE OF MARIJUANA

Under the US Controlled Substances Act of 1970, marijuana is classified as a schedule I drug, meaning that it has potential for abuse and no recognized medical use (therefore, it cannot be prescribed). The Controlled Substances Act makes it a federal crime to purchase, possess, or prescribe marijuana; however, it does include a mechanism for the Drug Enforcement Administration (DEA) to decontrol, reclassify, reschedule, or add substances to a schedule.

Efforts have failed to reclassify marijuana as a schedule II drug, the class of drugs that have a potential for abuse but are prescribable because of their therapeutic effects for very specific indications, although tightly regulated. Interestingly, dronabinol, a synthetic form of THC, which has been approved by the US Food and Drug Administration (FDA) for cancer chemotherapy- induced nausea and vomiting and AIDS wasting, was originally classified as a schedule II drug and is now a schedule III drug (these drugs, which include anabolic steroids, are considered even less dangerous and have a potential for abuse lower than that of schedule I or II drugs; abuse of these drugs leads to only moderate or low physical dependence).

The opiate morphine, which is the strongest pain-relieving drug available legally in the United States is a schedule II drug. "If marijuana were converted to a schedule II drug, with established controls on medical use, we need not expect problematic abuse by patients," commented John Benson, Jr., MD, emeritus professor of medicine at the Oregon Health Sciences University of Medicine in Portland and co-principal investigator of a 1999 expert report by the Institute of Medicine (IOM) assessing the scientific basis for use of marijuana as medicine. Benson added, "In the 1950s there were concerns and worries about the illicit use of morphine. We've learned that the fear of producing addicts through medical treatment is unfounded, primarily due to the regulated distribution system for approved narcotics and the sick patient's lack of interest in abuse."

DRUG REGULATION ISSUES AND DRUG POLICY

The opposition to moving marijuana to a less restrictive category (schedule II) is largely based on the fears that its illicit recreational use, already documented to be very high in the United States, would increase even further. Whether right or wrong, the recreational use of marijuana, the unquantified addictive potential of the smoked botanical product, and its perceived potential as an initiation into the use of "hard" drugs obfuscate the scientific and medical issues. "The driving force for the adoption of medical marijuana laws is the broad legalization of marijuana; it goes beyond reclassifying marijuana," noted Eric Votch, MD, clinical associate professor of medicine at the University of Kansas in Kansas City and chair of the Institute on Global Dru Policy. Votch emphasized that, "We should not have medicine by popular vote but by the tried-and-true FDA drug-development process."

Certainly, there is a wide division between persons fighting the war on drugs and those who espouse anti-regulatory principles. The latter includes groups that charge that a government conspiracy is suppressing data that unequivocally demonstrate marijuana's therapeutic efficacy. Whether the grass-roots efforts to petition the DEA to reschedule marijuana as a schedule II substance are wholly anti-regulatory is debatable. In the middle of the US drug policy and drug regulation tug-of-war are many scientists and physicians who agree that the classic pathway for drug development needs to be followed but also acknowledge that it may be nearly impossible to fulfil the FDA's requirement to demonstrate a measurable dose-response effect with smoked marijuana.

MEDICAL MARIJUANA

| BASIC AND CLINICAL SCIENCE |

Many scientists involved in marijuana research become emotionally aroused when weighing the medical benefits and toxic effects of marijuana, not necessarily because of scientific evidence but because of views on drug use and drug abuse. Nevertheless, the relevant scientific questions surrounding the issue of marijuana as a therapeutic agent presumably can be answered with collection and evaluation of data from controlled clinical trials.

With the release of two major scientific reports-from the National Institutes of Health (NIH) in 1997 and from the IOM in 1999- basic and clinical science evaluating the effect of marijuana has been elevated to the status of mainstream science. Equally important, marijuana research is now more easily funded. According to Steven Gust, PhD, special assistant to the Director of the National Institute on Drug Abuse at the NIH, one major outcome of the NIH and IOM summary reports was that the US Department of Health and Human Services (DHHS) broadened marijuana access for research purposes by formalizing its policy on making marijuana available to NIH-supported and non-governmental-supported research. Researchers can obtain marijuana for their studies by following the normal regulatory process for clinical evaluation of a drug by submitting an application for an investigational new drug with the FDA and registering the study with the DEA after the study protocol is reviewed for scientific merit by DHHS.

Surprisingly, only six proposals for marijuana research have been submitted to the DHHS since 1999 and, according to Gust, all six are in some state of approval. He commented, "This tells us that there is a lack of interest in the research rather than the argument we frequently hear about the government stonewalling efforts in marijuana research." Another likely explanation is that researchers are reluctant to work in an area that is murky and emotionally charged. Patients, too, may be reluctant to participate in clinical trials evaluating marijuana because of the sensitivity of the issues.

Most of the clinical research efforts are ultimately seeking to evaluate the safety and efficacy of smoking marijuana relative to oral administration of synthetic THC (dronabinol), existing noncannabinoid therapies, and placebo. For example, Donald Abrams, MD, along with his colleagues at the University of California, San Francisco, are investigating the drug-drug interaction between marijuana and two HIV protease inhibitors, nelfinavir and indinavir. Marijuana is metabolized by the hepatic cytochrome P450 system, as are protease inhibitors. A 21-day randomized trial involving pharmacokinetic sampling of plasma drug levels found that dose adjustments of the antiretrovirals are not needed because of marijuana's probable effect on the cyotchrome enzymes. Although no clinically significant difference was shown, observed changes in pharmacokinetic measures were greater among the participants who smoked marijuana compared with the two other treatment groups that received either dronabinol or placebo capsules. Abrams noted that whereas marijuana use among HIV-infected persons is primarily limited to appetite stimulation for AIDS wasting, there is also a potentially therapeutic role for the pain of HIV-related peripheral neuropathy.

Efforts in basic science research range from identification of the active ingredients in marijuana to characterization of the neurophysiologic and neuropathologic pathways involving the cannabinoid receptors CB1 and CB2 and the endogenous cannabinoids in the body. In the search to identify the substances responsible for marijuana's desirable therapeutic effects, most scientists consider THC to be the main active ingredient. However, some researchers and advocates of alternative medicine (along with entrepreneurial agripharmacologists) argue that the THC cannot be separated from other cannabinoids in the hemp plant; that some or all of marijuana's clinical benefit results from the combination and balance found in the natural leaf product.

Basic science research on the cannabinoids hit full stride with the identification in the 1980s of CB1 receptors in the brain and the parallel discovery that endogenous cannabinoids (notably, anadamide and sn-2 arachidonylglycerol) activate these receptors. The early research findings on endogenous cannabinoids and cannabinoid receptors made it abundantly clear that cannabinoids are involved in numerous normal physiologic processes namely, control of movement, coordination and balance, pain modulation, pain perception, pleasure sensation, learning and cognitive functions, and memory. The distribution of cannabinoid receptors in specific brain areas- the cerebellum, hippocampus, hypothalamus, and basal ganglia, for example is consistent with the known physiologic and behavioural effects of marijuana and cannabinoids. Such insight will prove invaluable in determining or exploiting the therapeutic potential of purified cannabinoid drugs, a recognized priority by NIH and IOM. "The hottest area right now," said Martin, "is identifying the basic signalling process for the synthesis and release of the endogenous cannabinoids; it could involve a neurotransmitter, a hormone-it could be anything." Several researchers point out the similarity between the cannabinoid and opiate pathways.

Without question, the most heated aspects of the medical marijuana debate in the scientific community centre around, but are not limited to, the undesirable and potentially harmful effects of marijuana. Indeed, the key scientific arguments against the therapeutic use of marijuana are the following: availability of other, less toxic medicines to treat the same symptoms at least effectively; potential for addiction; negative health effects of smoking (limited data suggest bronchial epithelial toxicity); mind-altering or mood elevating property and other related adverse effect (the "high" experienced with marijuana use is undesirable for many patients); drug tolerance; difficulty in measuring relief of symptoms ("Is the pain less, or is your mood better and you don't mind the pain?").

The concern about marijuana's addictive potential is frequently countered or dismissed with arguments highlighting greater addictive potential of other schedule I (for example, heroin) and schedule II (for example, morphine) controlled substances.

The issue of smoking is also damning for marijuana, as Janet Joy, PhD, a neuroscientist by training and an IOM senior program officer, noted, "There's no future in smoking marijuana as a conventional medicine," In a recent book she co-authored, 'Marijuana as Medicine? The Science Beyond the Controversy', one chapter subheading, "Where There's Smoke, There's Harm," summarizes the scientific community's hesitation for outright support of medical marijuana. Joy added, "However, at this time, until there is an alternative for that small segment of the population with un-met needs, referring to patients who have unsuccessfully tried other normally effective FDA- approved medications for their symptoms, we acknowledge the modest clinical benefit of smoked marijuana."

PHARMACEUTICAL AND AGRICULTURAL SCIENCE

Researchers are exploring several alternative routes of drug delivery to harness the therapeutic effects of marijuana and natural purified or synthetic THC, with or without other cannabinoids Oral administration of synthetic THC has already revealed some pharmacokinetic drawbacks. The time to maximum plasma concentration (Tmax) and decay rate are long. Synthetic THC administered orally takes approximately 30 to 60 minutes to achieve an effect, compared with 3 to 5 minutes for smoked marijuana. (Also, key side effects of oral THC include central nervous system events, including dysphoria rather than euphoria.) Newer formulations of synthetic THC in development should have more favourable pharmacokinetic and safety profiles.

Novel drug delivery methods that are in development include the transdermal patch, rectal suppository, nasal spray, and smokeless inhaler devices. These drug- delivery mechanisms are especially needed by patients who are unable to swallow or who have obstructions due to oesophageal and other gastrointestinal cancers.

With funding provided by the American Cancer Society, Audra Stinchcomb, PhD at the University of Kentucky College of Pharmacy in Lexington is investigating the controlled-release rates of approximately 12 different synthetic cannabinoid compounds through a transsdermal patch system. "We are at the in vitro stage right now, where we measure drug concentrations over time. The next step is animal studies, where in vivo blood levels will be measured," Stinchcomb said.

Agricultural science is also involved in exploring the therapeutic effects of marijuana. GW Pharmaceuticals (Wiltshire, United Kingdom) has an impressive government- approved facility at which cannabis plants are hybridized to yield the maximal concentration in the leaf is roughly 3% to 4% through the cross-breeding plants, the yield has increased to nearly 25%.

POLITICS AND EMOTIONS

Medical use of marijuana for persons with certain conditions is rarely discussed without some consideration of the social context. The two basic and diametrically opposed ideologies underlying the debate on making marijuana a prescribable drug appear straightforward-compassion for the suffering versus prevention of increased illicit drug use-although the divide is not just between those for or against drug relation and government control. For all the controversy, the patient population for whom medical marijuana is indicated is quite small.

SUMMARY

Recent scientific reports summarizing the current knowledge base and evaluating the benefit -to-risk ratio of marijuana have cautiously recommended smoking marijuana as a last and experimental resort for relief of chemotherapy-induced nausea or vomiting, life- threatening loss of appetite, muscle spasticity, glaucoma, or chronic pain. The legal and political implications of this recommendation of marijuana from a schedule I to a schedule II substance by the biomedical community are under scrutiny. The societal consequences of this action need to be systematically measured to allay the longstanding fears of drug policy-makers and the public; meanwhile, the medical profession needs to implement a system of checks and balances on these uses of marijuana, the volume of marijuana prescribed, and the prescribers of the drug- and intervene, when necessary.

Note added in proof: On 14 May 2001, the US Supreme Court ruled 8-0 that the manufacture and distribution of marijuana are illegal under any circumstances. Justice Clarence Thomas said " Marijuana has no medical benefits worthy of exception." The medical and legal implications of that decision are still being debated.

APPENDIX 6

BOOKS PUBLISHED ON MARIJUANA BY JAMAICAN AUTHORS

1. W. Barrett. *'Ganja.'* (Kingston: The Government Printing Press), 1951

2. Harry Lepinske. *'Jamaican Ganja: A Report on the Marijuana Problem.* (New York: Exposition Press), 1955.

3. Farquharson Institute of Public Affairs. *'Statement on Ganja.'* (Kingston: The Institute of Jamaica), 1970.

4. Michael Beaubrun. *'The Pros and Cons of Cannabis Used in Jamaica.'* (Mona, Jamaica: University of the West Indies), 1971.

5. Timothy Harding and F. McKnight. *'Marihuana- Modified Mania.'* (Chicago: American Medical Association), 1973.

6. John Rosevear. *Pot: A Handbook of Marijuana.* (Secaucus, New Jersey: The Citadel Press), 1973.

7. Terry Eunice. The Ganja Gang. Edited by John & Alison Tedman. (London: Oxford U.P)., 1973.

8. Michael Beaubrun. *'Cannabis or Alcohol: The Jamaican Experience.'* (The Hague, Paris: Molton Press), 1975.

9. Lambros Comitas. *' The Social Nexus of Ganja in Jamaica.'* (The Hague, Paris: Molton Publishers), 1975

10. Vera Rubin. *"The Ganja "Vision" in Jamaica."* (The Hague, Paris: Molton Publishers), 1975.

11. Vera Rubin and Lambros Comitas. *'Ganja in Jamaica: A Medical anthropological Study of Chronic Marijuana Use.'* (The Hague, Paris: Molton Press), 1975.

12. Vera Rubin. Cannabis and Culture. (The Hague, Paris: Molton Publisher), 1975.

13. Joseph Schaeffer. ' *The Significance of Marihuana in a Small Agricultural Community in Jamaica.'* (The Hague, Paris: Molton Press), 1975.

14. Vera Rubin. *'Ganja in Jamaica: The Effects of Marijuana Use.'* (Garden City, New York: Anchor Press), 1976.

15. M.C. Dreher. *'Getting High: Ganja and the Socio-economic Milieu,'* in *Caribbean Studies.* Vol. 16, No.2, 1976.

16. Melanie C. Dreher. *Keep off the Grass: A scientist's Documented Account of Marijuana's Destructive Effect.* (New York: Reader's Digest Press), 1976.

17. John Commissiong. 'Ganja.' (Kingston : University of the West Indies), 1978.

18. Jamaica Library Service. *'A Select listing on Ganja.'* (Mandeville: The Parish Library), 1979.

19. Melanie Dreher. *'Working Men and Ganja: Marijuana Use in Rural Jamaica.'* (Philadelphia: Institute for the Development of Human Issues), 1982.

20. Aaron Segal. *'Cross-cultural Gold: Cannabis in the Caribbean'* in *Caribbean Review,* Vol. 11, No.4, Fall 1982.

21. Melanie Greagan Dreher. *Health Care in the Caribbean & Central America-Maternal-Child Health and Ganja in Jamaica.* (Williamsburg, Va: Dept. Of Anthropology, College of William and Mary), 1984.

22. Kenneth Bilby. *'The Wily Herb: Notes on the background of Cannabis in Jamaica.'* (Kingston: University of the West Indies), 1985.

23. Dennis Forsythe. *'The Law against Ganja in Jamaica.'* (Kingston: Zacka), 1993.

APPENDIX 7

SELECTED JOURNAL ARTICLES PUBLISHED ON GANJA

1. Lozano, Indalecio, *The Therapeutic Use of Cannabis sativa (L.) in Arabic Medicine*. J of Cannabis Therapeutics. November 1, 2001; 63-70.

2. Gettman, Jon, *Cannabis and the U.S Controlled Substances Act*. J of Cannabis Therapeutics. November 1, 2001; 1: 95-110.

3. McDonald A., Duncan N. D., Mitchell D. I: *Alcohol, cannabis and cocaine usage in patients with trauma injuries*. West Indian Med. J. December 1999; 48 (4): 200-2.

4. Figueroa J.P., Fox K., Minor K., *A behaviour risk factor survey in Jamaica*. West Indian Med. J. March 1999; 48 (1): 9-15.

5. Simeon D. T., Bain B.C., Wyatt G.E., Le Franc E., Ricketts H., Chambers C., Tucker M.B. *Characteristics of Jamaicans who smoke marijuana before sex and their risk of sexually transmitted disease*. West Indian Med J., March 1996; 45 (1): 9-13.

6. Simeon D.T., Bain B.C., Wyatt G.E., Le Franc E., Ricketts H., Chambers C., Tucker M.B. *Smoking marijuana before sex: a high –risk behaviour in Jamaica?* AIDS.,November 1995: 9(11): 1293-4.

7. Broad K., Feinberg B. *Perceptions of ganja and cocaine in urban Jamaica*. J Psychoactive drugs. July- September 1995; 27 (3): 261-76.

8. Dreher M.C., Nugent K., Hudgins R. *Prenatal marijuana exposure and neonatal outcomes in Jamaica*. Paediatrics, February 1994; 93(2): 254-60.

9. Hickling F.W., Griffith E.E. *Clinical perspective on the Rastafari movement*. Hosp Community Psychiatry. January 1994; 45(1): 49-53.

10. Dreher M.C., Hayes J.S. *Triangulation in cross-cultural research of child development in Jamaica.* West Indian Med J., April 1993; 15(2): 216-29.

11. Hayes J.S., Lampart R., Dreher M.C., Morgan L. *Five-year follow-up of rural Jamaican children whose mothers used marijuana during pregnancy.* West Indian Med J., September 1991; 40(3): 120-3.

12. West M.F. *Cannabis and night vision. Nature,* June 27, 1991; 351 (6329): 703-4.

13. Dreher M.C. *Poor and pregnant: perinatal ganja use in rural Jamaica.* Adv Alcohol Subst Abuse, 1989; 8(1): 45-54.

14. Hayes J.S., Dreher M.C., Nugent J.K. *Newborn outcomes with maternal marihuana use in Jamaican women.* Pediatr Nurs. March-April 1988; 14(2): 107-110.

15. Nahas G.G. *Critique of study on ganja in Jamaica.* Bull Narc. October-December 1985; 37(4): 37-49.

16. Murthy N.V.A, Vassell M., Melville G.N., Wray S.R., Wynter H.M., West M. *Long-term effects of marihuana smoke in uterine contractility and tumour development in rats.* West Indian Med J., December 1985; 34(4): 217-284.

17. Golden K.D., Kean E.A. *Chemical analyses of some Jamaican preparations of cannabis.* West Indian Med J., March 1985; 34(1): 8-10.

18. Fraser H.S., Doston O.Y., Howard L., Grell G.A., Knight F. *Drug metabolizing capacity in Jamaican cigarette and marijuana smokers.* West Indian Med J., December 1983; 32(4): 207-11.

19. Parshad O., Kumar M., Melville G.N. *Thyroid-gonad relationship in marijuana smokers. A field study in Jamaica.* West Indian Med J., June 1983; 32(2): 101-5.

20. Wray S.R., Murthy N.V.A. *Review of the effects of cannabis on mental and physiological functions.* West Indian Med J., December 1981; 36(4): 197-01.

21. AMA Council on Scientific Affairs. *Marijuana: Its health hazards and therapeutic potentials.* J Amer Med Assoc 1981; 248: 1823-1827.

22. Murthy N.V.A Vassell M., Melville G.N., Wray S.R., Shantha Ram N.V., Hari Haram N.V: *reproductive toxicity of marihuana smoke-a-three generation study in female wistar rats.* West Indian Med J., June 1980; 35(2): 73-144.

23. Fraser H.S. *Ganja: (Marijuana).* West Indian Med J., June 1979; 28(2): 65-6.

24. West M. E., Lockhart A.B. *The treatment of glaucoma using a non-psychoactive preparation of Cannabis sativa.* West Indian Med J., March 1978; 27(1): 16-25.

25. Lockhart A.B., West M.E., Lowe H.I.C. *The potential use of Cannabis sativa in ophthalmology.* West Indian Med J., June 1977; 26(2): 66-71.

26. Marshman J.A. Popham R.E., Yawney C.D. *A note on the cannabinoid content of Jamaican ganja.* Bull Narc., October- December 1976; 28(4): 63-8.

27. Comitas L. *Cannabis and work in Jamaica: a refutation of the a-motivational syndrome.* Ann N Y Acad Sci. 1976; 2282; 24-32.

28. Hall J. *Preliminary studies on ganja smoking in Jamaica.* Practitioner. September 172;209(251): 346-51.

29. Davis W.G., Persaud T.V. Recent studies on the active principles on Jamaican medicinal plants. West Indian Med J., June 1970; 19(2): 101-10.

30. Persaud T.V.N., Ellington A.C. *The effects of Cannabis sativa on developing rat embryos-preliminary observations.* West Indian Med J., December 1968; 17(4): 232-37.

31. Stuart K.L *Ganja (Cannabis sativa L.)* West Indian Med J., September 1963; 12(3): 156-167.

APPENDIX 8

SELECTED ARTICLES PUBLISHED IN THE DAILY GLEANER ON MARIJUANA

ARTICLE NAME	DATE PUBLISHED
Majority want ganja legalised -- Chevannes	
US backlash against ganja - *Embassy official warns of decertification for Jamaica*	Friday, August 17, 2001
The rights of Non-Ganja Smokers	Thursday, August 23, 2001
Ministry Studying Ganja Commission Proposals	Thursday, August 23, 2001
A drug addict's triumph	Tuesday, December 25, 2001
'Street children hooked on ganja'	Sunday, March 24, 2002
American professor fined for marijuana	Tuesday, December 31, 2002
Ganja and crime	Sunday, November 27, 2005
The effects of ganja on sexual performance	Wednesday, April 12, 2006
Editorial - Mexico's marijuana decision	Sunday, April 30, 2006
Kingfish strikes - Luxury vehicles seized in counter-narcotics operation	Thursday, August 17, 2006
Drugs and Endless Sex	Sunday, September 18, 2006
'Ganja keeps Jamaica on US narco list' published:	Friday, September 21, 2007
Big ganja bust	Wednesday, October 24, 2007
Sperm goes up in smoke - Pollutants, marijuana linked to low fertility	Wednesday, January 2, 2008
Smugglers hunted - Police search for ganja plane crash survivors published:	Monday, February 25, 2008
Jamaica, land of sun, sea and weed - The United States Department of State hits at drug trafficking and political corruption	Monday, March 3, 2008
Fire bun!	Sunday, March 9, 2008
Marijuana - What role in Jamaica's future?	Monday, June 23, 2008
Rid us of Ganja, Guns, Gangs & Garrisons	Wednesday, July 23, 2008
Students held for weed, weapons seized	Saturday, November 15, 2008

Talking sex: Sex and drugs - dangerous cocktail	Saturday, December 20, 2008
Ganja boom - Farmers will turn to crime if sugar industry crumbles - study	Monday, February 9, 2009
Ganja linked to testicular cancer	Tuesday, February 17, 2009
Ganja linked to testicular cancer	Tuesday, February 17, 2009
Drug mules increase as economic crisis worsens	Sunday, February 22, 2009
Ganja raids increase in St Bess	Wednesday, March 11, 2009

THE BEST OF 2013
ARTICLES PUBLISHED IN THE DAILY GLEANER ON MARIJUANA

Marijuana Not On Minister's Agenda	June 27, 2013
St Vincent PM Wants Regional Governments To Discuss Legalising Marijuana	September 10, 2013
'Decriminalisation Of Marijuana Is Irresponsible'	February 11, 2013
Narcotics Board Rejects Marijuana Legalisation	March 7, 2013
EDITORIAL - Allow Free Trade In Marijuana	December 7, 2012
Let's Debate Marijuana - Pryce	January 23, 2013
Jamaica Must Resist American Influence On Marijuana Laws	June 25, 2013
Jamaica Risks Losing Out On Benefits Of Weed, Warn Advocates	September 1, 2013
Professor Calls For Government To Legalise Marijuana	
School Of Marijuana - Research Facility To Be Established	September 2, 2013
Give Me Credit For Early Work On Canasol	September 11,2013
Sun, Sea, Sand And Ganja - Local Farmers Offer Ganja Tours To Tourists	September 10, 2013
Can Ja Control Medicinal Ganja Distribution?	September 02, 2013
Ganja Has Potential To Attract High-End Tourists	September 02, 2013
Ganja On A New High - Jamaican Researcher Welcomes CNN's Celebrity Doctor's Late Endorsement Of Medicinal Properties Of The Weed	August 18, 2013

Justify The Weed - Justice Minister To Make Constitutional Case For Revising Ganja Law

Published: Saturday | October 26, 2013

WITH JAMAICA'S Ministry of Justice positioning itself to seek approval from Cabinet for the decriminalisation of marijuana, government Senator Mark Golding said the country is to advance constitutional justification to its international partners for the revision of the law.

Golding, the country's justice minister, said his ministry is giving active consideration to reforming the law relating to ganja in Jamaica.

Responding to questions posed in the Senate by Robert Montague yesterday, Golding said the revised law would permit the possession of small amounts of ganja, about two ounces, for recreational use.

However, the Attorney General's Department provided the justice ministry with a legal opinion indicating that Jamaica would have to advance constitutional justification to its international partners for the decriminalisation of marijuana.

PARTY TO TREATIES

Golding said Jamaica is a party to at least two international treaties which criminalise certain forms of conduct, such as the production, cultivation, sale, and distribution of any narcotic drug or substance.

"It is being considered whether such justification may be made based on the right of freedom of religion and the right to have respect for and protection of private life and privacy of the home," Golding said.

The United Nations Single Convention of 1961 - one of the treaties to which Jamaica has signed - requires parties to limit exclusively to medical and scientific purposes, the production, manufacture, export, import, distribution of, trade in, use and possession of drugs.

HOUSE SPLIT ON ISSUE

Earlier this month, the House of Representatives gave the nod to a private member's motion calling for the decriminalisation of ganja, following weeks of rigorous debate, which saw members on the government side split on the issue.

North East St Elizabeth Member of Parliament Raymond Pryce, had moved a motion in the House saying the decriminalisation of marijuana was a human-rights issue.

Pryce said criminal records haunt thousands of Jamaicans and their families and suggested that the Parliament debate the practicality of a prescribed amount of marijuana, below which there would be no criminal prosecution for the possession for personal use.

In the Senate yesterday, Golding said his ministry is considering to permit the use of ganja for medicinal use and to make it legal for persons to smoke ganja in private places.

"These considerations do not yet represent government policy as they have not been considered by Cabinet," the minister said.

He told the Senate that careful considerations were being given to the implication of the reform, including the Government's international obligations.

In the meantime, opposition Senator Alexander Williams, in his contribution to the State of the Nation Debate, said Jamaica was missing out on a multibillion-dollar medical marijuana market. In lending support to the call for decriminalisation of marijuana, Williams said Jamaica would have a natural advantage in the industry

SELECTED HISTORICAL ARTICLES PUBLISHED IN THE DAILY GLEANER

1. Richards, Dennis. 'The Leaf of Death'. April 23,1950, p. 3-8

2. 'Ganja smoking at the mental hospital.' July 1,1950,p. 3-4

3. Horner, John. 'Can we beat Ganja?' November 29, 1950, p.7-8

4. Johns, Vere. 'We must stamp out Ganja.' June 4, 1951, p.1

5. 'Major vice. The Menace in our midst.' June 17, 1951,p.1-5

6. Gleaner Western Bureau. 'Survey'.' June 22, 1951,p.1-2

7. Burns, H.S. 'Ganja-Weed of lunacy, murder.' June 28, 1951,p. 6-7

8. 'Court ruling on Ganja possession.' March 25, 1952,p.5

9. Johnson, Donald M. 'Indian Hemp a social menace.' August 20, 1952,p. 6-8

10. HPJ. 'Sober and sensible views on Ganja.' May 11, 1956,p.4-6

11. Milliner, H.R. 'Ganja-Letter to the Editor'. August 7, 1958,p.1

12. 'Pangola-like ganja, the new craze in St. Ann.' August 22,1958,p.2

13. Scotter, G. 'Pangola-Today.' August 23, 1958, p.3

14. Editorial. 'Pangoladdicts.' August 25, 1958,p.3

15. Virtue, Cliff. 'Pangola (Letter to the editor)' August 28, 1958,p.5

16. Walleer, Dan. 'Pangola Grass'. September 2, 1958,p.7

17. Editorial. 'Ganja.' October 13, 1958,p.2

18. Sunday Gleaner Special Article. 'Is Ganja really a dangerous drug?' November 16, 1958,p.1-6

19. Psychiatric Correspondent. 'Ganja is dangerous' November 23, 1958,p.1-4

20. Editorial. 'Ganja Puzzle'. November 26, 1958,p.3

21. 'Solicitor claims ganja in rum is medicine.' June 20, 1959,p.3-4

22. 'Heavier penalties planned for Ganja.' November 1, 1960,p.7

23. '150,000 ganja plants found at Roswell.' July 7, 1960,p.3

24. 'House passes law amendment stiffening ganja penalties.' January 6, 1961,p.1-7

25. The Native. 'A slander on Jamaicans.' January 10, 1961,p.3

26. Editorial. 'Ganja.' January 11, 1961,p.2-3

27. 'Debate on bill stiffening ganja penalties.' January 13, 1961,p.1-9

28. The Native. 'Jottings.' February 7, 1961,p.9

29. Gordon, Albertina. 'Wins appeal against ganja conviction.' February 14, 1961,p.5-6

30. '800 ganja plants destroyed.' April 12, 1961,p.4

31. The Native. 'The ganja menace in Jamaica.' April 26, 1961,p.8

32. Defense Counsel urges enquiry...Ganja accused dismissed.' May 6, 1961,p. 2-4

33. Strong Matthew. 'Ganja in get it right.' June 21, 1961,p.1

34. 'How to kill ganja.' June 21, 1961,p.3

35. 'United Nations told of new smuggling technique...dope from Jamaica posted to the United Kingdoms.' July 8, 1961,p.5-9

36. Raymond, Lauriston. 'The law and ganja.' August 4, 1961,p.4-5

37. The Native. 'Jottings.' August 19, 1961,p.6

38. Police shot at from ambush.' September 16, 1961,p.7-8

39. 'See no reason to disturb ganja conviction.' September 19, 1961,p.9

40. Thousands of Ganja plants destroyed.' October 24, 1961,p.1-4

41. 'Ganja bill back in house today.' February 18, 1964, p.1

42. Editorial. 'The ganja bill.' February 18, 1964, p.2

43. '2,000 ganja trees destroyed.' May 19, 1964, p.3

44. 'Charles Ganngadeen gets 2-year term for ganja possession.' May 20, 1964, p.6-7

45. 'Police stoned in raid.' November 29, 1964, p.1

46. 'Use of ganja does not cause people to commit crime.' January 6, 1965, p.3-5

47. 'Anti-ganja drive in Portland.' May 20, 1965, p.6

48. 'Banana boat takes ganja to the United Kingdom.' June 21, 1965, p.6

49. 'Ganja raid.' August 18, 1965, p.7

50. 'Two year old found in hut after ganja raid by police.' October 14, 1965, p.7

51. Davis, Allan. 'Jailed for possession.' November 8, 1965, p.3

52. 'Ganja seen as a medical boom-hopes stirred by synthesis of active ingredients.' March 9, 1966, p.1-4

53. 'No Indian weed.' June 23, 1966, p.3

54. The Native. 'Ganja-orama.' December 19, 1966, p.9

55. Levy, Eric. 'Ganja (Letter to the Editor).' October 16, 1967, p.2

56. Gregory, Colin. 'Of this and that.' July 3, 1968, p.1

57. Wright, Thomas. 'Pot of pregnancy.' August 30, 1968, p.5-6

58. Editorial. 'Goats and ganja.' October 19, 1968, p.3

59. Editorial. 'Pipe dreams dispelled.' November 2, 1968, p.3

60. Wright, Thomas. 'Ganja: Criminal activity.' November 9, 1968, p.6

61. Editorial. 'Hidden Industry.' February 17, 1969, p.3-4

62. 'Ganja: female plant more deadly than the male.' February 16, 1969, p.1-5

63. The Native. 'That pernicious weed.' February 3, 1969, p.4

64. 'Marijuana induces habit of using anything to escape reality, says United States expert on psychosomatic medicine.' January 17, 1969, p.1-6

65. Simpson, Walter. 'Male and female ganja plant.' March 10, 1969, p.2-3

66. 'Views on ganja.' March 19, 1969, p.8-9

67. Wright, Thomas. 'Ganja.' March 21, 1969, p.6-7

68. Wright, Thomas. 'The Farquharson Institute and ganja.' April 9, 1969, p.6-7

69. Wright, Thomas. 'Ganja.' July 4, 1969, p.4

70. Justice Parnell. 'Ganja is ganja.' August 6, 1969, p.5-7

71. Wright, Thomas. 'How to abolish ganja.' November 25, 1969, p.7

72. 'Farm labour scheme-a channel for ganja to the United States.' January 22, 1970, p.5-7

73. 'Police seize 538 lbs. Ganja shipment that was being sent as lumber to U.S.A.' February 22, 1970, p.1-5

74. 'Ganja traffic: The view from Florida's frightening teenage drug problem.' February 22, 1970, p.1-9

75. 'A panel on youth and ganja.' March 1, 1970, p.5-7

76. Ascencio. F. 'Use of Ganja.' March 6, 1970, p.7

77. 'U.S.A. to invite Prime Minister for discussions on ganja problem.' March 11, 1970

78. '77,000 seized, six held in police drive.' October 17, 1975, p.1

79. Anderson, J. 'Ganja and Firearms.' March 28, 1976, p.17

80. Broderick, P. 'Legalize it.' March 3, 1977, p.1B

81. 'Broderick calls for the legalization of Ganja.' March 06, 1977, p.1F

82. Henry, B. 'Trench Town ideology and Ganja.' March 10, 1977, p.6A

83. Heapne, J. 'Encouraging news at last.' March 11, 1977, p. 10A

84. Steele, J. 'Weekend reflections.' March 13, 1977, p.6A

85. 'Joint House and Senate team to study ganja.' March 23, 1977, p.1C

86. D'Costa, D. 'Ganja is miracle drug.' March 29, 1977, p.8A

87. Dias, H. 'Search-light on Ganja.' March 29, 1977, p.8A

88. Persadsingh, N. 'Ganja.' March 29, 1977, p.8G

89. Gordon, E. 'Ganja, Rum and Socialism.' March 29, 1977, p.3A

90. Lloyd, J. 'I and I must use the herb.' July 20, 1977, p.20A

91. Rubin, V. and I. Mouton. 'Studies on the weed.' July 24, 1977, p.2D

92. Brooks, H. 'Legalizing ganja.' August 9, 1977, p.08G

93. Taylor, G. ' A Benevolent alternative to alcohol.' August 14, 1977, p.13E

94. 'Cessna plane seized.' August 18, 1977, p.2E

95. ' Ganja revolution.' September 7, 1977, p. 3G

96. McNeil, Ken. 'Research into ganja needed.' September 9, 1977, p.1H

97. Wright, Thomas. 'Ganja trade.' October 1, 1977, p.12

98. 'Ganja haul in St. Thomas.' January 14,1978, p.2B

99. 'Ganja being used to make eye drops.' January 27, 1978, p.1A

100. Ritch D. 'Third World Dilemma.' February 23, 1978, p. 6A

101. Commissiong, J. 'All about ganja.' October 1, 1978, p.6A

102. Ritch, D. 'Discouragement or neutrality.' October 12, 1978, p.6A

103. Russell, H. 'Weekend reflections.' March 11, 1979, p.12A

104. 'Indictment of Ganja.' March 21, 1979, p.8C

105. Hickling, F. 'Ganja research.' March 25, 1979, p.17A

106. Maxwell, J. 'Still indicted.' April 8, 1979, p.27F

107. Ritch, D. 'Business as usual.' April 26, 1979, p.8A

108. Lampart, R. 'Ganja and the Police.' May 13, 1979, p.10C

109. 'Ganja...a medicine and recreation.' May 14, p.3G

110. 'Methodists take a stand against ganja.' June 17, 1979, p.8C

111. London, A. 'Colombians waging intense battle against ganja.' November 11, 1979, p.1

112. 'Final report on ganja sent to the House.' December 6, 1979, p.1D

113. Tulloch, V. 'A change in attitude.' December 14, 1979, p.8A

114. Beckford, S. 'No to ganja reform.' December 17, 1979, p.8A

115. Holness, C. and S. Beckford. 'Controversy.' December 24, 1979, p.6C

116. Blake, B. and C. Reid. 'Your letters do matter.' December 30, 1979, p.19D

117. Kitchin, A. 'The Mary Jane Connection.' December 31, 1979, p. 8A

118. Blake, B. 'The ganja debate.' January 6, 1980, p.13B

119. Kitchin, A and P. Maxwell. 'Ganja.' January 5, 1980, p.8G

120. French, J. 'Those airstrips.' March 23, 1981, p.6A

121. Reilly, J. 'Coptic pair on trial for ganja in Miami.' May 28, 1981, p.1A

122. 'Police probing Coptics.' May 30, 1981, p.1B

123. 'Focus on Ganja.' June 7, 1981, p.10A

124. Editorial. 'Ganja and the Coptics.' June 10, 1981, p.6A

125. Blake, E. 'Ganja and Marley's death.' June 19, 1981, p.12G

126. 'Ambivalence towards ganja smoking.' June 27, 1981, p.1B

127. Williams, L. 'Ganja trade a billion dollar operation.' June 28, 1981, p.1B

128. Kitchin, A. 'Down the ganja pipeline.' July 4, 1981, p..6A

129. Williams, L. 'Big men faceless but influential.' July 5, 1981, p.7A

130. Seaga, E. 'USA-Jamaica ganja trade curbed.' July 11, 1981, p.1C

131. Stone, C. 'Ganja money.' July 15, 1981, p.6A

132. Gentles, H. 'Money shock.' July 20, 1981, p.6F

133. Stone, C. 'That ganja debate.' July 20, 1981, p.6A

134. Perkins, W. and C. Stone. 'Ganja again.' July 21, 1981, p.6A

135. Gregory C. 'No morality with ganja.' July 22, 1981, p.p. 8A

136. Dunstan, D. 'JLP Government supporting the ganja trade.' July 23, 1981, p.17B

137. Egan.D.' The real ganja issue.' July 24, 1981, p.16C

138. Cargill, M. 'What's to be done about ganja.' July 26, 1981, p.5A

139. Stone, C. 'Understanding ganja.' July 29, 1981, p.10A

140. Egan, D. 'Facts v Opinion.' August 9, 1981, p.8C

141. Stone, C. 'No to ganja.' August 15, 1981, p.10G

142. Gabbidon, A. 'Ganja trade probe...Tinson Pen as ganja centre.' August 16, 1981, p.1B

143. Gabbidon, A. 'Two heads were packed in ganja.' August 17, 1981, p.1A

144. Gabbidon, A. 'Tackling ganja and cancer.' August 18, 1981, p.1A

145. Baugh, K. 'Ganja and rural problems.' September 7, 1981, p.1A

146. McKnight, F. 'Ganja and tourist.' September 22, 1981, p.3A

147. Reid, C. 'Can a responsible society treat ganja so lightly.' September 27, 1981, p.5A

148. 'Jamaica's flourishing underground trade.' October 13, 1981, p.3F

149. 'Coptics imprisoned in ganja traffic.' December 5, 1981, p.1F

150. Gabbidon, A. 'Coptics under fire in the United States.' December 13, 1981, p.36A

151. Gabbidon, A. 'The Ganja trade.' Jamaica 31, 1982, p.7A

152. Schwartz, B. 'Prosecutor goes after...' January 31, 1982, p.7A

153. 'Agricultural business knows that ganja says United States study.' February 11, 1982, p.1A

154. 'Illegal airstrips increase.' May 3, 1982, p.1A

155. Editorial. 'Illegal airstrip.' May 5, 1982, p. 8A

156. Williams, L. 'Putting pressure on ganja traffic.' May 16, 1982, p.9A

157. Virtue, W. 'A Lesson from the ganja trade.' March 17, 1982, p8C

158. Gregory, C. 'This ganja Business' May 19, 1982, p.10A

159. Edwards, D. 'Ganja.' June 3, 1982, p.8G

160. Morgan, G. ' Customs man held in big ganja haul.' May 21, 1985, p.1F

161. 'USA Drug Enforcement Agent testifies in ganja trial.' May 31, 1985, p. 32C

162. 'Pro-Ganja demonstrations at trial for Montego Bay-13.' June 1, 1985, p.1A

163. 'Coast Guard makes $US5M in ganja haul.' June 5, 1985, p.1B

164. 'DEA gives evidence at trial for Montego Bay-13.' June 6, 1985, p.4A

165. 'Tapes played at trial for Montego Bay-13.' June 12, 1985, p.3C

166. 'Americans on ganja charge.' June 14, 1985, p.3A

167. 'Twenty-two recordings played at trial of 13.' July 2, 1985, p.3A

168. Ritch, D. 'Ambivalence and Ganja.' July 7, 1985, p.12A

169. ' Skill Cole on ganja charge.' July 27, 1985, p.1A

170. Ritch, D. 'Ganja.' August 1, 1985, p.8B

171. 'USA seizes Air Jamaica plane.' August 8, 1985. p.1A

172. 'Air Jamaica security tightened.' August 9, 1985, p.1E

173. 'Air Jamaica and US customs in seven point pact.' August 25, 1985, p.1A

174. Dorman, AD. 'Seizing our airplane.' August 8, 1985, p.8E

175. Lampart, R. 'Health dangers of ganja.' August 31, 1985, p.8A

176. Wint, C. 'This ganja business.' September 3, 1985, p.8A

177. 'JLP Government seems to have the upper hand in the fight against ganja.' September 11, 1985, p.1A

178. Cargill, M. 'Drug Abuse-The American Connection.' September 15, 1985, p.12A

179. 'Ganja boat held.' January 11, 1986, p. 11A

180. Charles, P. 'Crackdown on ganja export from wharves.' February 16, 1986, p.1A

181. 'Ganja raiders get tough this year.' February 28, 1986, p.11A

182. Lampart, R. 'Eradicating ganja, time to review.' March 2, 1986, p.19A

183. 'Severe crackdown on ganja.' March 6, 1986, p.1A

184. Sears, J. 'Eradicating ganja.' March 6, 1986, p.8D

185. 'Policeman freed of ganja charge.' July 11, 1986, p.3A

186. 'USA customs moves to curb ganja shipment.' July 12, 1986, p.1B

187. '80 homes destroyed in ganja blitz.' August 23, 1986, p.1A

188. 'Another ganja crack down.' August 23, 1986, p.1D

189. 'Lightening kills four boys in ganja field.' September 5, 1986, p.1A

190. 'Anti-marijuana drive leaves some broke and bitter.' September 14, 1986, p.9A

191. 'USA nabs another ganja shipment.' September 19, 1986, p.1A

192. 'Ganja drama at illegal airstrip.' September 23, 1986, p.1A

193. Mais, S. 'Ganja and mail.' January 1, 1987, p.3A

194. Witter, W. 'All out ganja drive at Ports.' January 2, 1987, p.8B

195. Webster, A. 'Are we overpricing?' January 4, 1987, p.9A

196. Grant, J. 'Air Jamaica and ganja.' January 5, 1987, p.8C

197. Toyloy, N. '$215M of ganja goes up in smoke.' January 8, 1987, p.1B

198. Henry, C. 'Legalize ganja for medicinal purpose.' September 6, 1987, p.9A

199. 'Ganja act amended.' September 10, 1987, p.2E

200. 'Senate passes ganja bill.' September 15, 1987, p.2E

201. '807 ganja drive launched.' September 17, 1987, p.1A

202. King, P. ' Exports, a major channel for ganja.' September 18, 1987, p.1A

203. 'Rastafarians prepare statement on ganja.' September 20, 1987, p.1A

204. Seaga, E. 'Jamaica poised to eradicate entire ganja threat.' October 9, 1987, p.2D

205. Stephenson, G. ' Army targets ganja plane-type of weapon still under study.' October 9, 1987, p.1D

206. Shearer, H. '41 companies face exporters list axe.' October 12, 1987, p.1a

207. Shearer, H. 'Serious charge.' October 16, 1987, p.8A

208. 'Watchdog council on ganja set by exporters.' October 17, 1987, p.3B

209. 'Seminar cites devious ways of ganja smugglers.' October 23, 1987, p.2C

210. Thompson, L. 'DEA man warns bosses of ganja.' October 24, 1987, p.21A

211. 'Exporters facing the axe.' October 27, 1987, p.20D

212. 'Use of ganja in worship.' October 29, 1987, p.1A

213. Editorial. 'No to ganja.' November 4, 1987, p.8A

214. 'Jamaicans 16 years fined $165,000 for trafficking ganja.' November 17, 1987, p.2B

215. Francis, D. 'What do you call this ganja.' November 19, 1987, p.9A

216. Stephenson, G. 'USA grabs Jamaican ganja.' December 16, 1987, p.1C

217. 'Drug smugglers still try despite warning.' December 16, 1987, p.3C

218. Cargill, M. 'Coming home to roost.' December 17, 1987, p.6A

219. Wray, S. 'Regional approach to drug problem.' December 23, 1987, p.8A

220. Stephenson, G. 'Jamaican boat still in USA custody.' December 24, 2987, p.1A

221. Morgan, S. 'Ganja bane.' January 3, 1988, p.10A

222. Hibbert, R. 'Musicians promote ganja.' January 8, 1988, p.9A

223. 'Ganja find locks down 807 garment factory.' January 11, 1988, p.1E

224. 'After ganja find, USA firm pulls 807 contract.' January 19, 1988, p.3A

225. Editorial. 'Another ganja blow.' January 21, 1988, p.8A

226. King, P. 'Ganja was with the undies.' January 22, 1988, p.1A

227. King, P. 'Despite ganja trouble, Hanes print label stays with 807 business.' January 28, 1988, p.3A

228. Charles, P. 'And now its American Airlines $9.3M fine after ganja was found aboard aircraft.' February 3, 1988, p.1A

229. Charles, P. 'Ganja Collusion.' February 4, 1988, p.8A

230. Charles, P. 'Top level talks on ganja smuggling.' February 5, 1988, p.1A

231. Broderick, P. 'Ganja in coffee to Japan.' February 8, 1988, p.3A

232. Charles, P. 'Anti-drug fight, USA fines upset Jamaica.' February 12, 1988, p.1A

233. Forrest, R. 'Ganja trafficking and USA custom.' February 19, 1988, p.10C

234. 'Ship slapped with £566M. Weed was waist deep as crackers in container.' March 8, 1988, p.1A

235. 'Jamaica halves ganja production.' March 11, 1988, p.1A

236. Anderson, E. 'Government targets ganja airstrips.' March 17, 1988, p.1A

237. 'McKay cites some success in ganja eradication.' March 18, 1988, p.3C

238. McKnight, F. 'No helicopter for ganja eradication.' March 27, 1988, p.2A

239. Edwards, G. 'Threat to transshipment.' March 29, 1988, p.20A

240. 'Congressional hearing in Washington. Ganja eradication efforts praised.' April 7, 1988, p.1A

241. Vogel, M 'But top politician said stashing money in Cayman Islands.' April 7, 1988, p.1A

242. Simmonds, D. 'JDF destroyed fewer ganja fields in '87. After '86 fewer fields left to destroy.' May 3, 1988, p.3E

243. Cargill, M. 'Ganja shipment.' May 12, 1988, p.12A

244. 'Crackdown on ganja farmers, British magazine says it could cause Seaga the elections.' May 18, 1988, p.1A

245. 'Manley totally opposed to ganja legalization.' May 24, 1988, p.32D

246. Cargill, M. 'Result of Folly.' July 17, 1988, p.10A

247. 'Harding outlines finding of survey on ganja .' July 28, 1988, p.23A

248. Anderson, E. 'No let up on ganja spraying.' August 6, 1988, p.1A

249. 'Ganja in the Bammies.' August 11, 1988, p.2A

250. Williams, L. 'Ganja business now stronger than ever.' August 21, 1988, p.8C

251. Williams, L. 'The ganja business.' August 22, 1988, p.15A

252. Williams, L. 'State of the illegal ganja industry in Jamaica.' August 23, 1988, p.13A

253. Stair, M. 'Odd happenings in the country.' August 27, 1988, p.8A

254. Balfour, R. 'Hurricane Gilbert ravages ganja trade.' September 19, 1988, p.1A

255. Browne, C. 'Hurricane Gilbert and ganja.' October 12, 1988, p.9B

256. Browne, C. 'Baseless, untrue information.' October 21, p.8F

257. MacFarlane, C. 'Survey shows that ganja crop not hard hit by hurricane.' October 22, 1988, p.2A

258. 'Marijuana invades Olympic games.' November 6, 1988, p.3C

259. 'Eight found guilty on ganja charge.' November 12, 1988, p.15D

260. 'SeaLand services fined $528M for ganja.' December 12, 1988, p.1E

261. 'SeaLandservice suspend s service system. Review follows massive ganja fine by USA.' December 31, 1988, p.1A

262. 'Ridding Port Bustamante of ganja smuggling.' December 31, 1988, p.3A

263. Prendergast, A. 'Contractor denies knowing the ganja was in container.' January 10, 1989, p.2E

264. Prendergast, A. 'Container inspected by snifter dogs.' January 12, 1989, p.19C

265. 'Air Jamaica slapped with another big fine for ganja.' January 26, 1989, p.3A

266. Balfour, B. 'Hash oil, ganja found on Air Canada.' March 21, 1989, p.1A

267. ' USA seizes Air Jamaica plane for ganja.' April 5, 1989, p.6A

268. 'Biggest ever ganja find on Air Jamaica.' April 6, 1989, p.3A

269. Chen, J. 'Ordeal of passing check points.' April 7, 1989, p.2B

270. 'Air Jamaica wants bond reduce.' April 8, 1989, p.1A

271. Fitzwarren, E. 'Drugs fine sinking Air Jamaica.' April 9, 1989, p.4B

272. 'Shake up after Air Jamaica scandal.' April 9, 1989, p.1A

273. 'Get the plane back and sell the thing.' April 9, 1989, p.3A

274. Bowie, S. 'Jamaicans ashamed.' April 10, 1989, p.18A

275. 'A chronology of cases.' April 10, 1989, p.1A

276. Reynolds, S. 'The big caper.' April 10, 1989, p.6A

277. 'Washington offers no penalty pact.' April 11, 1989, p.1A

278. Pickersgill, E. 'Fried airbus flies again. Air Jamaica posts 2m bond for ganja plane.' April 11, 1989, p. 1A

279. 'How the Air Jamaica scam worked.' April 14, 1989, p.1A

280. Caine, T. 'Of apples and nurses and ganja.' April 14, 1989, p.6A

281. Brown, V. 'Defying the government.' April 14, 1989, p.6C

282. Hearne, J. 'The cost of sovereignty can be ruinously expensive.' April 16, 1989, p.7D

283. Stone, C. 'Some other drugs issue.' April 17, 1989, p.7B

284. Davidson, W. 'Eradication of ganja wishful thinking.' April 17, 1989, p.1A

285. 'USA gang clashes over ganja.' April 21, 1989, p.1A

286. 'How they shipped two tons of ganja.' April 22, 1989, p.1A

287. Cargill, M. 'Air Ganja, or is it Air Cocaine.' April 23, 1989, p.8A

288. Lampart, R. 'Who are the drug barons.' April 23,1989, p.6B

289. Cargill, M. 'The search for honesty.' April 27, 1989, p.6A

290. Simpson, V. 'Perspective of the marijuana war.' April 28, 1989, p.6B

291. 'Air Jamaica ganja issue.' May 9, 1989, p.1A

292. 'Air Jamaica ganja case may fizzle.' May 9, 1989, p.1B

293. '1985 ganja was larger.' May 20, 1989, p.1D

294. '4 convicted in Savanna-La-Mar Ganja case.' June 1, 1989, p.3B

295. 'Ganja found on ship and at airport.' June 9, 1989, p.2E

296. 'Since security measures, big cocaine and ganja finds at airports.' July 22, 1989, p.1C

297. 'Mair and Shaw to face USA court drug trafficking ganja.' July 29, 1989, p.3B

298. Ritch, D. 'Suppression of ganja trade blamed for national poverty.' August 6, 1989, p.8C

299. Dalley, M. 'Take the crime out of ganja.' August 29, 1989, p.7D

300. Irons, A. 'Ganja a blessing, a curse, who are we defending.' August 31, 1989, p.2E

301. Reynolds, C. 'Beyond cocaine and ganja.' September 1, 1989, p.6C

302. Chin, A. 'Jailed for two years.' September 5, 1989, p.1A

303. Huges, S. 'Aids relief in Marijuana cited.' July 31, 1990, p.3B

304. Dyer, O. 'Cocaine demand soars, minimum amount of ganja available.' November 17, 1990, p.1A

305. Spencer, E. 'Ganja eradication blamed for imbalance.' December 8, 1990, p.21A

306. Stone, C. 'Study shows that Jamaican are ganja users.' December 27, 1990, p.1A

307. Dreyer, M. 'Ganja effects on babies, survey done on Jamaican mothers.' January 28, 1991, p.3B

308. Bent, O. 'Ganja is our old friend.' February 21, 1991, p.14F

309. Lampart, R. 'Is ganja smoking really harmful.' March 17, 1991, p.7A

310. Harper, M. 'Ganja in molasses in Air Jamaica.' April 5, 1991, p.1B

311. 'Ganja smell, then weed found aboard American Airlines.' April 6, 1991, p.1A

312. 'USA spending more to eradicate ganja there.' May 6, 1991, p.3B

313. Burgess, C. 'Up with law and order.' May 26, 1991, p.6A

314. 'Huge ganja haul made on wharves.' July 5, 1991, p.1B

315. Campbell, Y. 'Ganja farmers want to plant coffee.' August 10, 1991, p.1A

316. Williams, R. 'Coffee for ganja.' August 11, 1991, p.6A

317. Campbell, Y. 'The ganja problem.' August 18, 1991, p.8A

318. Gentles, E. '16,000 kilo of ganja seized this year.' September 14, 1991, p.1E

319. Mullings, S. 'Farmers against aerial spraying of ganja.' December 21, 1991, p.3E

320. Gentles, E. 'Drug trafficking reduced.' January 5, 1992, p.1D

321. Ritch, D. 'Ganja as a necessary evil.' January 12, 1992, p.1D

322. West, M. 'Legalize personal use of ganja.' February 9, 1992, p.8C

323. Blanchard, D. 'Marijuana plantation uprooted.' February 15, 192, p.4C

324. 'Ganja farmers willing to grow food crops.' February 15, 1992, p.12A

325. 'No aerial spraying of ganja jet.' February 23, 1992, p.2A

326. Seiters, R. 'No to legalizing ganja in Germany.' March 2, 1992, p.3C

327. 'Glyphosphate best herbicide for marijuana.' March 8, 1992, p.2D

328. 'Ganja growing slashed.' April 3, 1992, p.1A

329. Davidson, W. 'Aerial spraying of ganja is very dangerous thing.' April 5, 1992, p.3A

330. 'Ganja was disguised as salt.' April 21, 1992, p.1A

331. Stanley, L. 'Ganja case postpone.' April 27, 1992, p.2E

332. 'USA ganja growers forced to grow indoors.' June 16, 1992, p.3C

333. 'Ganja found on wharf.' June 20, 1992, p.1A

334. Cargill, M. 'Ridding the Brits. of their ganja prejudices.' August 2, 1992, p.9E

335. 'Cops tell court she witnessed ganja deal.' September 19, 1992, p.19A

336. 'Ganja for AIDS.' September 23, 1992, p.1A

337. Williams, I. 'Cop transferred pending ganja probe.' September 27, 1992, p.2D

338. '2000 pounds ganja burnt.' October 3, 1992, p.1

339. 'Ganja users prone to high risk activity study show sex and cess, bad mixture.' June 4, 1996, p.2A

340. ' Closing the trade gap.' June 24, 1996, p.4A

341. 'Ganja threatens export trade.' July 7, 1996, p.1A

342. 'Legalize the weed.' July 15, 1996, p.4E

343. Forsythe, Dennis. 'Legalize ganja campaign.' August 14, 1996, p.8C

344. Cargill, Morris. 'On legalizing ganja.' August 22, 1996, p. 4A

345. Douglas, Luke. 'Free up the weed PNP, NDM to discuss issue, legalize ganja group formed.' September 2, 1996, p.1A

346. Wint, Carl. 'This ganja nonsense.' September 3, 1996, p.4A

347. Chang, Paul. 'Ganja as a natural plant and herb.' September 20, 1996, p.8A

348. Thompson, MacPherson. 'Coffee beans turned out to be ganja.' September 23, 1996, p.1C

349. Campbell, Leroy. 'Facts on Hemp.' September 26, 1996, p.5A

350. Gifford, Anthony. 'Legalize ganja take root.' October 16, 1996, p.1D

351. Clarke, Lavern. 'Criminals must retreat and legalizers too.' October 17, 1996, p.3A

352. Lampart. Ronald. 'Tobacco kills, herb heals.' October 22, 1996, p.1D

353. Cargill, Morris. 'The ganja campaign.' October 27, 1996, p.9A

354. Cargill, Morris. 'Two short letters.' October 31, 1996, p.4

355. Deyal, Tony. 'Waiting to exhale.' November 1, 1996, p.2A

356. Silvera, Ras. 'Rasta's defense of God-given herb.' November 1, 1996, p.10A

357. Lampart, Ronald. 'Links to your motor vehicle accidents.' November 1, 1996, p.10A

358. Walsh, James. 'Legalize it.' November 1, 1996, p.4E

359. Hall, John. 'Ganja burns brains.' November 1, 1996, p.10A

360. Cobham, Jeffrey. 'A true ganja story.' November 7, 1996, p.5C

361. 'Optimism towards legalizing ganja.' November 8, 1996, p.10B

362. Ritch, Dawn. 'Citizen's right to choose.' November 10, 1996, p.9A

363. 'Ganja dealers changing image.' November 12, 1996, p.2A

364. Reynolds, C. Roy. 'A weed worse than ganja.' November 12, 1996, p.4A

365. Cargill, Morris. 'A great ally.' November 28, 1996, p.4A

366. Forsythe, Dennis. 'Compassionate use of ganja.' December 18, 1996, p.4A

367. 'Privy Council denies Moore's weed appeal.' February 26, 1996, p.1A

368. 'No rest until herb us free. Rastas vow to continue ganja legalization fight.' March 24, 1996, p.2A

369. Forsythe, Dennis. 'Ganja rights ruling tomorrow.' May 15, 1997, p.1A

370. Forsythe, Dennis. 'Ganja challenge turned down.' May 17, 1997, p.1A

371. Stair, Marjorie. 'Narcotics, not an option.' June 5, 1997, p.1A

372. Hylton, Madge. 'The shiprider and marijuana.' June 9, 1997, p.5A

373. Reynolds, C. 'Scrap this crazy deal.' June to, 1997, p.4A

374. Barrett, Michell. 'Ganja-The green gold.' March 3, 1998, p.1A

375. Sinclair, Glenroy. '5,000 lbs. of ganja in apparel shipment.' September 7, 1998, p.2A

376. Frater, A. 'Hemp Beer: new use for ganja.' August 14, 1999, p.2A

377. 'Marijuana compounds ease tremors in mice.' March 2, 2000

378. 'Increase in heart attacks risk after smoking pot-study.' March 2, 2000

379. 'Big ganja find at Kingston Wharves.' January 1, 2001, p.1A

380. Anderson, Omar. '$1.5B ganja find.' January 10, 2001, p.1A &3A

381. Notice, Raymond. 'Ganja in the prisons.' January 20, 2001, p.6B

382. 'Fisherman arrested over ganja.' January 28, 2001, p.4A

383. Thompson, Eulalee. 'Seeing through ganja.' January 29, 2001, p.1A & 3A

384. Hyatt, Stephen-Claude. 'The ganja reality.' January 31, 2001, p.9D

385. Thompson, Eulalee. 'No market yet for ganja-based eye drop.' February 1, 2001, p.2A

386. Sinclair, Glenroy. 'Big drug bust in January.' February 7, 2001, p.2A

387. 'Marijuana theory challenged.' February 11, 2001, p.12C

388. 'Training leads to ganja grabs.' March 9, 2001, p.10C

389. Mills, Claude. 'More adolescent turning to ganja.' March 11, 2001, p.12B

390. 'Ganja-like substances in brain trigger appetite.' April 23, 2001

391. "NCDA, MAJ Supports ganja decriminalization." August 18, 2001, p.1A

392. "Majority want ganja legalized." May 23, 2001, p.1A

393. "US backlash against ganja.' August 17, 2001, p.1A

394. Letter to the Editor. "It could be ganja to the rescue." August 18, 2001

395. "Gov't can't pay ganja cutters." July 8, 2001

396. Letter of the Day "Ganja boat and rotten apples." August 6, 2001

397. Andrew Clunis. "California USA is reputed to be ganja capital." August 9, 2001

398. Commentary. "According to statistics more than half of ganja..." May 16, 2001

399. Eulalee Thompson "The forbidden herb-Is ganja bad for your health." August 22, 2001, p. B7

400. Klao Bell. "US unhappy with ganja eradication efforts." June 17, 2001, p.1A

401. Dr. R. G. Lampart. "The marijuana prohibition." August 22, 2001, p. B9

402. "US Pastor decries ganja propas at bishop's instalment." August 20, 2001, p. A3

403. L. Duperouzel. "Ganja makes you stupid, careless lazy." August 20, 2001, p. A5

404. "What the ganja commission recommends." August 19, 2001, p.10F

405. "Backing for ganja." August 16, 2001, p. A1

406. "Ganja found in cargo boxes." July 10, 2001, p. A8

407. "Weedless' stage shows Wednesday." June 6, 2001

408. "Police tighten net on drug smugglers-...But large percent." June 3, 2001

APPENDIX 9

SELECTED ARTICLES PUBLISHED IN THE JAMAICA OBSERVER ON MARIJUANA

ARTICLE NAME	DATE PUBLISHED
"Canada Placing Certified Marijuana into pharmacies	March 22, 2004
"Ganja-Gateway or exposure drug"	May 12, 2004
"Is salvia the next marijuana – Eight US states ban inexpensive, easy-to-obtain plant?"	March 12, 2008
"Girls aged 2 and 4, in hospital after marijuana overdose."	
"Ganja still the drug of choice"	April 28, 2003
"Don't ignore medicinal value of ganja – Chevannes"	October 30, 2001
"The Ganja debate – another perspective"	December 2, 2001
"Prof. Manley West honoured for ganja research"	September 28, 2001
"Theology and ganja"	
"A rational decision on marijuana, please"	December 12, 2003
"Healing Herb" – cannabis may be the 21st Century aspirin, study shows.	April 20, 2003
"Bill to legalise ganja for private use soon, say Nicholson	
"Law makers propose ganja research agency"	July 18, 2002
"Marijuana fails to boost appetite in cancer study"	May 14, 2001
"Marijuana users consume more calories"	June
"Belgium allows ganja for personal use"	Jan 20, 2001
"Could marijuana be the cure for arthritis	August 17, 2000
"Can ganja make you mad?" – Local doctors challenge marijuana myths	
"Obama opposes legalizing marijuana"	March 26, 2009

"Rastafarians want looser marijuana laws, reparations ..."	August 04, 2005
" 'Skill' Cole gets 18 months, fined $1 million-"	July 2, 2007
"JA cannot legalise ganja"	January 14, 2009
"Mo-Bay 4 in Florida drug bust	March 21, 2005
" Some things for the Prime Minister to do -	May 30, 2005
"Deportees get a reception with a difference"	September 2, 2006
"Stephen, Julian Marley arrested on marijuana charges"	February 14, 2002
"Jamaican sentenced for leading Mexico – US drug trafficking ring"	March 23, 2009
"Gang violence stuns Canada's Olympic city"	March 29, 2009
"Cops probe attacks on two customs officers"	March 28, 2009
"Hundred of offensive weapons, drugs seized from students"	November 14, 2008
"I wouldn't wish this on my worst enemy"	January 7, 2007
" Air J drug bust"	July 03, 2008
"Drug Council warns financial crisis could feed addiction"	March 28, 2009
"Ganja seized at wharf, airport"	March 2, 2009
"Big Potential for health tourism"	July 23, 2005
"Two Glengoffe cops taken off the frontline"	November 7, 2007
"Jah Cure scheduled for July release"	March 10, 2007

Ganja the wonder weed of questionable benelovence

15 | OPINION

Anthony GOMES

In his wisdom, Karl Marx believed that "religion is the opiate of the people". Indeed, in times of trouble, churches are full of the faithful seeking assistance of the Almighty to spare them from impending disaster. Similarly, with ganja, in times of national stress — whether due to the unacceptable level of crime or the grave state of the economy — the pro-ganja lobby again comes to the fore. The perennial arguments are once more advanced attempting to persuade the Government to decriminalise and ultimately legalise cannabis. This accounts for the recent plethora of pro-ganja articles and commentart in the media.

Before addressing the numerous views in circulation, a critical clarification is necessary: Medical marijuana, which contains proven beneficial medicinal properties, differs from smoked marijuana that is decidedly injurious to human health. This distinction is essential to consider when assessing the merits and demerits of marijuana. In Jamaica, it is well known that a leading use of medical marijuana are the medicines produced by Drs Albert Lockhart and Manley West, ie Asamasol, Canasol, and Antimol for the treatment of glaucoma and asthma; in association with Dr Henry Lowe and Mr Hawthorne Watson who contributed through research related to the nature of cannabis.

In the preparation of those medicines, the psychotic drug Tetrahydrocannabinol (THC) has been extracted, rendering the users immune from any psychoactive reaction. Untreated marijuana is known to contain about 30 active ingredients collectively known as cannabinoids, which are harmful to human health.

The likelihood of decriminalising untreated addictive ganja so it can be smoked or used in various foods and drinks cannot be described as a positive step in the improvement of the national health. In addition to alcohol and cigarettes, that contain addictive nicotine, the availability of another addictive substance that becomes easier to obtain, less expensive and more socially acceptable will induce more individuals of all ages to use them. Would such action be progressive and in the beneficial interest of Jamaica's national health?

The number of politicians and others calling for decriminalising of ganja is astounding given the parlous state of the country's economy. Such time spent should be devoted to creating jobs and stimulating growth instead of relishing the thought of what types of "spliffs" could soon be on the "high" street downtown and elsewhere.

Dr Dayton Campbell, MP for St Ann North Western, must be commended for revealing some of the detrimental effects of smoked cannabis, and warned against the ill and wide-ranging negative defects of decriminalising marijuana. It should be noted that in the United States it is medical marijuana that has been liberalised in certain states. Possession and use of the drug remains a federal offence.

Reference is frequently made to the Dutch experience and their control of what they categorise as "soft" and "hard" drugs, so called depending on the level of the health risks involved with their use. The possession of soft drugs is limited to 30 grams, but was recently reduced to five grams, for personal use, is a summary offence rather than an indictable offence. Soft drugs may be sold in coffee shops under strict conditions. In answer to the question, have drugs therefore been legalised in the Netherlands? The answer is "No," and importing or exporting, selling, producing, and possession of either hard or soft drugs are an offence in Dutch law.

The maximum quantity of soft drugs the coffee shops may sell, has been reduced to prevent tourists from purchasing drugs for export, a practice frequently encountered in Jamaica. The cost of addiction is a significant factor, as drug addicts are not left to their fate in Holland. Addiction being first and foremost a health problem, it is the aim of the various care services to reach as many drug addicts as possible. With the expected increase of ganja users following decriminalisation, the cost of health care in the public domain would rise. Minister of Health Dr Fenton Ferguson needs to give serious consideration to this potential liability. The Dutch are planning to commit addicted offenders to a special prison facility for addicts.

It is recommended that before changing the Jamaican law, Dr Ferguson contact the Dutch Ambassador in Cuba, and enquire about the latest drugs management techniques in Holland where it has been reported, that the system had to be modified in the light of rapidly rising costs relative to the care for the burgeoning numbers of addicts which have resulted from the liberalised system. Furthermore, it would be prudent to get the press to conduct a poll on the subject of decriminalising ganja to check the national validity of such a controversial decision.

Again the question must be asked, why are the domestic Drug Courts, with one in each parish, not used to bring about the same result sought by changing the domestic law? A first offender caught with a "spliff" and taken before the Drug Court is given a warning and released without charge or criminal record. A second offender, when again before the Drug Court, is asked to participate in a rehab programme. In the event the offender is unrepentant, they would then have to attend the Magistrate's Court for a hearing which could result in a verdict and create a record if found guilty.

The medicinal use of marijuana one thing, but the jamaican Government must contact other jurisdictions to see what drugs management techniques are in place. (PHOTO: AP)

The views expressed on this page are not necessarily those of the Jamaica Observer

THE DAILY OBSERVER Wednesday, October 16, 2013

SPECIALLY SELECTED HISTORICAL ARTICLES FROM THE JAMAICA OBSERVER ON MARIJUANA

1. '353 kilos of ganja seized: three arrested.' October 15, 1998, p.4

2. 'Three women, man fined and jailed for ganja.' February 4, 1999, p.2

3. Williams, Lloyd. 'KRC boss says ganja arrests troubling.' March 15, 1999, p.2

4. 'British teen held for drugs in Montego Bay.' March 16, 1999, p.4

5. 'USA report backs medical use of ganja.' March 18, 1999, p.3

6. '$576-m ganja haul.' March 25, 1999, p.1

7. 'Big ganja haul in Westmoreland.' March 27, 1999, p.11

8. 'Ganja worth $23M seized.' March 31, 1999, p.4

9. Walters, Basil. 'Rastas want ganja referendum.' April 4, 1999, p.2

10. Observer Correspondent. 'Two Americans fined for ganja.' April 7, 1999, p.2

11. 'California police forced to return marijuana.' April 24, 1999, p.2

12. 'Four on $21-m ganja bust, remanded in custody.' April 27, 1999, p.1 & 3

13. 'Big drug find at wharves.' May 14, 1999, p.5

14. 'Marijuana washes ashore Grand Cayman.' May 16, 1999

15. '8,000 lbs of ganja, hash oil seized in Canada.' June 23, 1999, p.2

16. Williams, Lloyd. 'Keep off the grass, Knight warns hemp growers.' June 27, 1999, p.4

17. 'Jamaican group launch pro-marijuana lobby.' July 1, 1999, p.4

18. Munroe, Norman. 'Munroe calls for ganja research institute.' July 24, 1999, p.3

19. Moyston, Louise. 'The resurrection of the ganja debate.' July 29, 1999, p.7

20. 'Jamaican man jailed for drugs in Barbados.' September 1, 1999, p.3

21. Chang, Kevin. 'Weed of wisdom or woe.' September 13, 1999, p.6

22. 'PNP delegates pass resolution for ganja commission.' September 19, 2001, p.4

23. Walters, Basil. 'Rasta wins ganja case in Guam.' September 21, 1999, p.6

24. 'JDF Coast Guard can't confirm Americans found ganja from Colombian boat.' September 23, 1999, p.3

25. Whyte, T.K. 'Where is the ganja?' September 23, 1999, p.1

26. Moyston, Louise. 'The law and ganja-a history.' September 29, 1999, p.9

27. 'Forbes believe big money behind ganja lobby.' October 1, 1999, p.1&3

28. Chang, Paul. 'Disproving the ganja myth.' October 2, 1999, p.7

29. Munroe, Norma. 'Senate says yes to ganja commission.' October 9, 1999, p.3

30. Forsythe, Dennis. 'Jamaica's marijuana blindness.' October 9, 1999, p.7

31. 'Judges in Rasta drugs storm.' October 11, 1999, p. 4

32. Whyte, T.K. 'US in secret anti-ganja mission here.' October 12, 1999, p.1&3

33. 'Ganja not a gateway drug to violence, says Harvard professor.' October 18, 1999, p.4

34. Observer Correspondent. 'Cops vow to stop ganja cultivation in parish.' October 20, 1999, p.4

35. Williams, Peter. '72-y-o Englishman fined for ganja.' December 30, 1999, p.3

36. 'Grandmother on trial for ganja-drug found in grandchildren's luggage.' January 13, 2000, p.5

37. 'Cops burn ganja.' January 16, 2000, p.3

38. 'US psychologist fined for ganja in MoBay.' February 3, 2000, p.2

39. 'Four held for drugs at Sangster airport.' February 6, 2000, p.3

40. 'Two Britons fined, jailed for ganja.' February 23, 2000, p.5

41. 'UN body calls for scientific research in marijuana.' February 24, 2000, p.1

42. Edwards, Claudienne. 'Study shows ganja is more significant cause of auto crashes than alcohol.' February 27, 2000, p.3

43. 'St. James salesman on ganja charge.' March 2, 2000, p.6

44. 'The wayward weed.' March 5, 2000, p.17

45. 'Big ganja haul in MoBay.' March 8, 2000, p.5

46. 'Ex-guards fined $1M for drugs-third man jailed for 18 months.' April 8, 2000, p.6

47. 'American fined $140,000 for ganja.' April 8, 2000, p.16

48. 'Calls for legalizing marijuana increase.' April 14, 2000, p.31

49. 'Court backs German Rasta's bid to grow ganja.' May 13, 2000, p.2

50. 'Inmates grow ganja in prison's garden.' June 27, 2000, p.1&3

51. Walters, Basil. 'Abuna tells why Rastas should be free to use ganja.' July 30, 2000, p.10

52. 'Ontario rules ganja prohibition unconstitutional.' August 1, 2000, p.3

53. 'Pungent garlic masks Miami ganja shipment.' August 4, 2000, p.3

54. Williams, Petre. 'Briton convicted for ganja in breadfruits.' August 4, 2000, p.5

55. Observer Correspondent. 'Sumfest vendors on ganja charges.' August 12, 2000, p.12

56. 'Could marijuana be the cure for arthritis.' August 17, 2000, p.18

57. 'Trinidad senator regrets legalize marijuana call.' August 24, 2000, p.9

58. Chang, Paul. 'Ganja and God not current fad.' August 30, 2000, p.7

59. 'Analysing ganja-is it any good?' September 7, 2000, p.10

60. Moyston, Louis. 'Where I stand.' September 11, 2000, p.7

61. 'PM announces national commission on ganja.' September 15, 2000, p.5

62. 'Chevannes to head ganja commission.' October 1, 2000, p.5

63. 'PM, ganja commission head to meet this week.' October 8, 2000, p.3

64. 'More Europeans smoking ganja.' October 12, 2000, p.9

65. Sankey, Pete. '$130-m ganja find.' October 18, 2000, p.1&3

66. Medley, Huntley. 'Two-thirds of Briton want ganja legalized.' October 19, 2000, p.5

67. 'Ganja ship had no legal cargo.' October 20, 2000, p.2

68. 'American fined minutes after arriving in Jamaica.' October 21, 2000, p.16

69. 'Ganja commission starts hearings November 6.' October 27, 2000, p. 5

70. Gomes, Anthony. 'The 'ganja' commission.' November 5, 2000, p.21&22

71. 'Call for boycott of ganja commission.' November 6, 2000, p.1&3

72. 'Man held at airport on drug charges.' November 6, 2000, p.3

73. Powis, Marjorie. 'Ganja commission not entirely public.' November 7, 2000, p.3

74. 'Chevannes hopes National Alliance will attend ganja hearings.' November 7, 2000, p.4

75. 'He came in defense of his rights.' November 8, 2000, p.5

76. ' Jamaica alone cannot legalize ganja.' November 13, 2000, p.4

77. 'Four drug arrests at airport in 14 hrs.' November 15, 2000, p.5

78. 'US Supreme Court to rule on ganja.' November 28, 2000, p.9

79. Gifford, Anthony. 'Human rights aspects of the prohibition and legalization of ganja.' November 30, 2000, p.7

80. 'British woman fined $229,000 for ganja.' December 19, 2000, p. 5

81. 'Canadian mine to produce legal marijuana.' December 23, 2000, p.12

82. Ward, Lincoln. 'St. Catherine woman imprisoned, fined for ganja.' January 4, 2001, p.4

83. Buckley, Byron. 'Can ganja make you mad-local doctors challenge marijuana myth.' January 4, 2001, p.5

84. 'Belgium allows marijuana for personal use-joins growing trend in Europe.' January 20, 2001, p.12

85. 'Big ganja haul-2, 000 kilos of weed at $15m seized at port.' February 1, 2001, p.1

86. 'Another big haul-ganja and hash oil valued at least $1.2 b seized.' February 12, 2001, p.12

87. McCormack, Karelle. 'Forensic experts called in to probe $1.2-b drug haul.' February 13, 2001, p.3

88. 'Ganja seized at MoBay Freeport Pier.' March 3, 2001, p.3

89. 'AMA refuses to back ganja as medicine.' June 20, 2001, p.13 Jamaica Observer (Reuters Chicago, June 19)

90. Petre Williams. "Co-operative gardener spared jail sentence for ganja." June 27, 2001, p.5

91. Huntley Medley. "UK police relax ganja laws." June 26, 2001, p.3

92. Letter to the Editor. "Don't be intimidated by US ganja warning." August 23, 2001

93. "US issue ganja warning" August 17, 2001, p.4

94. "British youth fined $230,000 for ganja.' August 21, 2001, p.4

95. "...Another Britain remanded on ganja charge." August 21, 2001, p.4

96. "American pastor warns against decriminalizing ganja." August 20, 2001, p.3

97. "Conscience vote expected on ganja." August 19, 2001, p.4

98. "Decriminalise it, say ganja commission." August 16, 2001, p.1

99. "Briton saved from prison." August 15, 2001, p.5

100. "Ganja report ready," says Patterson, August 9, 2001, p.3

101. "The ganja raid in CedarValley." August 3, 2001, p.6

102. "Home at last." August 2, 2001, p.2

103. "Four St. Elizabeth farmers held for ganja." July 25, 2001

104. Letter to the Editor. "For a new ganja law." July 4, 2001

105. "Henry wants it legalized." June 28, 2001

106. Louis Moyston. "Back off the weed, Mr. Knight." June 22, 2001, p.6

107. Michael Dingwall. "Ganja use and Abuse." June 9, 2001, p.7

APPENDIX 10A-B

10A | WEED OF MANY NAMES

Bag	Bhang	Brain Food	Cannabis	Cash Crop
Cess	Chalice	Col-I	Collie	Collie Weed
Cotton	Devil Weed	Di Ting	Exotic Godsen	Weed Grass
Green Gold	Half Hashish	Hashish	Hemp	Herb
High Grade	Holy Herb	Iley	Indian Hemp	Ischenc
Jamaica Gold	Kalli	Kalli Weed	Joint	Kal-I
Kiki	Kronic	Kushumpeng	Lamsbeth	Lamsbreath
Lamsbred	Mad Weed	Marijuana	Material	Mary
Mary Jane	Nyah Man's Bush	Portion	Pot	Quarter
Reefer	Sacrament	Sensi	Sensimillia	Shit
Skunk	Spliff	Stic	Tampi	The Thing
Thyme	Weed			

10B | LEGALIZE IT - SONGS WITH LYRICS THAT CALL FOR THE LEGALIZATION AND OR THE GLORIFICATION OF MARIJUANA

1. Buckingham Palace - *Peter Tosh*

2. High Grade - *Bounti Killa*

3. Legalize It - *Peter Tosh*

4. Mark of the Beast - *Peter Tosh*

5. Nah Go A Jail - *Peter Tosh*

6. Police Inna Helicopter - *John Holt*

7. Tired Fi Lick Weed Inna Gully - *Jacob Miller*

8. Wanted — Dead or Alive - *Peter Tosh*

APPENDIX 11A-B

11A | ARTICLES PUBLISHED IN THE DAILY NEWS ON MARIJUANA

1. 'Backyard ganja flourishing in New York.' October 3, 1973, p.6

2. 'Ganja, radio link snapped.' November 1, 1973, p.1

3. 'Ways of injustice.' November 2, 1973, p.1-2

4. 'This was the scene.' November 10, 1973, p.1-4

5. 'Held on Ganja charge.' November 10, 1973, p.3

6. '13 arrested on drug charges.' November 13, 1973, p.1-2

7. 'Ways of injustice.' November 13, 1973, p.4-5

8. 'Ganja, men seized on board ship.' November 30, 1973, p.2

9. 'Export of Ganja.' August 13, 1974,

11B | WEBSITES RELEVANT TO MARIJUANA

www.mpp.org (Marijuana Policy Project)

www.norml.org (National Organization Marijuana Laws)

www.marijuana.com

www.marijuana.org

www.marijuana-as-medicine.org

http://books.nap.edu/html/marimed for the Reform of Institute of medicine's 1997 study: Marijuana and Medicine: Assessing the Science Base)

www.4THC.com

http://bizone.8m.com/ (Pictures)

www.medmjscience.org

www.druglibrary.org

www.nih.org	www.legalize.com
http://www.nih.gov/news/ memarijuana/MedecineMari- juana.htm	www.health.org/medmarj.htm
www.yahooka.com	www.wonderweed.com
www.peretto.com/1010420/ index/html	http://pharmacology.about.com/health/ pharmacology/library/weekly/aa970906.htm (Medical Uses of Marijuana)
www.420.search.com (Links to other sites)	www.cheeo.com
www.420times.com	www.cannabis.net
www.Marijuana-Hemp.com	www.marijuanafacts.org
www.ganja.org	www.drugwatch.org
www.medicalseeds.com	http://www.healthcentral.com/Centers/ OneCenter.cfm?Center=Marijuana
www.marijuana.com	www.drugfreeamerica.org
www.ganjaland.com	http://www.commonlink.com/~oslen/
www.marijuanaheaven.com	www.hightimes.com
www.levellers.org/cannabis	www.hempnation.com
www.crrh.org	www.cannabis.com
www.cannabisnews.com	www.marijuananews.com
www.marijuanamagazine.com	http: marypics.freeservers.com
http://www.paston.co.uk/ users/web-book/chronol.htm (Chronology of Cannabis)	http://www.nidanih.gov/Marijintro.html (National Institute of Drug Abuse, USA)
http://www.erowid.org/plants/ cannabismedical info3.shtml (History of the Medical Use of Marijuana	http://www.erowid.org/plants/cannabis culture3.shtml (History of the Intoxicant Use of Marijuana)
http://books.nap.edu/html/ marimed/Institute of Medical Use of Marijuana	

GLOSSARY

ANABOLIC
Building, synthesizing.

ANTAGONISTS
Counteractive, acting against.

ANTHELMINTIC
Kills worm infections.

ANTIBIOTIC
Kills micro-organisms.

ANTIEMETIC
Prevents vomiting.

ANTINEOPLASTIC
Fights new growths and cancer.

ANTIPYRETIC
Controls fever.

ANTITUSSIVE
Controls cough.

ANXIOLYTIC
Controls anxiety.

APHRODISIAC
Stimulates that 'loving feeling'.

BARBITURATES
Sleep inducing chemical compounds.

BENIGN
Not harmful.

BHANG
Indian terminology for marijuana.

CACHEXIA
Severe weight loss.

CANNABIS SATIVA L.
Botanical name for the plant from which marijuana is derived.

CANNABINOIDS
Chemical extracts from Cannabis plant.

CARCINOGENS
Cancer-producing agents.

CARMINATIVE
Chemical extracts from the cannabis plant that promote belching.

CEREBROVASCULAR
Relating to blood vessels in the brain.

CHOREAS
Disorder of the nervous system characterized by jerky limb movements.

CHROMOSOME
The genetic material in the cell.

CYTOKINES
Chemical messengers that are involved in the regulation of almost every system in the body and are important in controlling local and systemic inflammatory response.

DYSPEPSIA
Poor digestion after a meal.

DIURETIC
Promotes passage of urine.

EUPHORIANT
Mood lifter.

FLATULENCE
Gaseous, full of wind.

GANJA
Jamaican and Indian terminology for marijuana.

GOITRE
Swelling of the thyroid gland in the neck.

EXOPHTHALMIC
Bulging or protruding eyes.

HALLUCINATION
Apparent perception of an external object not actually present.

HALLUCINOGEN
A substance that induces hallucination of a visual or auditory nature.

HEMATURIA
Blood in the urine.

HAEMORRHAGE
Bleeding.

HERBACEOUS
Remaining soft and non-woody. (in reference to a plant)

HYDROPHOBIA
Fear of water.

KINETICS
The movement characteristic of metabolites.

MELANCHOLIA
Sadness.

METABOLISM
Chemical processes in the body.

METABOLITES
The molecular structures, which take part in the chemical processes

of the body; for example glucose, fatty acids, amino acids.

NARCOTIC
Sleep inducing

NEPHRITIS
Disease of the kidney.

NEURALGIA
Pain along a nerve distribution in the body. Tic douloureux is an example of neuralgia.

NEUROTRANSMITTER
Substances that transmit nerve impulses to the brain.

OPIATES
Morphine-like Compounds with morphine-like action.

ORTHOSTATIC
Relating to posture.

PARANOIA
Undue fear, unwarranted accusations.

PHENOTYPE
Physical appearance.

PISTILATE
Female flowering plant.

POLYPLOID
Having many sets of genes.

PROPAGATED
Replanted, increasing in numbers.

PSYCHOACTIVE
An agent that affects the psyche at a conscious or unconscious level.

RECEPTORS
Recognition sites on the surface of the cells.

STAMINATE
Male flowering plants.

TAXONOMISTS
One who names plants.

THC
The chemical name for the most psychoactive chemical in marijuana.

VERMICIDE
Kills worm infections.

VERMIFUGE
Expels worms.

VERTIGO
Dizziness.

VISCERAL
Pertaining to internal body organs.

BIBLIOGRAPHY

1. Armentano, Paul. *NORML Statement on the Medical Use of Marijuana Science Supports Amending Federal Law'*. NORML Medical Marijuana, January 1997 (Online).

   a. **Available FTP:** http://www.norml.org/medical/index. shtml, www.norml.org/medical/index.html

2. Biskupic, Joan. *Medical Marijuana Use Challenged.* USA Today. March 29, 2001, p.3a

3. Blumenthal, Mark. *Government stops legitimate medical use of marijuana.* Herbalgram, #26, 1992, p.44

4. Cannabis. Amsterdam, TheNetherlands: Harwood Academic Publishers, 1998.

5. Commissiong, John W. *Ganja.* Kingston, Jamaica: Department of Extra-Mural Studies, 1978.

6. Dreher M.C., J. Nugent and R. Hudgins. *Prenatal marijuana exposure and neonatal outcomes in Jamaica: an ethnographic study,* 1994.

7. Eunice, Terry. *The Ganja Gang.* London: OxfordUniversity Press, 1973.

8. Facklemann, Kathleen. *Marijuana on Trial. Is marijuana a dangerous drug or a valuable medicine?* Science News, March 1997. (Online).

   a. **Available FTP:** http:// www.sciencenews.org/sn_arc97/ 3_22_97/bob1.htm

   b. www.sciencenews.org/sn_arc97/3_22_97/bob1.htm.

9. Fox, Kristin. *Situation Analysis of Drug Abuse in Jamaica.* USAID: Jamaica, November 1993.

10. Gwynne, Peter. *Marijuana*. The Scientist 11[7]: 1, March 1997. (Online)

   a. **Available FTP:** http://www.the-scientist.comwww.the-scientist.com.

11. Institute of Medicine News, National Academy of Sciences, March 17, 1999.

12. Iversen, Leslie L. *The Science of Marijuana*. New York, New York: OxfordUniversity Press, 2000.

13. Joyce, C.R.B. and S.H. Curry. *The Botany and Chemistry of Cannabis*. London: J & A Churchill, 1970.

14. Kambiz, Akhavan. *Marinol vs. Marijuana: Politics, Science and Popular Culture,* March 1999. (Online).

   a. **Available FTP:** http://www.commongroup.net/~oslen/MEDICAL/marinol.html

15. Lowe, Henry . "Give Me Credit For [Kingston] 11 Sept. 2013: n. pag. *Jamaica Gleaner*. Web. 16 Sept. 2013. Early Work On Canasol." *Jamaica Gleaner*

16. Lowe, H., A. Payne-Jackson, S. Beckstrom-Sternberg, J. Duke. *Jamaica's Ethnomedicine. Its Potential in the Healthcare System*. Kingston, Jamaica: Canoe Press, 2000.

17. *Marijuana and Medicine: Assessing the Science Base*. Institute of Medicine, Washington, DC: National Academy Press, 1999. (Online).

   i. "http://www.norml.org/medical/IOM_Report/iomlv.htm"

   ii. http://www. Norml.org/medical/IOM_Report/iomlv.html

18. Marijuana Policy Project.' Questions about medical marijuana answered.

   i. Institute of Medicine's Report. (Online)

   ii. Available FTP: http://www.mpp.org/science.html

   iii. www.mpp.org/science.html

19. Mathre, Mary Lynn. *Cannabis in Medical Practice: A Legal, Historical and Pharmacological Overview of the Therapeutic Use of Marijuana.* Jefferson, North Carolina: McFarlane and Company, Inc., 1997.

20. Mechoulan, R., A. Shani, B. Yognitinsky, Z. Ben-Zul, P. Brown and Y. Gaoni. *Some aspects of cannabinoid chemistry. In the Botany and Chemistry of Cannabis,* C.R.B Joyce and S.H. Curry, eds, pp 93-117. Churchill, London: CIBA Foundation Conference, 1970.

21. *Medical use of Marijuana.* Institute of Medicine, Washington D.C.: National Academy Press, 1999. (Online).
    a. **Available FTP:** http://www.books.nap.edu/html/marimed/
    b. www.books.nap.edu/html/marimed/

22. Murthy, N.V., G. Melville and H. Wynter. *Contractile response of uterine smooth muscle to acetylcholine and marijuana extract.* 1983.

23. Myers Jr., John. "Ganja Has Potential To Attract High-End Tourists." *Jamaica Gleaner* [Kingston] 2 Sept. 2013: n. pag. Jamaica Gleaner. Web. 16 Sept. 2013.

24. Nahas, G.A. *Marijuana in Science and Medicine.* New York: Raven Press, 1984.

25. Parasram, R. *Patterns of Cannabis Use in Jamaica.*

26. Robinson, Rowan. *The Great Book of Hemp: the Complete Guide to the Environmental, Commercial and Medicinal Uses of the World's Most Extraordinary Plant.* Rochester, Vermont: Park Street Press, 1996.

27. Rosenthal, Ed et al. *Marijuana Medical Handbook: A guide to Therapeutic Use.* Oakland, California: Quick American Archives, 1997.

28. Rubin, Vera and Lambros Comitas. *Ganja in Jamaica. The Effects of Marijuana Use.* New York: Anchor Press, 1976.

29. Service, Lloyd. *Marijuana: The contemporary situation.* The Jamaica Herald, July 17, 1993, p.6

30. Stuart, K.L. *Ganja (Cannabis sativa L.)* West Indian Medical Journal. X11 No.3 (115-160), 1963.

31. "Sun, Sea, Sand And Ganja - Local Farmers Offer Ganja Tours To Tourists." *Jamaica Gleaner* [Kingston] 10 Sept. 2013: n. pag. *Jamaica Gleaner.* Web. 16 Sept. 2013.

32. The, Editor. "Can Ja Control Medicinal Ganja Distribution?." *Jamaica Gleaner* [Kingston] 2 Sept. 2013: n. pag. *Jamaica Gleaner.* Web. 16 Sept. 2013.

33. Thompson, Eulalee. *Seeing through ganja.* The Daily Gleaner, January 29, 2001, p.1A&3A.

34. Virtue, Erica. "Ganja On A New High - Jamaican Researcher Welcomes CNN's Celebrity Doctor's Late Endorsement Of Medicinal Properties Of The Weed." *Jamaica Gleaner* [Kingston] 18 Aug. 2013: n. pag. Jamaica Gleaner. Web. 16 Sept. 2013.

35. Ward, A. and B. Holmes. *Nabilone a preliminary review of its pharmacological properties and therapeutic use.* Drugs (30-127-144), 1985.

36. Washington D, C. *The War on Drugs: First, inhale deeply.* Editorial: The Economist. September 2, 2000.

37. Wolstenholme, G.E.W. and Julie Knight. *Hashish: Its Chemistry and Pharmacology.* London: J & A Churchill Ltd, 1965.

38. Zimmer, Lynn and John P. Morgan. *Marijuana Myths, Marijuana Facts: A Review of the Scientific Evidence.* New York, New York: Lindesmith Centre, 1997

REFERENCES

Anderson B.J and M. D.Stein. *A behavioral decision model testing the association of marijuana use and sexual risk in young adult women.* AIDS Behav. 15(4):875-84. 2011.

Assaf F., M. Fishbein, M. Gafni, O. Keren and Y. Sarne. *Pre- and post-conditioning treatment with an ultra-low dose of Δ9-tetrahydrocannabinol (THC) protects against pentylenetetrazole (PTZ)-induced cognitive damage.* Behav Brain Res.1:194-201. 2011.

Avraham Y, N. Grigoriadis , T. Poutahidis, L. Vorobiev, I. Magen, Y. Ilan , R. Mechoulam and E. Berry. *Cannabidiol improves brain and liver function in a fulminant hepatic failure-induced model of hepatic encephalopathy in mice.* Br J Pharmacol. 162:1650-8. 2011

Bélanger R. E. , C. Akre , E. Kuntsche, G. Gmel and J. C. Suris. *Adding Tobacco to Cannabis—Its Frequency and Likely Implications.* Oxford Journals 13(8): 746-750. 2011.

Bergamaschi M.M., R. Queiroz, M. Chagas, D. Gomes de Oliveira, B. Spinosa De Martinis, F. Kapczinski, J. Quevedo, R. Roesler, N. Schröder, A. E. Nardi, R. Martín-Santos, J. Hallak, A. Zuardi and J. S. Crippa. *Cannabidiol Reduces the Anxiety Induced by Simulated Public Speaking in Treatment-Naïve Social Phobia Patients.* Neuropsychopharmacology. 2011

Capasso R., G. Aviello , F. Borrelli, B. Romano, M. Ferro , L. Castaldo, V. Montanaro, V. Altieri and A.A. Izzo . *Inhibitory effect of standardized cannabis sativa extract and its ingredient cannabidiol on rat and human bladder contractility.* Urology.4:1006.

Crean R.D., N.A. Crane and B.J. Mason. *An evidence based review of acute and long-term effects of cannabis use on executive cognitive functions.* J Addict Med.1:1-8. 2011

Cunha P., A. M. Romão, F. Mascarenhas-Melo, H. M. Teixeira and F. Reis. *Endocannabinoid system in cardiovascular disorders - new pharmaco-therapeutic opportunities.* J Pharm Bioallied Sci 3:350-360. 2011.

Demirakca T, A. Sartorius , G. Ende , N. Meyer, H. Welzel, G. Skopp, K. Mann and D. Hermann. *Diminished gray matter in the hippocampus of cannabis users: Possible protective effects of cannabidiol.* Drug Alcohol Depend. 114:242-5. 2011.

Genetic Risk and Outcome in Psychosis (GROUP) Investigators. *Evidence That Familial Liability for Psychosis Is Expressed as Differential Sensitivity to Cannabis: An Analysis of Patient-Sibling and Sibling-Control Pairs.* Arch Gen Psychiatry 2:138-147. 2011.

Guindon, J. and A. G. Hohmann. *The endocannabinoid system and cancer: therapeutic implication.* British Journal of Pharmacology 163:1447-1463. 2011.

Gieringer, D., Cavanaugh, J., Maughs, R., American Alliance For Medical Cannabis, A. A., & California National Organization for the Reform of Marijuana Laws (CalNORML), C. N. (2009, August 28). What Are the Non-smoked Ways to Use Marijuana Medically? - Medical Marijuana - ProCon.org. *Medical Marijuana ProCon.org.* Retrieved August 5, 2013, from http://medicalmarijuana.procon.org/view.answers.php?questionID=000223

Gupta, S. (2013, August 9). Dr. Sanjay Gupta: Why I changed my mind on weed - CNN.com. *CNN.com International - Breaking, World, Business, Sports, Entertainment and Video News.* Retrieved August 9, 2013, from http://edition.cnn.com/2013/08/08/health/gupta-changed-mind-marijuana/index.html

Gupta, S. (Director). (2013). *"WEED": A Dr. Sanjay Gupta Special - CNN Documentary* [Documentary]. USA: CNN.

Hazencamp, A. and F. Grotenhermen. *Review on clinical studies with cannabis and cannabinoids 2005-2009.* Cannabinoids 5:1-21. 2010.

[My paper]Ho B., T.H.Wassink, S. Ziebell and N.C. Andreasen. *Cannabinoid receptor 1 gene polymorphisms and marijuana misuse interactions on white matter and cognitive deficits in schizophrenia.* Schizophr Res. 128 (1-3):66-7. 2011.

Honarmand K., M.C. Tierney, P. O'Connor and A. Feinstein. *Effects of cannabis on cognitive function in patients with multiple sclerosis.* Neurology 76:1153-60. 2011

Howden M.L., and M.T Naughton . *Pulmonary effects of marijuana inhalation.* Expert Rev Respir Med. 1:87-92. 2011.

Kwiatkoski M., F. Silveira Guimarães and E. Del-Bel. Neurotox Res. PMID 21915768. 2011

Large M., S. Sharma , M.T. Compton , T. Slade and O. Nielssen. *Cannabis use and earlier onset of psychosis: a systematic meta-analysis.* Arch Gen Psychiatry.6:555-61. 2011.

Luton, D. (n.d.). Narcotics board rejects marijuana legalisation. *Jamaica Gleaner News Online.* Retrieved August 5, 2013, from http://jamaica-gleaner.com/gleaner/20130307/news/news1.html

Luton, D. (2013, June 23). Marijuana not on minister's agenda. *Jamaica Gleaner News Online.* Retrieved August 5, 2013, from http://jamaica-gleaner.com/gleaner/20130627/lead/lead3.html

Morrison P.D., J. Nottage , J.M. Stone , S. Bhattacharyya, N. Tunstall, R. Brenneisen , D. Holt , D. Wilson , A. Sumich , P. McGuire , R.M. Murray , S. Kapur and D.H. Fytche . *Disruption of frontal theta coherence by Δ(9)-tetrahydrocannabinol is associated with positive psychotic symptoms.* Neuropsychopharmacology.4:827-36. 2011.

Miller J.B., M. Walsh , P.A. Patel , M. Rogan, C. Arnold , M. Maloney and M. Donnino . *Pediatric cannabinoid hyperemesis: two cases.* Pediatr Emerg Care. 12:919-20. 2010.

Naftali T., L.B. Lev, D. Yablekovitz, E. Half and F. M. Konikoff. *Treatment of Crohn's disease with cannabis: an observational study.* Isr Med Assoc 13:455-8. 2011.

Nogueira-Filho G.R., S. Todescan, A. Shah, B.T. Rosa, U. da R Tunes, J.B. Cesar Neto. *Impact of Cannabis Sativa (Marijuana) Smoke on the Alveolar Bone Loss: A Histometric Study in Rats.* J Periodontol. 2011.

Parker L.A., E.M. Rock and C.L. Limebeer . *Regulation of nausea and vomiting by cannabinoids.* Br J Pharmacol.7:1411-22. 2011.

Rajesh M., P. Mukhopadhyay, S. Bátkai , V. Patel , K. Saito, S. Matsumoto, Y. Kashiwaya, B. Horváth, B. Mukhopadhyay, L. Becker , G. Haskó, L. Liaudet , D.A. Wink , A. Veves , R. Mechoulam and P. Pacher . *Cannabidiol attenuates cardiac dysfunction, oxidative stress, fibrosis, and inflammatory and cell death signaling pathways in diabetic cardiomyopathy.* J Am Coll Cardiol. 25:2115-25. 2010.

Reid P.T., J. Macleod and J.R. Robertson . *Cannabis and the lung.* J R Coll Physicians Edinb. 4:328-3. 2010.

Ruggieri M.R. Sr. *Cannabinoids: potential targets for bladder dysfunction.* Handb Exp Pharmacol. 202:425-51. 2011.

Shukla, R. K. (2013). Inside the Gate: Insidersâ€™ Perspectives on Marijuana as a Gateway Drug. *Humboldt Journal of Social Relations*, n/a(ISSUE 35, 2013), 11, 19. Retrieved August 5, 2013, from http://www.humboldt.edu/hjsr/issues/Issue%2035/Issue%2035%20First%20Article%20Shukla.pdf

Schwilke E.W., R.G. Gullberg , W.D. Darwin , C.N. Chiang , J.L. Cadet , D.A. Gorelick , H.G. Pope and M.A. Huestis. *Differentiating new cannabis use from residual urinary cannabinoid excretion in chronic, daily cannabis users.* Addiction. 3:499-506. 2011.

Trabert B, A.J. Sigurdson , A.M Sweeney , S.S Strom and K A McGlynn. *Marijuana use and testicular germ cell tumors.* Cancer 4:848-53. 2011.

The *Gleaner-* Ganja legalisation gaining traction. (n.d.). *Jamaica Gleaner News Online.* Retrieved August 5, 2013, from http://jamaica-gleaner. com/gleaner/20130803/cleisure/cleisure1.html#.UgUGCkw4x2A.email

Jamaica could benefit from medicinal ganja. (2013, August 9). *Jamaica Gleaner News Online.* Retrieved August 5, 2013, from http://jamaica-gleaner.com/gleaner/20130809/news/news2.html

Wolff V., V. Lauer, O. Rouyer, F. Sellal, N. Meyer, J.S. Raul, C. Sabourdy, F. Boujan, C. Jahn , R. Beaujeux and C. Marescaux. Cannabis use, ischemic stroke, and multifocal intracranial vasoconstriction: a prospective study in 48 consecutive young patients. Stroke 42(6):1778-80. 2011

Zajicek J.P., Apostu VI. *Role of cannabinoids in multiple sclerosis.* CNS Drugs. 3:187-201. 2011

AUTHOR'S INTRODUCTION

HENRY I.C. LOWE

O.J., C.D., J.P., PH. D., F.R.S.H.

Dr. the Honourable Henry I.C. Lowe, a scientist who specializes in medicinal chemistry, has contributed approximately 50 years in the fields of science and technology, energy, the environment, wellness and health sciences nationally, regionally and internationally since graduating from the University of the West Indies, Mona. As a result of his outstanding work in these areas he has earned several recognitions nationally and regionally, including the Order of Jamaica in August 2012 and Commander of the Order of Distinction in 1982. He has also served on several public and private sector boards. Dr. Lowe is not only recognized as one of the regions outstanding scientists but also public servant, author, educator and successful entrepreneur.

Dr. Lowe was born in St. Andrew, Jamaica and was educated at Calabar and Excelsior High Schools, University of the West Indies, (B.Sc. Hons.), University of Sydney, (M.Sc.), Manchester University, (Ph.D.), Bolton Institute of Technology England, (Dip. Technical Education), Harvard University and M.I.T, U.S.A., (Post Doctoral Studies).

A former Permanent Secretary for the Government of Jamaica, Dr. Lowe researched and established the first Ministry of Science & Environment in the CARICOM region. He served as Chairman as well as President & CEO of Blue Cross of Jamaica. Dr. Lowe is founder and Executive Chairman of the EHF Group of Companies, which includes a private, not for profit organization, Environmental Health Foundation (EHF), established in 1992, to enhance the quality of people's lives in Jamaica. The Group also includes a commercial entity, EHF Resource Development Limited. This company has subsidiaries Pelican Publishers Limited (a boutique publishing house with an emphasis on wellness and health publications), Eden Gardens Wellness & Lifestyle Limited (a premier wellness & lifestyle centre), and Bio-Tech R&D Institute (a company engaged in the research, development and commercialization of health and wellness products from Jamaican plant-based materials). Dr. Lowe established the first science based Nutraceutical industry in the Caricom region with significant financial potential for import substitution and the export market, which is a multibillion market.

Dr. Lowe has discovered several bioactive molecules from Jamaican medicinal plants (particularly Jamaican Ball Moss) which are being developed for cancer therapy, diabetes and HIV/AIDS. He is also the holder of 8 patents based on the areas of his research in nutraceuticals and chronic diseases. Along with Drs. West and Lockhart, Dr. Lowe developed the first commercial product from Ganja for the treatment of Glaucoma.

Dr. Lowe has published over 22 books and has three in various stages of completion at this time. Dr. Lowe was the first Caribbean person to publish a science textbook series for secondary schools, which were not only used in Jamaica and the Caribbean, but also in Africa. Some of his more recent publications include *"Caribbean Herbs for Diabetes Management: Fact or Fiction?"*, *"Discovering the Future - The Emergence, Development and Future of Science and Technology in Jamaica"*, and *"Jamaica's Ethnomedicine – Its Potential in the Healthcare System"*. He has also published over 100 articles in the areas of science, technology and the health sciences for journals and the popular press.

Dr. Lowe holds many awards and accolades, including the Order of Jamaica (OJ) and the Commander of the Order of Distinction (CD) which are among the highest natural honours for his work in Science and Technology. He also won the *Jamaica Observer Business Leader Award* (2006) and the CCRP *Living Legend Award* (2012); and is the only Jamaican who is a member of the prestigious American Association for Cancer Research (AACR). Dr. Lowe is a member of the American Association for the Advancement of Science, Fellow, Royal Society of Medicine United Kingdom, Harvard Medical School Postgraduate Association, American Association of Pharmaceutical Scientists and the American Chemical Society and a Life Member of the New York Academy of Sciences.

Dr. Lowe is an Adjunct Professor in the Department of Medicine, University of Maryland School of Medicine, USA and Distinguished Adjunct Professor of Ethno-medicinal Chemistry, University of Technology, Jamaica.

DR. THE HONOURABLE ERROL YORK ST AUBYN MORRISON

OJ, HON. LLD, MD, PHD, FRCP (GLASG), FACP, FRSM (UK), FRSH (UK), FJIM.

In 1992, at the University of the West Indies, he was appointed Professor of Biochemistry and in 1994, Professor of Endocrinology. In 1999, he was made Pro Vice Chancellor and Dean, School for Graduate Studies & Research, University of the West Indies.

In 1993, he founded the University Diabetes Outreach Programme (UDOP), which now hosts the largest annual international diabetes conference in the Caribbean region. Since 2007, UDOP includes diabetes related activities in the University of the West Indies (UWI), the University of Technology, Jamaica (UTech) and Northern Caribbean University (NCU).

He was seconded as President & Chief Executive Officer of Blue Cross of Jamaica Limited from June 2005 to December 2006.

He is Co-founder and Hon (Life) President of the Diabetes Association of Jamaica; Co-founder and Executive Member of the Diabetes Association of the Caribbean; advisor to the Pan American Health Organisation (PAHO); and has served on several editorial boards of International Journals.

He continues to maintain an active research interest in medicinal plant extracts and their potential for therapeutic application and has authored over 200 articles in peer reviewed learned journals.